Track and Field:

An Administrative Approach to the Science of Coaching

Track and Field:

An Administrative Approach to the Science of Coaching

RALPH E. STEBEN,
Associate Professor Louisiana State University

SAM BELL,
Track Coach Indiana University

JOHN WILEY & SONS,
New York Santa Barbara Chichester Brisbane Toronto

Library of Congress Cataloging in Publication Data:

Steben, Ralph E.   1923-
   Track and Field.

   Includes bibliographies.
   1. Track-athletics coaching. I. Bell, Sam, joint author. II. Title.

GV1060.5.S67   796.4′2   77-22001
ISBN 0-471-02546-1

Printed in the United States of America

10 9 8 7 6 5 4 3 2

To the thinking coach.

preface

The key to coaching success in track and field and cross-country is the ability to scientifically plan a program and organize the working structure of a highly technical sport. Very few lines of professional endeavor offer the administrative, scientific, and leadership challenges of track coaching. It is not enough to be a charismatic individual with an abundance of public-relations ability, who will get many people out for the sport and then admonish them to "do better" or "try harder" when the competition gets tough. An effective coach must also have a working knowledge of the physiological and mechanical operation of the human body and the learned or innate ability to plan practice sessions and conduct a meet.

The European emphasis on technical know-how is making its mark felt in international competition. The Russians and East Germans have learned that they can train their athletes to perform optimally, coaching them with several specialists: (e.g., the psychologist who takes care of their sociological and psychological needs; the biomechanist who plans the training and conditioning program for each individual; and the trainer who conducts the workouts prescribed by the biomechanist). The trainer knows when to stop the athlete before physical breakdown and how to care for real or imagined injury when it occurs. In this country, most teams have a coach and perhaps one or two assistants who are generally (but probably not specifically) trained to fill the above needs. Some athletes and coaches rely on the natural ability of their athletes rather than on a studied approach. If natural ability is combined with a thoughtful understanding of the activity, performance should improve.

Track is a unique activity featuring individual and team events, and a great deal is required of the coach in terms of leadership, technical knowledge, and subjective experience. It is also a sport that may be inadequately understood, improperly managed, and poorly conducted.

Attention to the following items may assist progress toward the goal of continually improving performance.

1. An increased understanding of the biomechanics of track technique.

2. Fast-moving, well-planned practice sessions supervised by an enthusiastic coach able to make adjustments when necessary.

3. A season featuring meets that provides opportunity for more contestants.

4. An award and publicity system recognizing the efforts of many place winners, not just the top person.

5. An awareness of the team and individual nature of the sport.

6. Conduct of well-organized track meets by officials and coaches for the benefit of contestant and fan.

7. Guiding the athlete toward development of self-discipline and confidence in formulating race and event plans for competition.

8. An emphasis on the team aspect of cross-country where the seventh runner is as important as the front runner.

The broad basis of organization and administration on which the more sophisticated aspects of the sport ultimately depend is emphasized in this book. Each event is discussed under appropriate areas of physical categorization, with analysis of basic, biomechanical aspects. Illustrations, including sequence photographs capture some of these elements, and the attendant discussions emphasize critical, mechanical coaching factors. Training and conditioning sections stress specific yet diverse benefits, depending on application. **What** to teach the beginner, **when,** and **how** are incorporated in the sections on administration and the discussion of the various events.

The primary audience should be the college physical-education student and the track coach, interested in technically thorough, in-depth material governed by conciseness and brevity; although the track fan, interested in a sound basis for his or her observation and understanding of the sport, can benefit as well. Through a careful planning and delegation process, the coach can develop the security and self-assurance necessary for any ongoing program. When troubles arise, they should be formulated into problems that will be solved rather than dismissed with a "seat of the pants" approach.

We extend our grateful acknowledgment to the people who helped this book to reach its final form: coaches Eddie Cole and Pete Boudreaux and LSU trainer Tracy Ladd for their suggestions; Fred Wilt for his constructive criticism and friendly encouragement; Loren Henkel for layout artistry; Andrew Steben for contributions to the pole vault chapter, art work, and line drawings; and to Florence Steben for her patience, editorial, and secretarial help.

Ralph E. Steben
Sam Bell

contents

Section V.   Caring for the Athlete

Track and Field:

*An Administrative Approach to
the Science of Coaching*

section one

The Prerequisities for Coaching

Chapter 1

Philosophy

Although philosophy can mean many things, basically it is defined here as the substitution of simple sense, or a problem-solving approach to finding the best possible solution, for a "common sense" or "good enough" way of doing things. The belief that one must apply common sense to the urgencies of coaching, teaching, and managing a team is a mistake if it only means doing what someone else is doing, what has been done before, what takes the least amount of effort, or if it follows the current, popular fad. Some practices, which seem appropriate at the moment, may only delay or even prevent individual and team progress because they are philosophically incompatible with the achievement of long-range objectives.

LEADERSHIP
More than a cafeteria approach—selecting some of this and that brand of thinking about the world, the nature of humanity, and how people think—is required for the coach to competently answer questions about teaching methods and program content and to inculcate students with reason and purpose. A coaching

philosophy generally encompasses a set of professional values and an understanding of how knowledge is acquired and used. When we talk about coaching philosophy, we usually mean the leadership style of character traits that make up the personality of the coach, since he or she forms half of the team relationship, with the athletes making up the other half. Surround all of this with the interests, culture, morals, and resources of the school and community environment and you have a picture of the complex setting in which the coach and team work.

Art or Science

. Consider further the question of whether leadership is an art or a science. If it is a science and can be learned, then individuals should either be able to change their style to fit the situation, or they should know how to change the situation to fit their style. If neither of these conditions is feasible, successful leadership must be considered a time-and-place situation; or it is an art, and people with charisma will succeed anywhere, anytime.

Styles of Leadership

If we assume that increased understanding of leadership styles can reveal how ideal leaders should behave or how the situation can be changed to make it more compatible with their style, the styles of leadership and their philosophies should be reviewed.

1. *Laissez-faire—Nondirection leadership.* This is not an uncommon style for authoritarians who have lost their touch and accepted defeat or who cannot function properly because of restraints. Quite often a beginner who prefers to avoid contact with people and problems will adopt this marginal philosophy. This person adheres to convention and follows rules of conduct in a passive, unenthusiastic manner. When conflict that requires a course of action occurs, he or she tends to remain neutral and rarely gets stirred up by any problem. This basic attitude seems to reflect personal survival within the system by assuming no position at all. Like driftwood, these people move with the current rather than selecting a direction of their own.

2. *Paternalistic leadership.* In this humanistic style of leadership, the coach discovers what the team members want and, by gentle persuasion and manipulation, helps to achieve the goal. Coaches are so intent on being accepted as "good guys" that they are inclined to accept the opinions, attitudes, and ideas of others rather than pushing their own. There is a looseness of organization, with any deviation usually being overlooked. The coach is patient, friendly, paternalistic, likable, and not apt to exert positive leadership. By setting general goals that everyone can support, the underlying attitude is one of joining a comfortable and friendly country club. In order to avoid social rejection, conformity to team atmosphere and work tempo is essential.

3. *Compromise-democratic leadership.* This pragmatic style leans heavily on precedent and established rules. To emphasize this, the approach to any conflict relies on finding what has worked best previously. These persons try to be firm, but are interested in obtaining a fair solution, equitable to as many people as possible. They rarely innovate and wait for others to test something before adopting it. Because this is a political kind of leadership, they are likely to eventually win some measure of security, status, and prestige since they support the status quo.

4. *Autocratic-authoritarian leadership.* These leaders are not only achievement oriented but are also impervious to criticism, feeling that nice guys usually finish last. Aggressiveness is characterized by doing things their way. They have great confidence in their ability to get things started and completed, interpreting facts to support their own views. There may be some substitution of quantity goals for quality performance. Although these coaches may not always be right, they are never wrong. Since they believe that any decision is better than none, they never doubt their actions.

5. *Control leadership.* This style is oriented toward finding the best and most effective solution to problems in given situations, not necessarily the traditional "one best way." This coach has strong convictions, is not only a starter and finisher, but looks for a better way to reach the common goal of team success by working for and with the people involved. Open and candid communication allows any conflict to be dealt with by direct confrontation, out in the open where those involved can settle any differences honestly and rationally. Mistakes are not deliberately committed but are regarded as misunderstandings, which can be modified and corrected through teaching. No attempt is made to pressure, abandon, compromise, or buy effort to improve performance; instead, the key is to make things happen through involvement and participation.

Although it is convenient to classify coaches by their leadership qualities, very likely, the majority will reflect characteristics from each of the styles discussed. To summarize, most of them could be placed in the compromise-democratic category. Percy Cerutty, however, greatly simplified it by describing two categories, one identified as the prestige-seeking noncompetitor who demands respect by exhortation. These coaches are prone to guess at some readily convenient workout schedule and insist that their naive charges expedite it. The second category, by contrast, wins respect from the athletes by demonstrating techniques and scientifically developing schedules, guiding the athlete to learn and develop an inquiring attitude and personal philisophy (1).

Leadership Training
If one or two of these "styles" seem to be more appropriate or ideal for coaching, then we must either be able to change our style or naturally possess it. It is unlikely that you can change your philosophy of life just by wishing. Although predicated on teaching a person how to act, most education and physical-education teacher training programs include theory courses designed to help the prospective tea-

cher/coaches to better understand themselves and others. Since role playing, sociodrama techniques, and general courses in public and human relations probably lack the impact for serious personality changes, more sophisticated and drastic measures may be appropriate. Sensitivity, T-group, or laboratory-training sessions designed to help people learn more about themselves under the guidance of a change-agent psychologist are suggested. If you want to establish something more than an eclectic, "pick as you please" style of thinking, this procedure may be worth the time, money, and effort involved. Leadership training programs are designed to do, in a short period of time, what experience normally accomplishes. If they give the individuals involved greater confidence in their abilities and judgment, experience should come easier.

Leadership—Situation Engineering

On the other hand, those who resist change and feel that style is unique have the option of altering the situation to make it more amenable to their style or of choosing a situation that is right for them. Psychologists have experimental evidence supporting the contention that the more authoritarian, task-structured person is just right for either the most difficult or the most favorable coaching situation. In a difficult team situation, there is no alternative except to lay down rules and regulations and then work with those who are left in a well-organized manner. Any effort to be diplomatic would result in chaos. In a favorable situation, the team naturally consists of well-motivated people working within an accepted organizational structure. Coaches can allow themselves the luxury of being agreeable, since the group will not be diverted from their quest for success because of it (2).

The relationship-oriented coaches work better in moderately favorable groups where their skill in human relations is needed if anything is going to be accomplished. When things are running smoothy they can organize and structure if this is acceptable to the group. There may be situations where structuring would undo any moderate improvements that had been attained. Some coaches are quite effective at a new job, only to lose their influence as their objectives are realized. Other coaches improve with time as they or the group learn to adjust to each other. Generally, while working with "normal" and moderate groups, the untrained, inexperienced, human-relations coach will do better initially, while the task-oriented person will have some trouble getting started (3).

Although changing the situation is probably more plausible in business and industry, there are applications that can be used in education. School administrators can influence team-coach/staff relationships. They can allow coaches to pick their own assistants, or they can assign experienced hands who are their equals or seniors in job knowledge and age. This could decrease control over the group. On the other hand, coaches may be given, or personally seek, an assistant with skills they lack. The athletic director or principal can give coaches specific instructions on how the job is to be handled, providing them with standard operating instructions and guidelines, or these procedures may be left largely to the coaches and their subordinates.

The power of position or rank of the coaches can be altered by school administrators who either support all of the coaches' decisions, giving them the authority to mete out rewards and penalties or who intimate that the school's support is tentative, requiring coaches to consult with their superiors as well as team members on various issues. This manipulation should not be viewed as sabotage, but as an attempt to change the group situation and permit the individual to perform best. To some extent, it may be easier to design the job to fit the coach than the coach to fit the job.

WHAT THE PUBLIC EXPECTS

Almost everyone interested in sports expects a coach to provide material success with intrepid moral leadership. There is a worshipful attitude of a nonsectarian sort that permeates the coach/public relationship. A coach is imagined to be a master teacher who communicates by lecture, discussion, example, and without saying anything. Coaches are "kings of the hill," calling all the shots for better or worse and, in this day and age, must sell their sport and recruit, even on the high-school level. There are many times when they are asked to be a guidance counselor for contemporary as well as former clients, taking care that they never actually tell a person what to do. Since a counselor is rarely credited for things that work out, even good advice can result in discontent. Coaches are also expected to be diplomats and politicians, the latter role relating to less principled trade-off or compromise situations dealing with people or things. Sometimes, a coach is obliged to become an actor although, in this case, it is prudent to be sure that good judgment is used so that the benevolent intention is not betrayed. It is dangerous to operate with foreign behavior in front of adolescents who, although less organized, are said to be more perceptive and unaffected than adults.

Coaches are also psychologists, employing this science on problem athletes, the team, and themselves. Many a coach also becomes the probation officer for a wayward youngster, who is given another chance by the courts. For youngsters with or without parents, the coach becomes a substitute parent. This paternalist must also be a benevolent dictator and act as judge and jury when crucial, critical decision making is necessary. These decisions are rarely optimal, hopefully satisfactory, and occasionally not so good—but better than no decision. They are vital to the coaches job, as a strategist and director of the sport. Ultimately, this person is the leader of the staff—the team; influential and appreciated for unselfish cooperation in faculty and community activity—a model person.

WHAT COACHES EXPECT OF THEMSELVES

Can a coach be all that the public and faculty expect? Heroes are said to be people who do what they can, with the inference that they avoid imitating someone else or modeling themselves after a famous and respected coach. At this time, it is important that a distinction be made between popularity and effectiveness. Although the coach must certainly have a sincere and genuine interest in students and favorable personal association with school personnel, gaining respect should not be confused with conducting a popularity contest. It is actually possible to contend with the contemporary, social concept of doing one's own thing and still be firm, fair, and consistent. It is possible to be liked well enough, be a disciplinarian, command respect, and be successful. While a program should be holistic and everyone in it an important individual, a successful program cannot emerge without discipline and a rational approach to problem solving.

The Qualities of the Successful Coach

A successful coach is completely dedicated to the human and mechanical aspects of the sport, yet aware that perhaps a minority of the team share this concept. There are many reasons why youngsters report for a sport, either voluntarily or after being recruited, and the coach should realize that he or she has the sometimes impossible job or trying to instill the desire to excel in someone who is not apt to be a competitor. To complicate matters, the coach must develop the ability to recognize and understand the talent in relationship to the needs of the team. People should be placed where they *and* the team will prosper. Although the choice of events may not be to the candidate's liking, success often provides the incentive to cooperate.

Many computations have been made of the hourly rate of pay for coaching, with the related arguments concerning the legitimacy of paying extra for coaching when the extracurricular efforts of other teachers go unremunerated. Whatever the local outcome of such debates, the successful coach must expect to work "hard" with long hours and low pay. Certainly most coaches do not enter the field because they expect great financial return. The intrinsic reward of seeing students prosper and the related ego-seeking satisfaction of realizing that their efforts are appreciated play an important part in why people coach. Individuals who contemplate coaching as a career should honestly answer a basic question. Are they willing to work a 12-hour day, which includes class-room teaching and preparation for the majority of the school year so that they can coach or do they look on coaching as an extension of their own "playing" days? This is not the end. Ambitious coaches may affiliate themselves with local agencies during the summer months and continue the coaching effort in terms of a summer playground or recreation program. Granted, there is a brief recess from academic preparation and teaching, but the pay is still low and the hours long!

With the realization that these are ways of becoming successful under existing American-education philosophy and guidelines, there is the eventual recognition that talented athletes are the ultimate predictor of success. All of this work may be important but, in the final analysis, coaches may still be defeated if they cannot ever have the athletes the opposition has. Can they persist and insist on avoiding mediocrity, with the understanding that the average athlete is forever apt to settle for being "average"?

Coaches must expect that there can be no "degree" of honesty in their dealings with people. An in-depth philosophy is necessary to be honest, holistic (i.e., concerned with individuals in the whole program), and yet not an apparent, hypocritical role player or actor. It is philosophically important to have courage of conviction while employing good judgment consistently, fairly, and impartially; one should be constantly aware of individual differences and able to interpret this to the team and outsiders who expect that everyone should be treated the same way.

The nature of the profession provides challenges and not only presents but creates problems. It is certainly not a dull existence and offers the opportunity to become successful—only to be expected to continue producing or be quickly forgotten. The "Old Coach," who stays with the sport for his entire tenure, is rapidly disappearing. It is said that coaching is nomadic and a young person's "game." Perhaps there should be a resurgence of the leadership/philosophy concept that produces people prepared for the long haul, who are not inclined to retire on the job, so that young people may be given the advantage of experience, ambition, and expertise.

CONCLUSION

Leadership is based on a power/authority, leader/follower, situation/environment complex, which requires a philosophy or way of thinking about the elements of life. If leadership in coaching is an art or time-and-place situation, it may offer little opportunity. If it is a science and can be learned, personalities and behavior may be changed or the employer may be able to alter the situation to fit the style of a person appointed to a coaching position. If the administration is not interested in this approach, one is left with four choices: comply with the situation; realize nothing can be changed and adopt a check in/check out approach; become a zealous advocate of the bureaucracy of the institution; or go elsewhere.

Realistically, teachers tend to teach the way they were taught, and coaches have a tendency to coach the way they were coached. Occasionally a minor innovation may be instituted based on something observed or heard discussed on the coaching circuit. Fads and cycles appear in the coaching profession as well as in other facets of life. While most coaches claim they are not adverse to theories of coaching and problem-solving methods, their actual practices consist of examples, drill, advice, encouragement, and criticism. This approach is not without merit, but there should be an opportunity for athletes to learn from their own mistakes. One of the accepted responsibilities of a coach is to *teach* prospective athletes how and why to train and condition themselves, regardless of their inherent aptitude. If a problem-solving approach has been used, when a naturally endowed person is questioned about their contest skill, it may behoove them to reply, "It came naturally—but I had to learn it."

To adequately train young people to be athletes, a good coach must recognize the individuality of each person and that, even when the sport involves playing with others on a team, the finished athlete is also an individual. If bad advise and incorrect discipline can cause natural athletes to lose their initial advantage, it will cost an "average" athlete, who most coaches work with, much more—unless coaches are "made" by their athletes, regardless of the quality of the coaching.

Coaches must not only know the sport but the athletes as well. Although they are expected by onlookers to be "models" their greatest responsibility is to help their charges help themselves in competition, realizing that their competitors have similar intentions. Under these circumstances, any athletic endeavor is bounded by rules—hence the problem of coaching and being an athlete is the problem of simultaneous satisfaction and dissatisfaction. If young people profess an interest in becoming athletes, their intentions must transcend mere desire. Intention and commitment, logically sequenced, are appropriate precursors of the dedication that distinguishes the person "playing at" from the one "playing in" the game. The paraphrased philosophy of Willye White, a U.S. female Olympian since 1956, is most appropriate here: "Learn to lose, know why it happened, and then turn your ears off to an indulgent society and train to compete effectively with personal satisfaction."

BIBLIOGRAPHY

1. Cerutty, Percy, "Coaches and Coaching—World Roundup," *Track Technique, 62* (December 1975).

2. Fiedler, Fred E., "Style or Circumstance: The Leadership Enigma," *Psychology Today, 2,* 38 (March 1969).

3. Fiedler, Fred E., and Martin M. Chemers, *Leadership and Effective Management,* Scott, Foresman, Glenview, IL, 1974.

Chapter 2

The Organization and Administration of Cross-Country, and Track-and-Field Programs

Planning is deciding in advance what is to be done. It must precede organization and the assembling of the resources needed to carry out the program before action can be initiated, by directing and coordinating the efforts of staff members. Progress is controlled by the formulated plans. This process, predicated on a philosophy of service to others in the management of human behavior, requires technical, human, and conceptual skill and implies there are qualifications for success in terms of vitality for work, rational thinking ability, the willingness to accept responsibility, and the ability to work and communicate with people effectively.

Coaching personalities range from those with little executive ability operating on a laissez-faire basis to democratic coaches making full use of the power of their position to work with others for others; to the autocrats, inclined to be arbitrary and inflexible, seeing their position exclusively as one of power; to the paternalistic types, who usually lose the initiative and creativity of their constituents because they provide rewards before services are rendered. We can probably easily identify track coaches with these characteristics, while recognizing that some people are better equipped to deal with the technical aspects of the program than they are with the people in it.

State-subsidized programs, such as those found in the USSR or East Germany, partially solve this problem by providing teams with specialists in the areas of human relations, physiological assessment, training, and conditioning. Collegiate, physical-education programs of study in this country attempt to provide prospective coaches with basic background in all of these areas, which can be further developed through the curiosity and drive of the individual coach. Most American coaches who are successful have one thing in common, the desire to continue to learn and master all aspects of what has to be one of the most involved and complicated jobs in the athletic program.

Whether one is the first coach of the sport at a new school or has been recently employed to follow someone else, the entire program as well as seasonal and daily situations should be looked over, and decisions should be made in advance as to what has to be done—how, when, and by whom. Five time/range plans containing elements for consideration are presented in a priority order.

Time/Range Plan I

A. Outline a schedule for the use or development of facilities, and prepare an inventory for equipment and supplies.

B. Prepare a budget for any items that require financial outlay.

C. Plan to recruit, train, and educate assistant coaches, managers, and officials.

D. Adjust plans for the anticipated track program to the policies, procedures, and methods of the school and athletic administration, following the state and conference athletic association regulations.

E. Outline tentative policies, procedures, and methods unique to the program in accordance with the coach's personal philosophy and time/place considerations.

F. Plan an information procedure to obtain candidates for a team.

G. Outline a training and conditioning program.

After thinking through the program and its goals, the next logical step is to hold a meeting with appropriate school officials to determine if the following items are financially feasible and administratively possible.

Time/Range Plan II

A. Can an assistant coach and a cadre of officials be appointed by the administration or may they be recruited from the faculty, with or without remuneration?

B. Assuming there are no outdoor facilities what is the possibility of surveying and liming a grass track on the physical-education and athletic fields? A more ambitious approach might involve borrowing farm machinery to construct a straightaway, surfaced with locally acquired materials. Concrete platforms for the shot put and discus and a long, triple-jump pit can be built by the coaching staff with custodial and student help. Since high-jump and particularly pole-vault pits require a synthetic landing area of shock-absorbing material, will funds be available to purchase either the units or the materials for their construction?

C. The problem of equipment and supplies may be partially solved through prior agreement with the school metal-and wood-working instructors. Items such as jumping and vault standards; takeoff boards; wood or metal shot and disc platforms (if concrete platforms are not available); hurdles and starting blocks can be constructed as class projects.

D. Supplies such as crosspieces, shots, discuses, javelins, and vaulting poles must be purchased. It may be necessary to conduct a candy or magazine fund-raising program if the funds for the overall program are limited, providing that school policy permits such campaigns. Uniforms and sweat suits need not be ostentatious. Basic gym equipment can be purchased and stenciled with a name or symbol representative of the school.

E. How will the team travel, be fed, and housed for local, conference, and state competition?

Time/Range Plan III
The following points on the agenda relate exclusively to policy.

A. Can the hallways and other building space be used for practice after school, during the winter months, and when weather is inclement? The nature of supervised hallway work may involve shuttle-interval relays, sprint and hurdle work, and long-jump/triple-jump check-mark practice. Other areas will be used for rope vaulting, putting with an indoor shot, high jumping on mats, and net throwing with a rubber discus and a flanged, rubber-tipped javelin, with stubby or small one and one-and-a-half kilo shots.

B. What are state, conference, and local regulations regarding the legality of preseason practice? Is there a school policy relating to preseason activity or regulating the use of facilities simultaneously with seasonal sports activities?

C. Will the training rules and regulations established by the coach for his or her sport be compatible with school policy?

The policy and budget items discussed seem to reflect a considerable challenge, based on an austerity time place situation, but they represent, in part if not totally, some of the problems that may be encountered. Regionally, the financing of school athletic programs and the policies attendant to them range from diversified programs financed by tax funds to more meager offerings of football and basketball financed by gate receipts with the help of a Parent's Club. Nonrevenue sports may be sponsored by interested patrons, civic groups, and local colleges or universities working on a public-service concept.

Time/Range Plan IV
With the initial questions settled, the coach can now concentrate on the following items, which require the direction and coordination of planning with the staff.

A. Whether the coach is inclined toward a democratic philosophy or not, it is necessary to develop a set of guidelines for team rules, regulations, the conduct of practice, and the level of expectation. It is an accepted and expected administrative procedure to put these guidelines down on paper to inform and protect the coaching staff, parents, and team members. A successful program, regardless of how long it takes to develop, cannot emerge without direction that has been carefully thought out, discussed, and developed before the beginning of formal practice.

B. Thought must be given to the training and conditioning program itself. A survey of previous campaigns or a projected estimation of the number and availability of candidates will guide the coach in establishing a pyramid of testing, training, and conditioning for the season. Any such plan does not have to be adhered to in a rigorous manner but is considered a framework for actual needs.

C. The head coach should plan several meetings with appointed or recruited assistant coaches and managers to discuss, review, and revise the philosophy, policies, procedures, and methods of the program, as well as technical training and instruction relating to the track events. Prospective managers may be instructed in separate meetings in the matter of their training and responsibility for help in the conduct of workouts, caring for equipment and supplies, supervising phases of practice, recording practice data, attendance keeping, and other duties.

D. Plans should be made early, perhaps in conjunction with step C, for the development of an information system pertaining to the forthcoming season and the recruitment of candidates. Use of the public-address system, planned physical-education class instruction, improvised pentathlons or decathlons, intramural meets, the school and local newspapers, brochures, and other media all represent legitimate ways to channel talent and advertise the program. Liaison may be established with junior high-school, physical-education teachers and coaches, including them as part of a system for the development of seasonal and summer playground programs.

E. Home track meets require numerous trained officials and managers who must know and conduct their assignments with dispatch for the enjoyment of contestants, fans, and officials. Plans should be made and machinery devised to reach men and women within and outside the school and to compile a list of interested, available personnel. Meetings held before the first contest will acquaint people with the interpretation of rules, the proper conduct of a contest, and a schedule providing dates, starting times, and the order of events. It may be wise to draw up an alternate list and a system to verify those officials scheduled prior to each contest.

Time/Range Plan V

Now consider more specific tasks relating to practice sessions, track meets, junior high-school feeder meets, development of an awards and archive system, and a summer playground program.

THE CONDUCT OF PRACTICE. In conjunction with the coach's master schedule and framework of pyramidal training, a daily workout or practice schedule should be posted for all squad members to study before practice begins. The manager's record of the previous day's activity is also posted if it involves any measuring or time-trial activity. This material, also kept in a log book, allows each individual's progress to be determined, and it is particularly valuable when workouts or parts of workouts are repeated.

Indoor practice sessions begin with each athlete checking in with the manager for attendance before the squad assembles in a designated area for warm-up procedures. Ideally, running should precede other components of a warm-up, but if this cannot be done because of inclement conditions or unavailability of the gymnasium or hallways, step bench, running in place, or side straddle step exercises may be substituted. Stretching and flexibility exercises should be done with caution to avoid injury during warm-up.

After a 20 to 30 minute warm-up, the squad breaks up into groups for more specific work according to the foundation of training for each subdivision. The schedule may entail weight training, running, hurdling, shuttle relay, or check-mark work in the hallways or gym; and rope vaulting, high jumping, net throwing, or shot putting in other areas. A precise time schedule for activity in each area, with assistant-coach or student-manager supervision for each group, is necessary not only to develop a sense of efficiency in the athlete but also to meet school policies relating to proper use of facilities.

As the season progresses, it is advisable for the coach to have an inclement weather schedule worked out in advance. The concept of "practice every day" instills the perseverance necessary for serious and purposeful activity. The routine for attendance and warm-up outdoors is the same as that for indoors and is followed by training on a time schedule, as previously posted. The practice should allow time for sufficient rest between assignments and consultation with coaches, yet should be expedited as rapidly as possible. A well-organized workout can be conducted in an hour and a half, releasing the athlete for other obligations.

THE CONDUCT OF TRACK MEETS. The conduct of successful track meets is based on an understanding of the sport and the rules that govern it by coaches, athletes, officials, fans, and the press. The best way for a coach to indirectly influence the latter two groups is to set aside instruction time during squad and officials' orientation meetings, since each contestant and official *must* know the portion of the rules that pertains to them. Although the visiting team should be accorded every reasonable courtesy, their misfortunes must be considered part of the learning process if they occur because the team does not know the rules. The track meet itself is neither the time nor place for officials to be expected to train and educate uninformed coaches or contestants.

Although it is not necessary to repeat here what is readily available in rule books pertaining to rules, recommended standard color markings for tracks, starting mechanics, and track-meet management, some key problem areas warrant discussion. First, let me mention a philosophical point relating to the rules. There is a common misconception on the part of some educators regarding fairness, and a too common practice of allowing many "opportunities" for a student/athlete to learn what constitutes a violation or foul. It is true that there are contested calls in football and basketball, but track seems to be inordinately plagued with poor starting procedures and the overlooking of fouls, particularly in the running events. The rules were not written to be dismissed or ignored but to protect everyone involved. They should be understood by all concerned and discharged with intelligence, competence, and good judgment.

The meet director. In most instances, the director is also the track coach of the host school, except in a meet of large proportions when it may be more appropriate for someone else to coordinate the work of the games committee and attend to all technical, physical, and personnel needs of the meet in advance. The requirements, including promotional aspects, are spelled out clearly in the rule books.

Starting. Collegians have accepted the "no false start" rule as part of their normal routine, while interscholastic competition still allows one false or unfair start before disqualification. In spite of this difference, athletes should be coached for a sensory set, with the athlete motionless in the set position, concentrating on the sound of the gun for the stimulus, rather than on the motor set, which may encourage leaving the starting position prematurely, whether the gun has been discharged or not.

Both the starter and athlete have to be competent for the start to be fair to all, with the winner determined on the basis of who is the best runner. The starter should be pleasant, efficient, impartial, and objective in discharging his assignment. Although it is his job to display leadership and obtain the confidence of the athletes, the attention of the fans should be on the race itself and not on the starter.

Clerking. The clerk of the course and his or her assistants must escort and place each contestant in the proper position on the starting line. The meaning of "staggers" should be quickly and clearly emphasized regarding a breaking point at a designated place on the track. Knowledgeable relay-zone inspectors, who work in conjunction with the clerks, can assist runners who have been previously informed of their proper position on the track. This procedure is more efficient if relay runners go directly to their zones from the staging area instead of reporting to the starting line first. In larger meets, special instructions relating to clerking items that accompany the entry blanks should be reviewed by the coach with his athletes before the meet.

The announcer.   The progress of a meet can be facilitated by securing the services of a well-informed person with an engaging, authoritative voice who will issue calls, supply relevant information, introduce contestants, and announce results in the fewest words possible. If expedited with expertise, this procedure not only keeps a meet on schedule but also serves as a valuable, educational function. Announcers must be careful to center attention on the contestant and the meet, rather than on themselves. Good judgment must be used in narrating the progress of a race or "on stage" efforts in crucial field-event trials. Runners and the starter, ready for a race, should not normally be detained by lengthy introductions, and announcements concerning athletes at the award stand should not be a disruptive factor. In many meets the contestants are conducted to the award stand immediately after the contest to wait on cue for the presentation of awards at a discreet moment.

Head-finish judge and head-finish timer.   These people coordinate and supervise the work of the finish judges and timers whose duties must be handled with dispatch—every person doing their job in a consistently correct way. No matter how long a group has worked together, procedures should be seriously reviewed before the meet with alternate judges and timers present. After places have been picked and handed to the head judge, they are recorded and advanced to the head timer. Occasionally the result of a race may be held up after a close finish. In these cases, decisions should be made by the head-finish judge as quickly and fairly as possible, with or without the aid of photographic equipment. The liaison between the head-finish judge and the starter should be thoroughly understood, with no race being started until signal clearance is made by the head-finish judge. It is most discouraging and unfair for a group of athletes, ready to run, to be kept waiting at the starting line by disputes at the finish line or lack of coordination by the announcer, finish judge, and starter.

Referee.   A working, rather than honorary, referee should assume the responsibility of settling disputes relating to transactions of the rules. Assisted by marshalls and inspectors who are thoroughly acquainted with their jobs, the referee should handle this task with dispatch and objectivity. In larger meets, protocol requires that coaches' protests be handled by means of a protest-table procedure within a prescribed time period. A meet should not be inordinately held up by lengthy discussions on the track between coaches and officials.

Field-event judging.   Field events should not be dismissed as the orphan of the track-meet program. A competent, head-field referee should coordinate the work of all chief field-event judges. Each chief field-event judge in turn, is responsible for the conduct of his event, including the assistance of measurers and attendants who replace crosspieces, adjust standards, catch vaulting poles, level pits, and retrieve implements. This personnel should be recruited and trained prior to the season and not drafted from the stands just before or during the contest.

The conduct of the home track meet should be undertaken with the concept that it will be an enjoyable event, with all concerned anxious to return. It seems reasonable that good administration by the host school will encourage less-organized opponents to reciprocate. Well-run meets are the result of educative and administrative procedures practiced by hosts and visitors well in advance of contests.

JUNIOR HIGH-SCHOOL FEEDER MEETS. The development and continuing success of high-school track and cross-country programs can be strengthened by encouraging the development of intergrade, interschool, elementary, and junior high-school competition. A high-school coach can assist personnel from these schools, advising them of the procedures used to start or continue a program. It may be advantageous to conduct clinics to train coaches and reinforce the understanding that a proper foundation in the sport is of great value to young athletes as they advance to high school. The emphasis of the programs should be twofold: quantity participation rather than development of a few outstanding individuals; and instruction and experimentation in all events.

Regardless of whether there is a junior-high competitive season, a meet can be conducted for students by the members of the high-school track and cross-country teams at the conclusion of the respective seasons. This meet should receive the same careful attention given to promotion, administration, organization, and publicity of the high-school contests, and it should offer an excellent opportunity for team members to understand more fully the work and responsibility required in producing a well-run contest. If awards are given, they should be numerous and modest, emphasizing the participation concept.

PROMOTION ASPECTS. Successful promotion of a track and cross-country program includes the development of an honors system. Initially, this requires the approval of school authorities, including the athletic administration, the cooperation of various school departments, and the local press. Ideas for consideration include: construction and display of a record board; annual shield awards for the most outstanding individual in cross-country and each track-and-field event, with appropriate publicity in the local newspaper; team and individual state champion photographs in the trophy case or gym foyer; placing the names of relay team members on trophies won in meets where they are awarded; and, during the competitive season, weekly certificate awards for outstanding accomplishment. Since it is assumed that the common practice of awarding monograms and championship patches will be followed as finances permit, this will not be discussed.

Record board. Financed by the student council, Key Club, or other school-service organization, a plywood record board equipped with metal tracks can be

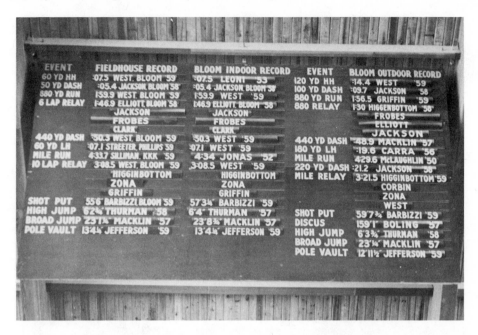

Figure 1. A student council financed record board for the field house or gymnasium.

constructed, painted, and lettered with the various events (Figure 1). Cardboard inserts, lettered by the art department, with the name of the record holder and the effort are placed in the metal tracks. Dimensions should be adequate for reading the board from a distance if it is hung in an indoor facility. When a record is broken and retired, the insert is removed and presented to the former record holder. The board should be prominently placed in the gymnasium, fieldhouse, or foyer of these buildings. Smaller, foyer-style record boards, complete with individual photographs are also currently popular.

Shield awards. With the help of the wood-working and art departments, wooden shields for each event may be constructed, finished, and lettered (Figure 2). The name and effort of the best annual performer are placed on the shield, which is hung in the hallways adjoining the gym. This information can be advanced to the press and announced at the annual-sports assembly or banquet. Since graduates have reason to return to their school, the prominently displayed shields can become a topic of discussion and serve as a valuable tradition builder.

Archive photographs. Dependent on the local, regional, and state success of a school, photographs of the most significant individuals and teams can be placed in the trophy case or hung in hallways. Data pertinent to the accomplishments of the team or individual can be included on or under the photograph.

Trophies. School awards won at relay meets may be engraved with the names

Figure 2. The shield award plaque for hallway or alcove.

of the members of the relay team before they are displayed in the trophy case. If finances do not permit engraving, the names may be typed on paper, placed in a glassine envelope, and fixed to the trophy. Alumni who return to their school appreciate this gesture, which, like the shield awards, helps significantly in the development and retention of tradition.

Weekly award certificates.   Throughout the competitive season, certificates may be presented by the coaches or captains to the previous week's outstanding performers. A balloting system may be used immediately after a meet to determine the recepients. This information should be forwarded, with photographs, to the school and local press for appropriate publicity.

Brochures and newsletters.   The use of brochures and newsletters is a very effective promotional device, as well as a morale builder and tradition developer. These brochures need not be as professional as the material coming from sports-information departments of large universities, with the degree of sophistication largely up to the ambition and resources of the coach. The brochure may feature highlights of the previous season, biographical prospects for the coming campaign, pictures of the leading candidates, records, and a schedule for the new season. A weekly or monthly newsletter mailed to alumni and interested fans may be of value if it is not precluded by preparation and mailing expense.

A cooperative press is most helpful in the development and maintenance of a program. Although the complete, objective results of all meets with occasional, subjective recognition is important, the promotional ideas discussed above represent more durable ways to foster tradition. The concepts presented here are based on giving *many* relatively inexpensive awards with long-lasting, personal value. The initial financing of this program may be modestly expensive, but the annual upkeep is nominal, and the results are enduring.

THE SUMMER PLAYGROUND PROGRAM.   In this program, local parks and playgrounds are used for the instruction of boys and girls in the basic mechanics of starting, running, relay racing, and selected field-event competition. Financial backing and sponsorship by a park board or recreation district are required, with public information, publicity, and promotion provided by local media. If a workable plan submitted to these agencies is accepted, the scope of the undertaking may take the following form:

Selection and training of staff.   The coach should select three or four talented track-and-field athletes who are familiar with the basic mechanics of the events to be handled and organize their efforts for demonstration and instruction, using the guidelines outlined and discussed in each chapter under "how to teach beginners."

Facilities, equipment, and supplies.   The initial budget may be of substantial proportions, but only nominal expenditures will be required thereafter for maintenance and replacement purposes. Large equipment would include a set (four or five) of junior-sized hurdles (.61 meters/24 inches), high-jump and pole-vault standards, long-jump takeoff boards, and pole-vault planting boxes for each park. Most of this equipment may be made and repaired in a park-board maintenance shop. Small shots, junior-sized discuses, and crosspieces have to be purchased from an athletic supply house. At this time a decision will have to be made regarding inclusion of the pole-vault event. Small diameter, nonflexible, 2.44 and 3.05 m (8 and 10 ft) poles are inexpensive and durable compared with their flexible counterparts, but they require a different technique.

Awards, promotion, and publicity. The sponsorship of service clubs (Lions, Kiwanis, Rotary, etc.) and the local press might be sought for financing the awards presented in the local playground and final meets. Inexpensive ribbons may be given for numerous places in each local playground meet, with medals and trophies awarded at a culminating meet held on the high-school track. The title of the program acknowledging the sponsors may be placed on the awards (e.g., Chicago Heights Park Board-Star-Kiwanis Track Meet, etc.) Displaying the awards in the window of the sporting goods dealer from whom they are purchased, along with posters advertising the program in other selected business houses (banks, supermarkets, park fieldhouses, etc.) helps to create community interest (Figure 3).

The plan, organization, and conduct of the program. On the basis of advance information placed in park field houses and advertised by local media, the staff circulates to each park in the city with instruction geared to youngsters in age groups ranging from 7 to 12 years old. The events covered in several visits may include starting, running, hurdling, baton passing, high and long jumping, pole vaulting (if this event is to be included), and shot and discus throwing. Each park should be provided with the necessary equipment and supplies, with the prepared facilities available to the youngsters on a daily basis under the supervision of the park attendant.

Suggested age groups and the disposition of events could take the following format:

Age 7 and 8:	50-m dash, 4 × 50 m relay, high jump, long jump;
Age 9 and 10:	60-m dash, 60-m hurdles, 4 × 50 m relay, high jump, long jump;
Age 11 and 12:	70-m dash, 70-m hurdles, 400-m run, 4 × 50 m relay, high, long and triple jump, pole vault, shot put, discus throw.

Preparation of running area. If the park area is sufficiently flat, a straightaway of 70 meters can be closely mowed and limed with lanes. A line 200 m in length encircles the lanes with exchange zones for the 4 × 50 m relay. If space does not

Figure 3. Awards for playground meets provide incentives when displayed prominently.

permit a circular track, a shuttle relay race without batons can be substituted, even though baton-exchange technique may be taught in learning sessions. As scheduled, the teaching staff arrives in each park to provide instruction under the supervision of the coach. After two or three visits over as many weeks, a neighborhood meet may be conducted with ribbon awards for five places in each event.

Culminating meet on the high-school facilities.   With sanction from the school board, the high-school track is prepared for an all-city meet, which features the same events that are conducted at the neighborhood parks, with the addition of age-group competition for junior-high, high-school, and open division.

The same careful and thorough preparation goes into this meet as in any high-school event but, since school personnel may not be available, park district or recreation board attendants and other personnel can be recruited and trained for the conduct of the meet. Entry blanks in the newspaper or those available at the park field houses should be filled out with the help of parents to verify age and sent to a post office box by a specified deadline date (Figure 4). The blanks are processed by a games committee, with heats and flights set up according to need. If several heats or flights are necessary for events in each age group, place winners can be determined on the basis of time, height, or distance. On the day of the meet, clerks, with the assistance of a well-informed announcer and a published order of events, will help keep the meet on schedule. Parents should be urged to attend. A fencing arrangement utilized around the field-event areas will permit a more intimate relationship with the competitors, while curtailing crowd interference with the administration of the event.

Junior-high, high-school, and open divisions.   An order of events comparable to the junior-high and high-school programs can be arranged, with open competition for older participants in previously publicized events.

Park championship.   Each entrant should be encouraged to affiliate with his or her local park, regardless of age group. The incentive for a neighborhood to win the all-city meet will encourage the park attendants, parents, and youngsters to respond, which will begin the development of a trend to augment the tradition of the high-school program.

CROSS-COUNTRY

Although there is some similarity between the distance runs in track and the sport of cross-country, the activity is significantly unique. The team approach in cross-country far transcends that in track and, in some instances, may require an adjustment in the philosophy of the track coach who doubles as the cross-country coach. The model for organization and administration of track and field (previously discussed) may be applied successfully, with attention directed to items characteristic to the singular nature of the sport.

The elements of administration should be applied to:

1. Sanction to conduct the sport.

2. A budget.

3. A place to run.

4. Scheduling.

PLAYGROUND
TRACK & FIELD MEET

SPONSORED BY THE CHICAGO HEIGHTS PARK DISTRICT

ALL EVENTS WILL BE HELD ON SAT., JULY 1
STARTING TIME AT 1:00 P.M.

AT BLOOM HIGH SCHOOL FIELD

ENTRIES MUST BE POSTMARKED TUESDAY, JUNE 27 . . . NO POST ENTRIES

DIVISION 1	**DIVISION 2**	**DIVISION 3**	**DIVISION 4**
Age 7-8	Age 9-10	Age 11-12	Age 13-14
☐ 50 Yard Dash	☐ 50 Yard Dash	☐ 75 Yard Dash	☐ 100 Yard Dash
☐ Broad Jump	☐ 60 Yard Hurdles	☐ 80 Yard Hurdles	☐ 100 Yard Hurdles
☐ High Jump	☐ High Jump	☐ High Jump	☐ 440 Yard Dash
	☐ Broad Jump	☐ Broad Jump	☐ High Jump
	☐ Pole Vault	☐ Pole Vault	☐ Broad Jump
		☐ Shot Put	☐ Pole Vault
		☐ Discus Throw	☐ Shot Put
			☐ Discus Throw

Name..

Street...

City...

Entrant's Age...................   Parent's Signature...

MAIL ENTRY NO LATER THAN JUNE 27th TO:

RALPH E. STEBEN
CHICAGO HEIGHTS PARK DISTRICT
POST OFFICE BOX 31   CHICAGO HEIGHTS, ILL.

—MEET REGULATIONS—

1. Entry blanks must be signed by Entrant's Parents to verify age.
2. Entrants are not limited to number of events, but must be present when name is called for event — no waiting.
3. Chicago Heights Park District Officials and Bloom Township High School assume no responsibility for injury or lost articles.
4. Track shoes may be worn on the track only.
5. Medals will be awarded for the first five places in each event.

The program officials reserve the right to request a certified birth certificate from an entrant and to deny participation to any person not complying with meet regulations.

Figure 4. Sample entry blank for playground meet.

5. Public relations, promotion, and motivational programs.

6. Training programs and practice planning.

7. Training rules and regulations.

8. Preseason meetings.

9. Programs for the junior high school.

10. Summer programs.

Unique elements emphasized in the cross-country section of the chapter on long-distance running relate to the team concept and the need to run as a "gang" to keep the spread between the first and seventh runners minimal. As odd as it might seem, it may be the seventh runner who emerges as the star of the team in the final analysis. It is the responsibility of this runner to maintain contact rather than to expect the lead runners to accommodate him by slowing down! This philosophy must be incorporated in planning items 6 thrrough 10. The actual training programs should include a well-engineered assortment of activities. Different places to train, largely independent of the home-competitive course, not only eliminate or reduce boredom but help bring the team to its peak for the championship meets.

Preparation for home and away meets must include items unique to the nature of the sport. Procedures that relate to marking the course, duties of officials, disposition of the chute, and scoring are spelled out clearly in the rule books. A map of the course should be available on arrival or sent in advance to any visiting team. Assuming that the teams will arrive well before the start of the contest, it should be a relatively simple matter for them to inspect the course, with or without a guide. In large meets, scoring need not be a problem if one of the various numbering plans described in the cross-country section (Chapter 15) is made known to the contestants and coaches in advance. A well-organized meet with knowledgeable contestants can be expedited rapidly, leaving all concerned anxious to return to the next meet on an exciting new course.

THE TEAM MEETING AND THE ITINERARY

Preparations for a home or away track or cross-country meet should include a team meeting the day before competition. Generally, the purpose of the meeting is to strengthen the team concept of the squad, revitalize individual and collective confidence, announce assignments, discuss strategy, and post a time schedule.

Specifically, and particularly in preparation for contests away from home, an itinerary should be distributed and briefly discussed with the squad. Suggested items may include the following.

1. A list of people making the trip and their assignments.

2. Personal, team equipment, and supply check.

3. Suggestions for the evening meal, activity after dinner, and when to retire for the evening.

4. Suggestions for awakening in the morning, what to have for breakfast, and a reminder to pack a lunch if necessary.

5. Arrival time, early enough to dress at home if this is planned, including taping, therapy, or other physical-training needs.

6. Specific instructions regarding the administration of the meet sent by the host school.

7. Brief reference to previously discussed policy regarding conduct on the bus or in private autos to and from the contest. If private autos are used, a plan should be developed for convoy mode of travel, with responsibilities clearly delineated regarding proximity, speed, and emergency stops.

8. Instructions regarding departure time from the host school after the contest, including another personal, team equipment, and supply check, and the time of arrival back home.

The agenda for the squad meeting should be largely objective, brief, concise, and complete, reflecting prior planning by coaches and team captains. Although dependent on the philosophy of the program, the meeting should be conducted in a manner that engenders a feeling of quiet confidence for the contest and the empathetic understanding that each athlete understands his or her responsibilities and has the self-discipline to discharge them.

If the team travels in a school bus, some items ordinarily reviewed in a team meeting can be postponed and discussed at the beginning of the bus trip. The return trip is often enhanced by reading the results of the meet to the squad, conveying congratulations for the performances, with suggestions for improvement in training, technique, and strategy. Quite often, win or lose, a "pep" talk of rational proportions at this time is more valuable to the squad than a fiery, unnerving oration before the contest. Preparations for the next meet should begin at this time, with positive emphasis on progressive improvement for optimum performance.

Chapter 3

Training and Conditioning

Whether a motivated individual trains primarily for physical fitness and its benefits or for competitive performance, the elements that influence success relate to improvement of the mechanisms that control energy output and neuromuscular function. Energy production depends on internal, chemical process or metabolic systems, while strength and technique depend more specifically on activity of the neuromuscular system. Measurable improvement of these factors can be attained with the degree limited by the initial condition of the individual and natural endowment. It is important to recognize that, although everyone can make some improvement through various training and conditioning programs, full development of an individual's capabilities may still leave him or her in an average category.

Scientists study the performance requirements of various events in specific environments and evaluate, amend, and develop improved systems of training and conditioning in relation to the age, sex, and body type of an individual. Not only can the capacity of human capability be improved but the power or rate at which this capacity is used can also be enhanced, primarily by improving efficiency.

An understanding of the basic language employed is preliminary to an investigation of the adjustments of the body during exercise. **Training** involves the development of an athlete for a specific event and deals equally with improvement of skill and conditioning. **Conditioning** refers to the adjustment of body chemistry or metabolism to stressful workouts for improvement of anaerobic and aerobic energy capacity of muscle tissue through exercise programs. **Anaerobic energy metabolism** is equated with intensity activity, yet initiates all activity. It functions in a deficit of oxygen, is the immediate precursor for all aerobic metabolism, and occurs simultaneously with it in most strenuous activities that require more than 10 seconds to complete (Table 1). **Aerobic metabolism** is particularly important for endurance and requires an understanding of the relationship between oxygen uptake and work. Oxygen uptake refers to the volume of oxygen taken up or consumed by body tissue per unit of time and increases as work output increases.

METABOLIC SCHEME

All of the chemical phases of anaerobic and aerobic metabolism are interlinked and interdependent. Initially, all of our energy comes from the breakdown of food. After digestion and absorption, the breakdown products are transported to tissues for reconstruction into human fat and protein or for further processing into the simple sugar, glucose. Both the liver and the muscles process this into glycogen for storage purposes, ready at an instant's notice to supply muscle and other tissues

Table 1

Relative Contribution of Anaerobic and Aerobic Processes to Total Energy Output During Maximal Exercise of Different Duration.[a]

Work Time, Maximal Exercise	Energy Output (kcal)			Relative Contribution (%)	
	Anaerobic Processes	Aerobic Processes	Total	Anaerobic Processes	Aerobic Processes
10 sec	20	4	24	83	17
1 min	30	20	50	60	40
2 min	30	45	75	40	60
5 min	30	120	150	20	80
10 min	25	245	270	9	91
30 min	20	675	695	3	97
60 min	15	1200	1215	1	99

[a]Based on the assumption of a maximal anaerobic energy output of 30 kcal and a maximal oxygen uptake of 5 liters/minute.

SOURCE. Philip D. Gollnick and Lars Hermansen, "Biochemical Adaptations to Exercise: Anaerobic Metabolism," in *Exercise and Sport Sciences Reviews,* Vol. 1, edited by J. H. Wilmore, Academic Press New York, 1973.

through a chemical reaction with the energy for production of phosphagen (adenosine triphosphate—ATP and phosphocreatine—PC), the ultimate energy chemical of the body. The combustion of glucose begins anaerobically and, if oxygen is lacking because the activity is very intense, the initial anaerobic reaction continues, leading to lactic-acid production.

It is convenient to think that ATP is supplied to each muscle cell in three ways, forming the foundation for sprint, middle-distance, and distance running, as well as the strength and power concepts of muscle used in field events (23).

1. *Phosphagen (ATP-PC) system.* ATP and PC are always present in muscle in limited amounts. At the onset of any exercise, but more particularly in conjunction with extremely short, intensive activity, the phosphagen system represents the most rapidly available source of energy. This system may also be thought of as the alact (without lactic acid) part of the anaerobic metablism, used primarily by athletes in quick, intensive performances lasting 5 to 6 seconds. It is not as dependent on the oxygen we breath or on a series of complex chemical reactions as are the other two energy mechanisms.

2. *Lactic acid (HLA) systems.* The next step in the energy scheme includes the phosphagen system but, since the activity in this case is not only intense but longer, the breakdown of muscle metabolism by this system will provide substantial energy for maximally paced events up to 5 minutes in length but will last only about 45 seconds if the activity is at maximum speed, as in the 400-m dash. Not only does the accumulation of HLA help the athlete continue intensive activity, but it finally accumulates in such quantities that exercise must cease so that an oxygen-debt phenomenon can effect its recycling during a heavy breathing period following the exercise.

3. *The oxygen (O_2) system.* Slower, less intense activity simultaneously engages the aerobic pathway, allowing further production of ATP with the availability of O_2 assuring little or no HLA production. This mechanism is more efficient than its two precursors and engages metabolic cycles and chains that provide for the complete breakdown of glucose into CO_2 and H_2O.

Most events in track and field require at least two of these systems at one time. Field events like the shot and discus require only the phosphagen system, but the jumps and the javelin may minimally invoke the HLA system as well. Running requires percentages of all of the systems, with the O_2 system participating in ever increasing proportions as the event gets longer.

Anaerobic Considerations

Work below an individual's maximum oxygen uptake produces little lactate (HLA), most of which is dissipated and oxidized by the muscle and its enzymes during the workout. Higher work rates produce greater concentrations of HLA in muscle and body fluids, which also level off, until work is supramaximal, in which case the continued increase in HLA leads to exhaustion. Environment plays a role in acid production, increasing it at high altitude and under warm weather conditions. Small muscle-group work of the variety encountered in upper-extremity weight training usually results in increased production of HLA as contrasted with larger muscle group work of the legs (1,15).

It is a paradox that fatique from intensive activity does not always deplete the body stores of ATP! Two-thirds of the available supply may remain unused, even when the work leads to exhaustion (8). Oxygen supply may be adequate for continued work, but HLA concentrations, sufficient to stop activity, may still be produced, indicating that there is an imbalance between aerobic and anaerobic capacity in the muscle itself (20).

THE EFFECTS OF TRAINING ON THE ANAEROBIC METABOLISM. It is unclear and somewhat disturbing that training does not seem to substantially improve either the capacity or the power of the enzymes that regulate anaerobic metabolism. Training is beneficial, however, because it improves one's ability to tolerate greater amounts of HLA (23). Also, lower acid concentration in trained individuals, working sub-maximally, may be due to improved oxygen uptake (8, 24). Physiologists continue to investigate this perplexing problem but, at this time, any increase in the amount of ATP and the ability to tolerate more HLA in trained muscle are attributed primarily to improved oxidative phenomena as a result of intensive training activities. It is interesting to note that Don Lash, outstanding Indiana distance runner of the late 1930's ran 4:07.2 and 8:58 for the mile and two-mile runs. Jim Ryun, of more recent origin, recorded 3:51.1 and 8:25.2 with a similar aerobic capacity (80 to 81 ml of oxygen/kilogram of body weight/minute). An examination of the sample training schedules of the two athletes during their prime reveals that Ryun's workout procedures were more demanding quanitatively and particularly in terms of quality. From this observation we might conclude that modern training and conditioning programs cannot enhance aerobic capacity any better than the less arduous programs of the 1930's Also, perhaps programs of middle-distance and distance runners should be structured to maintain that capacity with further concentration on the development of efficiency and anaerobic capability. The general concept of this approach would be to stimulate the important body factors by repeatedly challenging the metabolic mechanisms involved that do not depend on the slower delivery of oxygen to the muscles for energy release.

Aerobic Considerations

The metabolism associated with easily accomplished work loads requires less oxygen and, as intensity increases, more oxygen is required until a limit of uptake is reached. In most work a steady state of oxygen uptake is achieved—an indication that physiological adjustments and responses are in balance. Steady-state work may occur with a minimal production of lactic acid in the muscle tissues and blood stream at uptakes of 50 percent. Beyond this point, up to a maximum oxygen uptake, more lactic acid is produced but it can be tolerated, diffused, and oxidized during the workout. If work intensity is again increased, the oxygen uptake will not increase any further, which results in a final steady state and, with aerobic processes maximized, lactic acid accumulates in large amounts and fatigue finally slows or stops the effort. Following the exercise, there is a period of heavy breathing and rapid heart rate known as the oxygen-debt period, when the lactic acid is oxidized and the supply of oxygen in muscle tissue is replenished.

Progressive resistance-endurance exercises over some projected period of time will result in increased aerobic capacity. In other words, there will be improvement in the capacity or amount of oxygen that an individual can attain during rigorous work. Power, the rate at which capacity is used, can be obtained by escalating or continuous work rates, leading to the maximum heart rate attainable in the extended amount of time that invokes all of the aerobic metabolism.

It has been customary to equate improved aerobic capacity with increased transport of blood and oxygen to the working muscles, which is brought about by endurance training programs; most of the improvement is credited to increased heart output. However, recent research developments have prompted physiologists to attribute the slower glycogen depletion, lower lactate levels, greater endurance, and increased ability of the working muscles to extract oxygen from the blood in trained individuals to adaptations within the muscles (16). Physiologists now recognize that trained individuals, when compared with untrained, can work at a higher work rate using the same percentage of maximum oxygen uptake (VO_2 max) or work at the same rate and use less glycogen (16, 28). When the work rate is the same for all individuals, regardless of oxygen uptake, the aerobically trained person derives considerable energy from oxidation of fatty acids and less from carbohydrate for ATP and PC production (16).

THE EFFECTS OF TRAINING ON THE AEROBIC METABOLISM.   Based primarily on increases or enlargement of chemical factories (mitochondria) in muscle, endurance exercise helps to raise the level of some enzymes, increasing the capacity to generate ATP. Some researchers have reported that endurance exercise can adaptatively change anaerobic type muscle tissue to an aerobic variety by increasing the size and number of these components. However, this interpretaton is still under investigation, because of insensitive, analytical laboratory procedures.

While physiologists know that an increase in maximal cardiac output accounts for about half of the rise in VO_2 max that occurs with training, studies indicate that this merely delivers the oxygen to a larger mass of working muscle, rather than more oxygen to the individual cells. An increase in muscle mitochondria (able to extract a greater percentage of O_2 from blood) accounts for the other half of the improvement in VO_2 max. Not so strangely, this implies that there is apt to be less oxygen tension in both the muscle and in the venous blood (greater arteriovenous oxygen difference) of the trained individual during work requiring the VO_2 max.

Holloszy hypothesizes that:

(a) an increase in muscle mitochondria can result in an increase in VO_2 max even if O_2

supply is limiting, and (b) the increase in VO_2 does not have to be proportional to the increase in mitochondria (16).

This statement implies that, after training, a relatively large increase in mitochondria will extract more oxygen and increase the oxygen uptake (but to a lesser extent). This makes a relative degree of hypoxia in the muscles compatible with the increase in VO_2 max.

Aerobic and Anaerobic Muscle

The development of strength and endurance in muscle is made possible by corresponding improvement in the circulorespiratory and cardiovascular functions of the body. Although a limiting factor in any part of this overall system may determine the level of ability of a participant, different metabolic and contractile properties of an individual's muscle tissue ultimately set the limits of performance. Human muscle is a mixture of slow-twitch, red (slow oxidative) and fast-twitch, white types (fast glycolytic) and, although one may predominate in a given muscle group, this proportion may vary among individuals (10). A slow-twitch, red muscle demonstrates more aerobic capability and is better suited for endurance activity than its fast-twitch, white muscle counterpart (anaerobic sprints and field events) (6).

There is evidence that the percentage of the two fiber types cannot be increased by training, but it is not yet clear if one fiber type can be changed into another by the training procedure (3, 9, 10, 11, 25, 27). It is known that talented distance runners have greater proportions of the slow, oxidative fibers, while the fast, glycolytic variety responsible for power performances is more abundant in intensity athletes (5, 10, 12).

Foundations of Training

A broad foundation of quantity-oriented activities provides the base for a pyramid of conditioning before the season starts. As condition gradually improves in terms of weight loss, improved oxygen uptake, lowered resting heart rate, increased strength, power, and other factors that are more difficult to measure, the amount of work through the competitive season is gradually reduced in favor of improved quality.

Regardless of the event for which an athlete is training, general conditioning relative to the event precedes specific training. It is not necessary for athletes in intensity events like the shot put, pole vault, and sprints to run 10,000 meters of slow pace overdistance on a daily basis during the off-season, which may be required of 1500 and 3000 meter runners. Conversely, it is also not necessary for endurance-oriented people to include great amounts of weight training in their programs, as is customary and necessary for athletes in the intensity events. When we review the training procedures of outstanding athletes over the last half century, however, one observation is outstanding: the intensity, duration, and frequency of their work has increased significantly (26).

Intensity refers to the power or rate of doing work and is commonly thought of as the pace at which one runs or the explosiveness with which weights are lifted. In endurance events, heart rate is linearly related with physical work capacity and oxygen uptake. If they are to derive any conditioning benefit from the work, athletes must exercise at 70 to 80 percent of their age predicted maximum heart rate, corresponding to 57 to 78 percent of maximum oxygen uptake (14).

Duration of exercise refers to how long the workout is pursued at a given rate or pace. In interval work, this means the length of the workbouts, which are usually equal in terms of either distance or time [i.e., repeat distances are consistently run in a certain time or workbouts (calisthenics, lifting weights) are performed at a predetermined rate for a specified time]. Caution must be exercised when dealing with this variable, and it should be understood that it may take several weeks for normal, healthy individuals to adapt to the initial stress of training. An important criterion to remember for cardiovascular development is that initially the total work done is more important than the intensity of the endurance activity.

Frequency is how many times a day or week training sessions are undertaken. It may also relate to the number of repetitions in a set of exercises, as is common in weight training and interval workouts. Because of fatigue, frequency in repetitive activities such as in interval or intermittent training should be carefully controlled, particularly if duration and intensity factors are kept constant. The fact that training effects are both gained or lost rather quickly is of equal importance. Regular, continual stimulation is necessary to maintain efficiency, although modes of training can take many forms and variety is very important. Motivation will vary, however, and some athletes may become very disturbed if their habitual routine is altered.

Arguments regarding the relative merits of continuous and interval training continue despite the findings of physiologists. There does not seem to be any question that more work can be done intermittently, at a submaximal intensity sufficient to evoke improvement of oxygen transport and extraction, with negligible increases in HLA accumulation. The question is whether the intensity is sufficient for maximal improvement in performance. When intensity is maximal, the candidate has the choice of working continuously for a limited amount of time or of working intermittently, but cumulatively, over a much longer period of time, and evoke a greater training effect. The following general suggestions for various combinations of interval workout length, pace, and rest can stimulate development of strength, aerobic, and anaerobic processes related to the event (2, 7).

1. For strength and alact anaerobic (ATP-PC) capacity development, work maximally for 5 to 6 seconds, with considerable rest. Rest to work ratio —3:1.

2. For strength, alact, and lactic anaerobic (HLA) development, work at high intensity for up to 45 seconds or 1 minute. Rest to work ratio — 3:1.

3. For development of anaerobic-aerobic processes, decrease the pace and work for periods of 1 to 2 minutes. Rest to work ratio — 2 1/2:1 or 2:1.

4. For development of the aerobic capacity, work at lesser intensity for 3 to 5 minutes, with comparable and preferably shorter rest periods. Rest to work ratio — 1:1 or 1/2:1.

WEIGHT TRAINING FOR TRACK, FIELD, AND CROSS-COUNTRY

Physical and mechanical conditioning of human muscles is based on a synthesis of metabolic principles and elements of simple kinesiology. An example of a common misunderstanding about endurance may illustrate this point. Physical educators sometimes discuss cardiovascular endurance as though it were independent of muscular endurance. Can one exercise the muscles without using the cardiovascular system, or vice versa? Not likely!

Although it is recognized that endurance runners are not inclined to train exclusively with lightly loaded barbells and dumbbells, in a sense, that is what they are doing when they run over varying terrain. Another case in point relates to the sprinter, who is less inclined to visit the weight-training room than the more persevering and disciplined distance runner. However, doesn't the sprinter train for strength when sprinting uphill at challenging grades and for speed when sprinting down gentle, sloping stretches (4)?

Perhaps we erroneously equate the need for weight training with the athlete who uses an implement other than his or her own body (e.g., shot, discus, javelin, hammer, vaulting pole). Conversely, can a jumper, propelling the body as an implement, benefit from formal weight-training work, particularly of the lower extremities, to improve his vertical lift ability?

Evidently a few questions can evoke more questions than answers about the necessarily perplexing nature of strength, power, and endurance weight training. Perhaps in continuing the line of inquiry while examining a few basic principles, we should be reminded of a thought attributed years ago to Arthur Steinhaus, "is a strong man an athlete, or does the athlete become strong because he is an athlete?" (28).

Strength

There are a number of ways to increase strength, ranging from hard labor to handling one's own body weight to the use of isotonic, isometric, and isokinetic contractions. **Isotonic** contractions occur when the length of the muscles changes as the load remains constant. The length of the muscle may become shorter (concentric contraction) or yield under stress and become longer (eccentric contraction). Most strength-development procedures use this concept.

Isometric "contractions" occur when effort is exerted and no movement occurs. In other words, tension is developed but the length of the muscle remains unchanged. In most instances an athlete needs to develop a dynamic instead of this static variety of strength.

Isokinetic activity is a dynamic exercise expedited with the aid of a device that keeps the speed of movement constant throughout the full range of movement, consistently loading the muscle for maximal performance. Kuznetsov also refers to explosive exercises in which a formidable, static resistance is overcome to effect a rapid transition to concentric work (22). The Exer-Genie device is especially adapted to this, while the newer cam-operated Nautilus machines, Mini-Gym, and Cybex devices provide a challenging resistance equal to the changing force applied by the muscle throughout its joint excursion.

Specifically, muscular strength is the isometrically or isotonically measured tension produced by a muscle, and generally it is recognized as the contractile, neuromuscular, and mechanical ability of the body to apply force. The dynamic methods are preferable to static or isometric procedures for strength development. A few important factors that relate to strength are: (1) stretching a muscle slightly before using it results in a more forceful contraction; (2) the greatest anatomical strength occurs at the position offering the best combination of force, joint angle, and angle of muscle pull; (3) unless one is obese, there is generally a good relation between muscle girth and strength; and (4) maximal muscle strength seems to be voluntarily influenced by some psychological factors.

Training will cause muscles to undergo increases in mass and work capacity and is achieved and accompanied by hypertrophy of the thinner fibers, more capillaries per cross section, and more mitochondria. Attendant with the latter changes are increases in oxidative capacity and amount of protein and enzyme activity. Associated increases in glycogen and phosphocreatine are also affiliated with neuromuscular aerobic and anaerobic phenomena.

Power

The force-velocity (strength-speed) relationship of performance indicates that we should train for the speed component if the load to be lifted is small and, as expected, the force (strength) component is enhanced as velocity decreases. Correspondingly, if one is interested in power (force times velocity or the rate of doing work), optimal output is achieved when lifting between one-half and two-thirds of the maximum that can be moved or a load representing one-third of the maximum strength when measured isometrically (30).

Muscle power can be classified as continuous when it refers to running and sprint work and instantaneous, as seen in the explosive activity of the sprint start and the jumping-and-throwing events. It becomes apparent that strength and speed components are influenced by the nature of the implement and the event. Common sense also dictates that, while speed of movement is correspondingly increased as the load decreases when training with weights, it never completely simulates the required speed of movement with the throwing implement itself. This is the genesis of logic for general, off-season weight training, with greater emphasis on specificity as the season develops.

Endurance

It has become convenient to distinguish local muscle endurance—the ability to repeatedly use a specific muscle for a long period of time—from cardiovascular endurance—the ability to provide circulation of blood and oxygen to the muscles. Whether this distinction is helpful or not, endurance is important because both kinds depend on the same energy sources. Consequently, endurance training, whether done by lifting weights or running, primarily depends on and stimulates aerobic energy-release mechanisms.

When an individual lifts weights for muscular strength, endurance is also enhanced. There is a positive relationship between strength and absolute endurance. Absolute endurance is the amount of time an individual can work against a fixed resistance. However, when working against a proportion of one's strength, a strong person will display no more endurance than a weak person and, consequently, there is little correlation between strength and relative endurance.

How Much and What Kind of Weight Work

Although there are benefits for runners, sprinters, and hurdlers, weight training is generally pursued to greater advantage by jumpers and throwers. Notice that, while strength is an important criterion in all throwing events, brute strength will not substitute for rhythm, speed, flexibility, and technique. Soviet research recommends a distribution of power in weight training, emphasizing the importance of locating the correct point at which maximum application of power is required in an event, which usually precludes maximum starting speeds in training exercises as well as in the event itself (21).

Soviet coach, L. Ivanova, indicates a need for continued weight work throughout the season, dividing it equally between the preparation and competitive seasons in a cyclical manner, with changes in the training loads for motivation. In the discus, for example, Ivanova suggests power-oriented work for the arms and shoulders and strength-oriented work for the legs during the competitive season (17). This implies workouts that require technique and strength work on the same day. Most high-school coaches and athletes do not have time for morning and afternoon practices, which means these operations must be combined in one session. Many coaches believe the best way to implement technique in any throwing event is to throw (4), while others feel that drills and exercises emphasizing specificity are necessary. Whether this work can be synthesized into the whole movement may well determine the success in technique development.

The amount and nature of weight work necessary for various events is a continuing and perplexing question. Although it is known that progressive-resistance exercises greatly increase functional strength (with motivation and heredity setting the limits for improvement), it is less certain that the work actually helps the skills of throwing, jumping, or running. If enterprising coaches would keep a log book and frequently conduct tests and correlate improvements in strength, power, and endurance with event progress, it might be possible to proceed with more certainty.

FOUNDATION WEIGHT-TRAINING PROGRAM

There are countless methods of weight training. Many are used in an eclectic manner, with the hope that work-pattern variation will motivate the candidate psychologically to relate the weight work with the athletic event. In each of the following sections describing events, there are suggestions for weight training drawn from this foundation program, with sample weekly workout patterns including strength, power, and endurance exercises. The suggestions are made on the basis of the principles that are discussed in this section.

The recommended exercises should be assembled into a program scheduled for the individual and initiated with precautions relating to beginning loads, soreness, and injury. A good rule of thumb is to start with 50 percent of maximum lifting ability for several sets—15 to 20 repetitions per set—for the first week to help determine adequate starting loads. If lifting ability is unknown, starting with 50 percent of body weight for leg exercises, 35 percent for arm and shoulder exercises, and 20 to 25 percent for torso exercises is a safe recommendation. After determining the maximum, one set/one repetition lifting ability for an exercise with the correct technique, continue the routines with two-thirds to three-quarters maximum load. When it becomes apparent to the athlete and the coach that the load is too light, add 2.25 to 4.5 kg (5 to 10 lb) for big muscle lifts, and 1.0 to 2.25 kg (2 1/2 to 5 lb) for smaller muscle lifts at frequent intervals, until the load becomes reasonably challenging.

The exercises are a generous sampling of activities that can help develop movements and physiological systems needed by track athletes. They are suggested for transfer to the explosive nature of the events and to improve vertical jumping or lifting ability, stride length, leg speed, arm and shoulder power, and the stabilizing and torque (twisting) requirements of torso and hip muscles. All exercises should be worked smoothly, through a full range of movement, on a progressive-resistance basis for flexibility, endurance, power, and strength development.

There are many approaches to how this should be done in terms of number of sets, repetitions per set, and increases in load or repetitions. Several routines can be planned for lifting two to three days a week during off-, preseason, and early season, either working the same muscle groups every session or on an alternating variety basis. **Endurance** work is characterized by light loads, expedited rapidly with many repetitions for several sets and little rest. **Flexibility** is best attained by lifting through a full range of movement in all exercises and, specifically, with moderate weight and slower contractions, including isometric holding at the end of each repetition. **Power** work requires greater loads, with fewer repetitions for two to three sets expedited explosively, while **strength** lifting features the heaviest loads, with the fewest repetitions and sets.

Although heavy-load strength training is usually based on three sets, four to six repetitions per set, more repetitions per set should be expected for light and moderate loads. Additionally, the routines may be varied by using slightly lighter loads for each successive set to keep the number of repetitions the same; by employing an "up the ladder" routine, increasing the load and reducing the number of repetitions; and by countless other variations designed primarily to make the activity more interesting. It is important to stress the muscular system progressively over the length of the seasonal program.

Depending on the initial condition of the individual, improvement should be rapid, and challenging loads will soon be reached. Except where noted in previous discussions (flexibility), always lift explosively relative to the load, and return the weight eccentrically with a slower motion. Spotters are necessary for any presses, pullovers, and back-hypertension exercises. For safety and the best development, torso-twist and trunk-torque exercises should be executed with external resistance applied throughout the motion to avoid a ballistic movement. Avoid "cheating" or mechanical momentum tricks except when using the **plyometric principle** (see page 45). Work the muscle group that the exercise is designed for. Do not consciously employ other muscles—principally the stabilizers or anchor muscles—as synergists or helpers.

Each event requires overall body conditioning expedited during off-, pre-, and early seasons. During the competitive season, weekly weight-training sessions become less numerous, more specific, and quality oriented. All sessions should be preceded with a lightweight warm-up of the major segments of the body. Generally, strength workouts (few reps and sets with increased poundage) may be undertaken once a week with muscle groups that require them, particularly the legs. Power-training concepts (less weight, more reps and sets) should be reserved for the arms and shoulders. An alternating timetable can be worked out by coach and athlete, varying the program to assure recovery, variety, and emphasis for specificity.

The following exercises are generally recommended for the body segments indicated. There is some overlap of muscle groups, since it is rare that groups can be completely isolated.

Hip, Knee, and Ankle Exercises

The following exercises are recommended for improvement of: stride length and sprint cadence; the low pelvic approach or transition period of jumping and javelin events; the vertical lift and takeoff in jumping, vaulting and throwing; glide and drive phases of the shot; the thigh hang of triple jumping; development of the swinging (free) and supporting (takeoff) leg for hip swing, hitchkick, and piking in jumping; and for the rockback and hip lift in vaulting.

1. *Squats,* various percentages (25, 50, 66, 75).
2. *Jumping squats* with dumbbells.
3. *Bouncing split squats.*
4. *Heel rise.*
5. *Jumping heel rise.*
6. *Bent-leg dead lifts* using front, back, and combination grips.

7. *Knee rise* (Hip flexor or leg pull-up) exercise with knee flexed wearing an iron boot.
8. *Leg pull-up* with the knee extended wearing an iron boot.
9. *Hamstring curl* (leg curl or knee flexor) exercise on a bench, prone position.
10. *Knee extension* (quadriceps) exercise on a bench, supine position or sitting.
11. *Abduction leg raise* with an iron boot, while lying sideways on the mat.
12. *Leg press.*
13. *Bouncing split jumps.*
14. *Step up,* alternate leg bench or platform stepping.
15. *Gather* (sinking) exercises. Useful for events like the jumps and javelin, emphasizing the gather or sinking effect with forward hip movement.
    A. *Hip press.* From a clean position, press the barbell, driving the hips forward under the bar.
    B. *Hip split squat.* A squat in which the weight is dynamically dropped and held while in a split position, with and without the "post" leg extended.
16. *Hanging straight leg lift.* Exercise while hanging from a chinning bar. Start with the legs parallel with and resting on a table. Lift the legs up and lower slowly.
17. *Dead weight lifts* (behind-the-back and bent-leg dead lift).
18. *Medicine ball foot push.* Standing or sitting on the floor, push a medicine ball back and forth, using the inner side of the foot.
19. *Medicine ball leg throw.* Seated on the floor and from a bench, throw a medicine ball alternately with each leg and with both legs. The exercise may be executed with and without the arms supporting the body, by placing them behind the back in contact with the floor or bench.
20. *Swinging and supporting legs exercise.* This is weight training with leg weights. The suggestion to employ weights is preferential. The center of gravity of the limb is changed, and the momentum developed does alter natural motion and range of movement. This is true, of course, in using weights with any part of the body and would raise many embarrassing questions of how to develop strength and power!
    A. *Incline extension-flexion leg swing.* Lying face up with the head at the top of an inclined bench, swing the free leg from below the bench (hyperextended hip position) with the knee extended to a position above the bench with the knee flexed, simulating the forward-upward punch desired in the long jump takeoff. Repeat the exercise with the other leg for bilateral symmetry and carry-over value for the leg action found in the hang and hitchkick technique.
    B. *Gym rings extension-flexion leg swing.* The same exercise (A) may be executed from a bench parallel with the floor, hanging onto gym-

nastic rings with one leg resting on a gymnastic horse, or hanging onto stall bars with the inactive leg supported by the horse or a partner.

Exercises for Torque and Rotational Requirements of the Hip

The following exercises are recommended for torque and pretorque positions found in the throwing events, particularly the discus and the rotational shot. The emphasis here is repetition with less load than is generally used for large muscle groups of the lower extremities, stabilization to enlist the correct muscles, and mechanical devices or brakes to prevent possible injury by checking the momentum of ballistic movements while handling resistance.

1. *Leg lifter.* Lie on the floor with the arms horizontally outstretched, holding onto barbells or floor handles. Using loaded iron boots on the feet and with the knees extended, lift the legs up together rapidly and lower slowly.
2. *Double leg swingover.* With similar stabilization, swing the legs together from the right to left, rapidly on the upswing, and slowly on the downswing. Repeat in the other direction.
3. *Single leg swingover.* With similar stabilization and the iron boot on one leg at a time, repeat exercise 2. The unloaded leg is kept on the floor.
4. *Bench single leg swingover.* The same exercise may be done next on a bench to increase the range of movement. A buddy system can be used with one or two helpers restricting the amplitude of movement.
5. *Upright hip rotation.** In a standing position with a loaded barbell on the shoulders, alternately rotate the barbell clockwise and counterclockwise with the legs (i.e., hip rotation), not the torso. Again, either the buddy system or appropriately placed posts should interrupt the amplitude of movement to prevent injury to the hip, abdominal, and spinal rotators.
6. *Squat hip rotation.** Repeat exercise 5 from a squat to an extended position while rotating, emphasizing the hip prior to shoulder forward/upward movement. Again, the twisting should emanate from leg position (hip joint) and movement, not the torso.

Torso or Trunk Exercises

The following exercises are recommended for torque positions in throwing events—particularly the conventional shot put and javelin—and for stabilization of the arms and legs in all events requiring running.

1. *Bent leg sit-ups* with trunk twisting from the floor and on an inclined bench.
2. *Reverse sit-up* (rockback—hip lift) with leg weights on a bench incline or level.

*For best results, do these exercises isokinetically (see pp.37, 39–40).

3. *Straight leg sit-ups* with trunk twisting from the floor and on an inclined bench.
4. *Side bender* (lateral raises) with barbell or dumbbells. Stand with the dumbbell in one hand, lower the weight maximally by bending sideways, and lift by bending in the opposite direction maximally.
5. *Torso twist.* Employ a spotter to check excessive amplitude or swing.
6. *Back hyperextension* from a bench with resistance and stabilization to hold the legs down. Allow the entire trunk to extend beyond the edge of the bench. Lower slowly to the floor, while holding a barbell or plate behind the neck, and explode upward.
7. *Hang cleans* (erect back hyperextension). After a bent-leg dead lift, lower the weight to the extended knees, flexing at the waist with the back straight, and straighten up and lean back maximally.

General Exercises for Torso or Trunk

These exercises develop the trunk stabilizers for arm and leg activity in all events featuring running: staying away from, pulling and pushing off of the vaulting pole; the rockback and hip lift of the vault; and the arm strike in throwing events.

1. *Straight arm pullovers* while lying supine on a mat.
2. *Straight arm pulldowns* (slowly lower barbell to the thighs) while lying supine on a mat.
3. *Bent arm pullovers* while lying supine on a bench.
4. *Erect pulldown* (reverse press) from a machine while seated on a bench. This is the "opposite" of the bench press.
5. *Bent rowing*, also an "opposite" of the bench press.
6. *Supine pulldown* from a machine while lying supine on a bench.
7. *Bench press.*
8. *Incline bench press.*
9. *Hanging bent leg lift* exercise while hanging from a chinning bar. Emphasize lifting anteriorally (forward rotation) with the pelvis. Wear iron boots.
10. *Single and double erect pullovers* with a wall-weightmachine or dumbbells. Start with the arm(s) behind the back, elbows partially flexed, and pull the weight forward/upward over the shoulder, finally extending the elbows.
11. *Single and double erect pullunders* (armlifts). Repeat exercise 10, pulling the weight forward/upward under the shoulder, extending the elbows.
12. *Supine and prone flyaway* with laterally held dumbbells while lying on a bench.

*For best results, do this exercise isokinetically.

Exercises for the Shoulders, Arms, and Wrists

These exercises develop sprint and running arm action; vertical lift for jumping; staying away from and pushing off of the vaulting pole; and the arm strike and release in throwing.

1. *Conventional arm curls.*
2. *Reverse arm curls.*
3. *Military press,* seated and standing.
4. *Shoulder shrugs.*
5. *Back press,* seated and standing.
6. *French* (overhead or triceps) *curl,* seated, standing, or in a "post" position.
7. *Side bender,* with barbell or dumbells.
8. *Forward arm raises* with dumbbells.
9. *Arm swing* with dumbbells.
10. *Wrist roll,* with a roller, using an overhand grip.
11. *Conventional wrist curls.*
12. *Reverse wrist curls.*
13. *Wrist pronation,* from the supinated position, either with a dumbbell loaded ahead of the thumb or using a wrist pronator-supinator machine.
14. *Wrist adduction* (ulnar wrist flexion) from abduction (radial wrist flexion) with the loaded end of the dumbbell behind the little finger.
15. *Wrist abduction,* from adduction with the loaded end of the dumbbell ahead of the thumb.

Total Exercises

1. *Cleans, split and squat style.*
2. *Squat clean and jerk.*
3. *Split style clean and jerk.*
4. *Squat snatch.*
5. *Split style snatch.*
6. *Power dips.* Similar to a high pull-up or upright row with split or squat leg movement to help complete maxium pull-up distance.
7. *High pull-up.* A high, upright row from a squat position followed by a heel rise.

Recreative Sports and Games

Remember that training is a monotonous chore at times and needs to be interspersed with more enjoyable activities that feature running, flexibility, coordination, and agility. Unless the coach and athlete are apprehensive and anticipate injury, to ankles and knees in particular, activities such as basketball, volleyball, handball, paddleball, tennis, swimming, and perhaps surfing, skateboard, and snow or water skiing can occasionally be substituted for related motion experience. Considering the risks and advantages, the choice is elective.

Plyometrics

Plyometrics is a term recently coined by the Europeans for a concept of training that uses preferably overloaded, but extremely fast, eccentric/concentric muscle contractions, (facilitated by the stretch reflex) to obtain a better relationship, (particularly but not exclusively) between the strength and power requirements for explosive action/reaction requirements of intensity events. The phenomena of this principle occur also, albeit to a lesser extent, in the slower but fluid movements of the middle- and long-distance runner.

The plyometric principle purposely makes use of momentum to eccentrically stretch a muscle, with the intention of immediately rebounding and concentrically contracting the involved muscle groups while handling a load. Plyometrics utilize the old concept of weight men pumping an overweight implement with a pendulum motion before releasing it. They also apply the newer practice of depth jumping, useful specifically for jumpers but also used by other athletes; box drills for triple jumpers; and the relatively simpler bouncing, hopping, and bounding activities that are more suitable for sprinters and runners in general (13, 31).

All of these activities are valuable training procedures, but place unusual stress on muscles and tendons. To prevent injury, they should be introduced with caution in terms of quality, quantity, and frequency. Close supervision of novices and experienced athletes during the entire season is advised.

Other Performance Factors

Flexibility, running speed, and speed of movement and coordination are also important in the development of a track, field, and cross-country athlete.

Flexibility, while difficult to define, is highly specific to the event. Mobility of the joints involved may be directly enhanced by ballistic or slow-tension, muscle-stretching exercises. The slow variety is recommended because it can be done without invoking the stretch reflex that is observed in dynamic activity, whereby the body part is abruptly returned to a resting position. Slow stretching may be an excellent way not only to start a season but also to start each practice session, gradually following with the dynamic variety of stretching, which is more specific to the actual performance.

Speed may be loosely interpreted as acceleration, maximum velocity, speed of body segments, or the ability to change direction quickly. The simplest way to develop speed is to become stronger while improving efficiency of movement. Although genetic disposition largely determines ultimate improvement in speed, attention directed to purposeful repetition of skilled movement, while correctly employing the mechanics of kinesiology, will net significant improvement.

Coordination, the ability to integrate the separate abilities in a skilled task, is also specific to the event. Primarily a function of the nervous system, improvement in coordination depends on analysis of the event and correct application of mechanics, while continually repeating the action phase. We might add the phrase, "all things equal," however, it is assumed that the subject is strong, enduring, unemotional, yet well-motivated and athletically intelligent. Shortcomings in any of these departments make the job of teaching more challenging, regardless of the theory of learning employed.

The Pyramid

A broad base of quantity-oriented training provides the bulk of preseason activity. Initially, a *distance* candidate will run many miles a day at a comfortable pace, with different geographical sites providing the main variation in the training regimen. As training continues, the volume of running gives way to more quality-oriented work wherein the pace is increased, or tempo changes of the Fartlek variety allow for a change in stress.

Weight training for intensity-oriented athletes is characterized by numerous sessions at reduced loads and by many repetitions per set, replaced after adjustment to initial trauma by heavier loads with fewer repetitions and sets. As the training progresses further, efforts are intensified to produce more explosive movements, even if this requires a slight reduction in the loads.

As the competitive season approaches, the pyramid shrinks. Continuous running is reduced in volume and supplemented by interval work, allowing numerous, repetitive efforts at specific distances, with either precisely timed recovery periods of walking or jogging or a resumption of work when the heart rate falls below 150 bpm (beats per minute) between repetitions or 120 between sets (7). Weight training becomes more specific, with perhaps one session a week directed to heavy-load strength work and another session to lighter-load, power-oriented work.

Sprinters and hurdlers are not likely to achieve their best performance by adopting either the endurance running programs or the strength and power weight training regimens during the competitive campaign. However, they will profit from both kinds of work, particularly in off-season and early-season work. Early in the season, these athletes seem to thrive on broad-base work featuring reduced quantities of the above which prepares them for ATP-PC- and ATP-PC-HLA-oriented interval work plus flexibility, agility, and explosive exercises and drills specifically oriented to their events. Many of the field events also require these parameters of motor fitness, and they must be included to assure a well-balanced training program.

During the competitive season, the pyramid continues to shrink, with quality effort and variety honing the edge of competitive sharpness. Frequent rest periods and days off should not be denied the individual and in addition, games designed to break the monotony of training without endangering the structure of the human body have a valuable place in the regimen.

Improvements in speed, strength, power, flexibility, agility, endurance, balance, coordination, and body control over several months are possible, but personal improvement may still fall short of the ability of others, trained or untrained, because of genetic differences. What Per-Olaf Åstrand said concerning a wise selection of parents may hold true not only for maximum oxygen uptake but also for other parameters of championship-caliber physical fitness. Furthermore, Åstrand suggests that:

> an increasingly larger number of naturally endowed individuals entering the ranks of competitive athletes may in part explain the gradual improvement of athletic records (2).

Certainly, improved efficiency of technique and motivation are necessary for performance, but basic potentialities cannot be altered with respect to the general population.

BIBLIOGRAPHY

1. Asmussen, Erling, and Marius Nielsen, "Studies on the Regulation of Respiration in Heavy Work," *Acta Physiological Scandinavica, 12,* 171 (1947).
2. Åstrand, Per Olaf, and Kaare Rodahl, *Textbook of Work Physiology,* McGraw-Hill, New York, 1970.
3. Baldwin, K. M., et al, "Respiratory Capacity of White, Red, and Intermediate Muscle: Adaptive Response to Exercise," *American Journal of Physiology, 222,* 373 (1972).
4. Carr, G., "Combining Weight Training and Throwing During Season," *The Throws: Contemporary Theory, Technique and Training, edited by Fred Wilt, Track and Field News Press, Los Altos, CA, 1974.*
5. Costill, D. L., "Championship Material," *Runners World, 9,* 26 (1974).
6. DeVries, H. A., *Physiology of Exercise,* Second Edition, Wm. C. Brown, Dubuque, IA, 1974.
7. Fox, E. L., and D. K. Mathews, *Interval Training: Conditioning for Sports and General Fitness,* W. B. Saunders, Philadelphia, 1974.
8. Gollnick, P. D., and L. Hermansen, "Biochemical Adaptations to Exercise: Anaerobic Metabolism," *Exercise and Sport Sciences Reviews,* Vol. 1, edited by J. H. Wilmore, Academic Press, New York, 1973.
9. Gollnick, P. D., et al, "Effect of Training on Enzyme Activity and Fiber Composition of Human Skeletal Muscle," *Journal of Applied Physiology, 34,* 107 (1973).
10. Gollnick, P. D., et al, "Enzyme Activity and Fiber Composition in Skeletal Muscle of Trained and Untrained Men," *Journal of Applied Physiology, 33,* 312 (1972).
11. Gollnick, P. D., et al, "Glycogen Depletion Pattern in Human Skeletal Muscle Fibers After Heavy Exercise," *Journal of Applied Physiology, 34,* 615 (1973).
12. Gollnick, P. D., K. Piehl, and B. Saltin, "Selective Glycogen Depletion Pattern in Human Muscle Fibers After Exercise of Varying Intensity and at Pedalling Rates," *Journal of Physiology, 241,* 45 (1974).

13. Grieve, D. W., "Stretching Active Muscles and Leading with the Hips," *The Royal Canadian Legion's Coaching Review, 7,* No.1 (1969).

14. Hellerstein, H. K., and R. Adler, "Relationships between Percent Maximal Oxygen Uptake and Percent Maximal Heart Rate in Normals and Cardiacs," *Circulation, 43–44, Supplement II (October 1971).*

15. Hermansen, L., and B. Saltin, "Oxygen Uptake During Maximal Treadmill and Bicycle Exercise," *Journal of Applied Physiology, 26,* 31 (1969).

16. Holloszy, John O., "Biochemical Adaptations to Exercise: Aerobic Metabolism," *Exercise and Sport Sciences Reviews,* Vol. 1, edited by J. H. Wilmore, Academic Press, New York 1973.

17. Ivanova, L., "New Strength Approach for Discus Throwers," *Track Technique, 50* (December 1972).

18. Jarver, Jess "Views on Development of Power," *Modern Athlete and Coach, 11,* No.4 (1973).

19. Karlsson, Jan, "Lactate and Phosphagen Concentration in Working Muscle of Man, with Special Reference to Oxygen Deficit at the Onset of Work," *Acta Physiologica Scandinavica Supplementum, 358* (1971).

20. Keul, J., et al, *Energy Metabolism of Human Muscle, translated from German by James B. Skinner, Vol.7, Medicine and Sport Series,* Baltimore, University Park, 1971.

21. Koslov, Vikor, "Application of Maximum Power in Throwing Events," *Modern Athlete and Coach, 8,* No.4 (1970).

22. Kuznetsov, V., "Speed and Strength," *Track and Field, 12,* 10 (1974).

23. Mathews, D. K., E. L. Fox, *The Physiological Basis of Physical Education and Athletics,* W. B. Saunders, Philadelphia, 1976.

24. Nagle, Francis J., "Physiological Assessment of Maximal Performance," *Exercise and Sport Sciences Reviews,* Vol.1, edited by J. H. Wilmore, Academic Press, New York, 1973.

25. Morehouse, L. E., and A. T. Miller, *Physiology of Exercise,* Sixth Edition, C. V. Mosby, St. Louis, 1971.

26. Pollock, Michael, "The Quantification of Endurance Training Programs," *Exercise and Sport Sciences Reviews,* Vol.1, edited by J. H. Wilmore, Academic Press, New York, 1973.

27. Saltin, B., "Intermittant Exercise: Its Physiology and Practical Applications," Lecture at Ball State University, January 20, 1975.

28. Saltin, B., and J. Karlsson, in *Muscle Metabolism During Exercise,* edited by B. Pernow and B. Saltin. Plenum, New York, 1971.

29. Steinhouse, Arthur, *Toward and Understanding of Health and Physical Education,* Wm. C. Brown, Dubuque, IA, 1963.

30. Travers, P. R., and W. R. Campbell, "The Organism and Speed and Power," *Fitness, Health and Work Capacity,* International Committee for the Standardization of Physical Fitness Tests, edited by Leonard A. Larson, Macmillan, New York, 1974.

31. Verchoshansky, J., and G. Chornowsov, "Jumps in the Training of a Sprinter," *Track and Field, 9,* 16 (1974).

section two

Coaching the Field Events (Jumps)

Each chapter in section two is divided into three parts: science/technique; teaching the beginner; and training and conditioning for the event. The science/technique part presents a simplified biomechanical analysis of the activity and is illustrated with sequence photographs of prominent athletes. Since no two athletes are identical in application of technique, the reader should understand that the biomechanical analysis is the basis for style in spite of minor differences.

Teaching the novice athlete is organized to concur with the analysis of part one and is fortified with illustration to emphasize and amplify more difficult aspects of drills, exercises, and technique. The third part presents a foundation of training and conditioning information for the event, followed by sample weekly programs for off-, early-, and later seasons. These suggestions are designed for the average high-school athlete and are NOT intended to be followed as a prescription, but to serve as a guide for the development of appropriate programs. Because of the singular nature of some of the events and the similarity of training over a longer portion of the season, the calendar breakdown is more general, emphasizing quantity initially and quality later.

Chapter 4

The High Jump

Whether using the straddle or the flop style, the most important phases of the high jump are the approach and takeoff. For success, an understanding of the basic science of these phases, including the mechanics of bar clearance, is necessary.

BASIC SCIENCE OF THE STRADDLE (Figure 5, frames 1–19)

In all interpretations of championship, straddle-style jumping, great leg spring and the innate or learned ability to convert forward momentum (through a flat takeoff into vertical momentum) is basic. Great strength of the extensor muscles of the body, particularly the legs, directed reasonably close to and through the center of gravity of the body in a short period of time, may be a challenge to the novice jumper. The added requirement of applying this force to the center of gravity through a range of motion from a lowered or gather position adds to the strength and time problem. Just as an individual in an upward-bound, express elevator experiences a sinking feeling as a result of the downward pull of gravity, the high jumper increases his or her body weight many times the force of gravity, projecting the body upward at takeoff. If the extensor muscles are not strong and

Figure 5. Rosemarie Ackermann, East Germany. Montreal Olympic record holder at 1.93m (6 ft, 4in.) executing a straddle. Courtesy of Helmar Hommel, West Germany.

fast enough for the explosive effort, the jumper will either buckle under the stress or compromise, using a slower and higher approach, thus taking more time to apply the force over a smaller range of motion.

To obtain an effective impulse or application of force for a short period of time, all available effort should be directed to raising the center of gravity of the body as high as possible before the takeoff leg precisely loses contact with the ground. It follows that, if the amount of time the force is applied is too long because of insufficient strength, the jump will suffer.

The Run (Figure 5, frames 1–3)

Within the physical limitations of the candidate, the purpose of the run is to develop optimum, horizontal velocity, which can be controlled for conversion to directing the body up faster than gravity can pull it down. This requirement applies to all jumpers, regardless of ability, and a seven to nine stride-accelerating run usually proves sufficient. In the straddle, the direction of the run is at an angle of 20 to 40 degrees to the crossbar, allowing enough room in relation to the standards for free or nontakeoff leg activity, as well as assistance in rotation over the bar

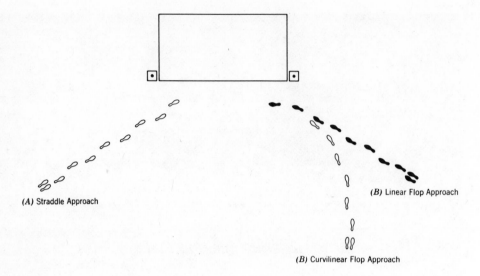

(A) Straddle Approach

(B) Linear Flop Approach

(B) Curvilinear Flop Approach

Figure 6. An eight-stride, high-jump run pattern for a left leg takeoff, straddle (A) or flop (B).

(Figure 6). The last few strides, with the pelvis lowered, are similar to a rapidly expedited "Groucho Marx" run.

The Takeoff (Figure 5, frames 4–10)

As the flexed, takeoff leg is planted ahead of the pelvis, the shoulders react away from the crossbar in a layback position. This puts an eccentric contraction, or a stretch, on the muscles to be used and provides for a greater distance through which to apply force vertically to the mass of the body.

Movement of the arms is coordinated with takeoff and free leg activity for a horizontal to vertical transfer of momentum within the limitations of impulse possibilities. In double-arm action, the laterally rotated arms are brought back together to prevent lean into the bar and then moved forward/upward as the takeoff foot is planted. The powerful push of the takeoff leg is coordinated with the upward drive of the free leg and the arms. The inside arm (closest to the crossbar) is stopped in its upward movement when just above the head, with the intention of bringing it into the body to assist the continued reach of the outside arm in promoting a roll over the bar.

Kinesiologists tell us that the free leg should be slightly flexed to bring it up rapidly, developing maximum velocity with the knee extended when the foot is waist high (2, 5, 16). Whether this comparatively straight leg, with its attendant mass, can continue to develop great velocity the rest of the way up depends on the overall strength of the jumper. Some jumpers keep the free leg flexed throughout the swing to move it up faster but may sacrifice momemtum or moving the body weight up rapidly. Within recent memory, world records have been set with both kinds of free-leg activity.

In sharp contrast to currently accepted straddle-takeoff technique, Ozolin contends that greater speed in the approach with less time for support, a higher takeoff posture, and a faster swing with a straight leg will return the world record to the straddle technician (9). He argues that conventional form, requiring a lowered body position with great leg flexion prior to takeoff, does not effectively "compress the springs" or muscles of the body because it takes too much time from an anatomical position that is unfavorable for work. His argument is supported by an analogy of the higher rebound of a steel ball as contrasted with that of a rubber ball from the same surface. It remains to be seen whether it is easier to adapt the athlete to the style or select a style for the physical characteristics of the athlete!

Crossbar Clearance (Figure 5, frames 10–17)

The impetus to roll over the crossbar after takeoff is acquired prior to this phase. The angle of run, placement of takeoff foot in line with the run, the checked, forward progress of the body with the solidly planted takeoff leg, the transfer of momentum from the free limbs to the center of gravity, and a slightly off-center direction of force through it provide sufficient rotation around a composite axis, running through the center of gravity. Imagine the simultaneous and varying spin of the body acquired at takeoff about all three primary axes of the body, summed up into one average or composite axis of spin that facilitates rotation over the crossbar.

It is possible to initiate movement in the air as long as another part of the body reacts equally in an opposite direction. If the straddle-clearance style is of an arch variety, the hips will move up while the head and legs move down, as the entire body rolls over the crossbar. Most jumpers raise the lead arm markedly while it is diving for the pit, to raise the trail leg enough to clear the bar while rolling over it. Brumel, for instance, cleared the bar with the head and shoulders first, virtually wrapping this part of his body about it, while the hips and legs, held in a froglike posture, were still facing the front side of the bar. At the precise moment the right arm and shoulder initiated a twist of the trunk facing the landing area, while the hips and legs now facing the back side of the bar, reacted in the opposite direction, swinging the trail leg out of the way. (3). While Wilt is quite emphatic that outward (lateral) shoulder rotation, rather than lead-arm lift, is responsible for effective trail-leg clearance, it is the arm action, no matter how slight, that initiates the rotation (17).

Landing (Figure 5, frames 18–19)

Landing is a problem of reducing the energy of falling by continuing to roll as contact is made with the pit, or by presenting as much body surface to the pit as possible.

Figure 7. The "flop" high jump technique of Dwight Stones, USA. PR 2.31 m (7 ft, 7 1/4 in.). Courtesy of Toni Nett, West Germany.

BASIC SCIENCE OF THE FLOP (Figure 7, frames 1–11)

The primary advantage of the flop is in triggering the stretch reflex of extensor muscles to a more sudden and thus more effective extent (17). Eldon Fix, without considering the stretch reflex, studied variables that contribute to high jumping and concluded that the flop is the better technique for candidates with a fast run-up but less leg spring; while those oppositely endowed would enjoy more success with the straddle (7). Carlo Vittori fundamentally agrees with this observation, noting that contact for application of force at takeoff for the flop is about .14 seconds compared with .22 seconds for the straddle (14).

It would seem that strength and time for application of force is necessary for the straddle, whereas the best candidate for the flop should have a naturally explosive neuromuscular system with unusual elasticity, characterized by the ability to react like a supercharged shock absorber. Although power, which can be developed through weight training, is important, the flop may be more applicable to youngesters who are not yet endowed with great strength and to women, in spite of their slightly lower center of gravity, who characteristically have more elasticity than strength. The back to the bar flop with adaptations and refinements, or a yet untested front flip, may be the techniques of the future, with the straddle becoming an endangered species.

The Run (Figure 7, frames 1–2)

The sensation of an outward-pulling, "centrifugal" force in the circular run-approach employed by the majority of floppers is somewhat similar to the feeling a sprinter has when attacking a tight turn on a small, flat, indoor track. The takeoff for the jump is almost perfectly vertical, just as is the reaction of the sprinter, who pulls a muscle while negotiating the turn. Some jumpers may purposely expedite what appears to be an accelerating, low, pelvic run during the last two or three

strides for a "gather," driving into the turn with the run while centrifugal force "pulls" the trunk toward the crossbar. It is important to note that the only way to lower the pelvis (hips) is to either take longer strides or run on bent knees. The latter alternative is detrimental to effective approach procedure.

The general plan employed by floppers using the circular run-approach is based on several circles of decreasing radii with a common point of tangency in front of the near standard, somewhat similar to an upside down letter J (|). Wagner contends that Fosbury, in initiating the style, employed an eight-stride circular run to encourage a mind-set for rotation about the long axis of the body and initiate presentation of the back to the crossbar (15). The curved run, however, does not turn the body about the long axis but, if executed properly, causes the body to land on the landing pad (17). Theoretically, the curved run may be responsible for producing some rotation, but it also reduces horizontal velocity. Consequently, individuals with more speed than spring, who use the circular run-approach, may be able to compensate for any loss of horizontal velocity by capitalizing on the fabled rotational advantages.

Previously arranged check marks (usually measured at right angles on the apron to a dimension, left or right of the appropriate standard) place the jumper in front of the near standard at a 25 to 45 degree angle to the crossbar going into the last three strides (Figure 6, page 56). The curved run is continued while some jumpers initiate a settle in the last two or three strides, bringing the arm closest to the crossbar across the body for development of further rotation.

The Takeoff (Figure 7, frames 2–5)

At three to four strides before takeoff, when there is a tendency to drive up into the crossbar, the tight, curved run is negotiated. At the precise moment of takeoff, the takeoff foot should be planted parallel with the crossbar, which places the jumper in a position between being parallel with and running away from the bar. There should be a definite emphasis on directing both legs along the immediate tangent of the curved running path (i.e., stay on the path, do not drift off!). The checking of the takeoff leg, in conjunction with the curved run and settle position of some jumpers, initiates forward acceleration of the upper part of the body.

The terms "gather" and "settle" should not imply reduction of approach speed, which would reduce the maximum effect of the stretch reflex. Although it is true that the settle flexes joints and stretches extensor muscles for the stretch reflex, there is obviously a point of diminishing return in overemphasized gathering. With few exceptions, close examination of world-class jumpers will reveal little settle in executing the takeoff of flop technique, unless they also have experience with the straddle, in which case it may be excessive and create problems. Coincident with checking the outside takeoff leg, rotation of the inside free leg toward it is countered by an opposite rotation of the shoulders and takeoff leg while presenting the back to the bar.

The impetus at takeoff is provided by powerful, eccentric contractions of the extensor muscles that results from the rapidly checked fast run and change of direction. Eccentric contractions may be described as decontraction, yielding, or stretching of concentrically contracted muscles, with the speed of their contraction contributing more to spring than the mass of muscle involved. Once the demands of the run and change of direction are served, these muscles contract with greater power and drive the center of gravity vertically. At this point, the takeoff may be loosely compared to the old, scissors-style high jump or a long-jump takeoff, but with the rotation about the long axis of the body.

As in the straddle style, arm action is important for lift at takeoff, and transfer of momentum is continued by driving one or both arms upward just prior to loss of contract with the apron. If single-arm action is employed, it is the outside arm that drives upward. Double-arm action would be used in a manner similar to that for the straddle takeoff. In either case, the arms are initially kept rather close to, or in a position parallel with the long axis of the body. This arm action, stopped when parallel with the ground, is coordinated with the powerful lift of the flexed free leg. This action directs the drive of the body up instead of at the pit. It is possible that single, rather than double-arm action, may be more effective. Wilt hypothesizes that double-arm action decreases approach speed, correspondingly reducing the speed of forced, eccentric contractions of leg muscles and proportionately lessening the effect of the stretch reflex (17).

Presently there is some difference of opinion among observers as to exactly what is responsible for the presentation of the back to the bar. Ulrike Meyfahrt, for instance, demonstrated little action with either the free leg or the lead arm. This would seem to support Wagner's contention from observation of Fosbury, that the curved run is sufficient for back to the bar presentation after takeoff. However, many floppers use a straight approach and are able to present the back to the bar. The explanation is simple and employs a basic understanding of the way muscles and joints work together. If a jumper uses the medial-hip, rotator muscles of the stabilized (grounded) takeoff leg, the pelvis and body will swing toward that leg, presenting the back to the bar. On the other hand, the motor-learning apparatus of the jumper may enlist the medial-hip, rotator muscles of the free leg, swinging it across the body, also presenting the back to the bar. The curved run may cause more travel along the bar, increasing the possibility of knocking it off. The straight approach could be the better of the two for some jumpers, allowing greater takeoff speed and less travel along the bar in clearance.

Clearance (Figure 7, frames 6-10)

Following the rotations at takeoff, the upward flight is characterized by a relaxed, passive extension of the entire body. The arms and legs are held close to the long axis of the body, encouraging the continued rotation necessary to turn the back completely to the crossbar. After this action, some jumpers hold one or both arms laterally to discourage further rotation, which otherwise might continue to turn the athlete over too far.

The jumper may look over the shoulder, with the chin tucked in on the free leg side, as the back is arched or kept flat. This head movement causes a shoulder movement that keeps the back parallel with the bar. As the trunk begins to clear the bar, an active phase begins, with the important axis for movement now the one that runs through the hips in a horizontal or bilateral manner. It is important to get the trunk over the bar first and, at the favorable moment, with the heels together, the knees bent, and the passively relaxed hips laterally rotated (to the outside), action/reaction is initiated about the hip axis to allow the legs to be raised out of the way of the crossbar. The movement probably begins in the legs and hips, with the more stable trunk reacting toward them in an equal and opposite manner.

Landing (Figure 7, frames 11-12)

The energy of the fall is reduced by presenting maximum body surface to the pit.

TEACHING THE HIGH JUMP

Since learning the event precedes training for it, initial emphasis should be placed on the style or technique, which will net the best future results for the candidate.

Figure 8A. The function of the takeoff leg is accentuated when the crossbar is low at the head end.

Considering that the arbitrary selection of one technique may not uncover the latent talent of an individual, it is expedient to either employ some test and measurement techniques to determine vertical-jumping ability and speed or to teach each style and leave the decision of which one to develop up to the candidate.

The Straddle

While there are variations of the straddle technique, the following itemized-organizational procedures for a group or an individual will acquaint the beginner with the essentials.

1). Provide a safe landing area with a crosspiece and standards adjustable for low heights. The standards should have pegs, set every 2 or 3 cm (1 in.) apart, on the back side to facilitate quick and easy placement.

2). Line up the candidates in front of the near standard, at an angle of about 30 degrees to the crosspiece, set at head height of the individual. This angle may be increased or decreased later to satisfy the particular needs of each individual.

3). Standing upright about an arm's length from the crosspiece, the candidate swings the extended free leg up as high as possible. The goal is to kick above the line of the crossbar

Figure 8*B*. A crossbar placed higher at the head end of the straddle emphasizes the importance of the roll action.

without losing one's balance. No attempt should be made to clear the bar. If, for psychological reasons, coaches are adamant about this procedure, the same objective may be served by heading or kicking at a ball suspended from a tree limb.

4). Leaning back, with the takeoff leg well stretched out ahead of the body, the candidate kicks above the crossbar with the free leg, coordinated with a forward/upward drive with both arms.

5). Drills emphasizing imitation of the takeoff, flight, and roll may precede or supplement the teaching procedure. A balance beam or rail may be used for one or two hand vaulting from a short run-up, giving the candidate the feeling of the takeoff, roll, and landing. A similar drill, without the rail for the pushup, requires that you take off, roll in the air, and return to the same area with the takeoff leg. When the candidate is ready for a crossbar, it may be set, diagonally low at the head end of the roll, to challenge the function of the takeoff leg. Correspondingly, when the bar is set diagonally higher at the head end, emphasis is placed on the roll action (1) (Figure 8A and 8B).

6). Initially without the crossbar or using a string held at very low heights, the candidate repeats step 4, driving the free leg and arms up vigorously rolling over the bar and landing on the takeoff foot, while rolling the trail leg over with the body. Attempting clearance is a critical phase of the instruction, and emphasis should be placed on the following items, in order, as candidates take their turns.

  A. Backward lean.

  B. Free leg kick and corresponding arm action along the plane of the standards.

  C. Roll over the real or imagined crosspiece or string. No attempt should be made to require kicking or lifting the trail leg up out of the way, which encourages an opposite reaction of the trunk, pushing it into the crosspiece. The feeling of rolling the leg with the rest of the body is important.

7). Substitute a crossbar with the candidate jumping from a standing position. Gradually raise the bar, emphasizing the basic principles learned in previous steps.

8). As a maximum height is reached for each individual, introduce a three-step running approach, emphasizing the settle and layback movements and vertical takeoff.

9). As progress is made over days and weeks, the length of the run may be gradually increased commensurate with the speed and strength of the individual.

Steps 2, 3, 4, and 5 employ the use of a standing, high-jump procedure. Other methods introduce a jump with the run during the first teaching period and may be preferential. In view of this, a brief review of the procedure is presented.

John Dobroth teaches beginners to high jump emphasizing the takeoff as a function of the run (4). This method may be taught in one or two sessions with the athlete employing the full motion of the run and jump in a short period of time. It may be organized in the following manner and is described for a right-handed individual using a left-leg takeoff.

1). Line up the candidates to the right of the landing pad, parallel with the crossbar and facing the apron. Instruct them to walk forward and, with their right foot, to step on a point (*a*) in front of the pit that will eventually represent the takeoff. Continue with three running strides while veering off at an angle of 25 to 30 degrees from the line of the crossbar, and end with a leap from the left foot without looking at that point (*b*) on the apron. Do this drill repeatedly until some consistency is gained regarding the first and second points.

2). Turn the jumpers around to approach the second point, hit it with the right foot, take three running strides toward point *a* (the high jump takeoff), and jump into the pit from a left-leg takeoff.

3). The remainder of the procedure is a phasic learning of bar clearance.

Phase I   A. Standing with the feet about 30 cm (1ft) apart, swing the right leg around the left leg without moving the left foot.
B. Repeat A, but now allow the left foot to leave the ground, empha-

sizing the transfer of weight from the left to the right leg as rotation is executed.

Phase II Similar to phase IB with emphasis on the right foot landing on the spot where the left foot was. Right-leg rotation should create the feeling that the left leg will follow.

Phase III From a lean-back position with the left leg 61 cm (2 ft) in advance of the right, swing the right leg up and around the left (leaving the ground), turn 180 degrees, and land half way between the original standing position. Look at the right foot landing, and swing the right arm in front and across the body.

Phase IV Repeat Phase III from a takeoff of 25 to 30 degrees over a crossbar that is placed on the ground, landing on the pad with the right foot and hand touching first.

4). Repeat Phase IV with the addition of one, two, and three steps, gradually raising the bar.

Frank Sharpley in a discussion of learning the straddle high jump emphasizes coaching points that might be included in Dobroth's approach (10).

1). Use the scissors technique from both sides to determine the preferred takeoff leg.

2). To avoid lean into the bar, lift both arms at takeoff.

3). At takeoff, lift the head and shoulders high and drive up, avoiding any crouched lean.

4). The outside arm (lead-leg side) goes over the crossbar before the inside arm, which should be locked in, close to the trunk.

The Flop

1). Line up the athletes in front of a crossbar set at head height. Have the candidates run a short circular path, accelerating as they negotiate the sharp turn, leaning toward the center of the circle, and running past the bar along the path of the circle. The last three to four strides to the anticipated takeoff point are negotiated at an angle of 20 to 45 degrees. Emphasis should be placed on ignoring the bar and avoiding any lean into it.

2). Repeat step 1, with a shorter run, and execute a pop-up takeoff, swinging the flexed free or inside leg up and across the takeoff leg. Emphasis should be placed on experiencing the rotation from the checked run, assisted by free leg action. Landing should be made on the free leg to emphasize the passive stretch-out of the flight phase.

3). If a straight run-approach is used, the angle of the run should be closer to the acute end of a 20 to 45 degree range. The back to crossbar presentation will depend more on contraction of the medial-hip, rotator muscles of the grounded leg or similar muscles of the free leg. Whether the straight or curved run is used, its speed must be fast to respond with an explosive stretch reflex when checked.

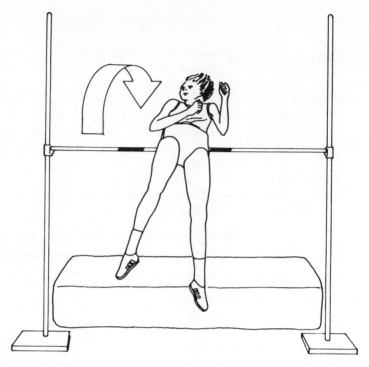

Figure 9. The reverse squat jump, keeping the pelvis high, may be used as a drill to overcome psychological problems of flight while learning flop high-jump technique.

4). Gradually lengthen the run, and continue the exercise without clearance.

5). Without the crossbar, repeat steps 2 and 3, taking off and landing on the back or in a sitting position in the pit. Emphasis should be placed on keeping the legs in a passive stretch-out position after takeoff, with the back flat or arched to discourage the habit of a premature jackknife.

6). Steiner suggests throwing a medicine ball back over the head and, by watching its flight, one should gain experience in the feeling of backward flight (11). Follow this exercise with a reverse squat jump into a pit, keeping the pelvis high (Figure 9).

7). As confidence in this manuever is attained, repeat step 5 with a string crossbar, raising it gradually from easily negotiated heights. The following essentials of technique should be emphasized.

    A.   Extend the takeoff leg and foot maximally, and drive the partially flexed free leg up and across it.

    B.   Keep both legs together after the takeoff in an extended position.

C. Bring both arms in alongside the body, moving them away as initial clearance is gained.

D. Turn the head to the opposite direction of rotation, and keep the chin down while going up and over the bar.

E. Either arch the back or keep it flat, with the legs passively extended, and expedite the back-to-bar or jackknife "frog-leg" position with flexed knees when the back clears the bar.

F. Land on the back in the pit.

8). If some candidates display a better horizontal-to-vertical-component conversion, they may have to be moved slightly closer to the far standard. This positioning is important for jumping over the lowest part of the crossbar.

Some coaches may prefer to start with step 5 initially and perfect the flight phase before teaching the run-and-takeoff procedures without clearance. The sequence can then be executed in its entirety, gradually lengthening the run with the gather characteristic of any vertical jump approach. This procedure is suggested with the understanding that techniques are important only if they can be used. Any procedures can be pragmatically varied to obtain more satisfactory results with individual or group instruction. Each candidate has variations that may seem just as controversial as the original style yet, if the jumping is productive, there will be a mechanical explanation.

FOUNDATION TRAINING PROGRAM FOR THE HIGH JUMP

The following suggestions assume that the beginner has mastered the essentials or basic technique by a learned or felt experience and is sufficiently mature, physically and mentally, to assume the responsibility of self-disciplined work. In many instances, regardless of the style employed, the training is similar but should be adjusted for the motivational needs of the individual.

I. Warm-up and Warm-down

Precede each workout with a warm-up run of 800 to 1200 m. Follow this run with 20 to 30 minutes of stretching and flexibility exercises.

The momentum associated with ballistic (uncontrolled, dynamic) stretching should be developed gradually and never be forced in quality or quantity. The majority of the stretching exercises may be performed statically, holding the gradually approached, tolerable, maximum limit for several seconds. Many coaches prefer this approach, particularly early in the season, to eliminate the possibility of overzealous, dynamic stretching, which results in muscle pulls.

Before weight-training sessions, a short lightweight warm-up that features a repetition exercise resembling the clean and jerk with a squat clean, sit-ups on an incline board without weight, and lateral bending with a light weight dumbbell should follow the general warm-up.

Conclude each session with a warm-down run of 800 to 1600 m.

II. Flexibility-Agility Exercises

Although flexibility can be improved by following good weight-training protocol, an assortment of exercises will be listed that can be used not only as warm-up stretching exercises and activities but also for prolonged flexibility-agility sessions during a workout. These exercises are a valuable supplement for increasing stride length and will also, hopefully, help reduce injury to muscles, tendons, and ligaments. A warm-up run should always precede their use. Not only should each exercise be started with caution at the beginning of a season, but the same precaution holds for the beginning of each session. It is suggested that the initial work be semistatic, slowly going throught the range of motion and holding the maximally attained position for several seconds. Ballistic work may follow as flexibility improves during the season and as warm-up is assured each session.

- **A.** *High kick.*
- **B.** *Hurdler's spread* or split on the floor, and the split also expedited while standing with the lead leg on a rail, followed with the trail leg on the rail.
- **C.** *Wrestler's bridge* from the back of the head. Do this exercise initially with the knees flexed and finally with the knees more extended as condition improves.
- **D.** *Floor touch, with knees and back straight as possible.*
- **E.** *Trunk flexion.* From a sitting position with the knees held down, flex the trunk and attempt to bring the forehead to the fists, which are placed on the floor in front of the exerciser.
- **F.** *Trunk extension.* Lying prone with the hips held down and the hands behind the neck, raise the chin 46 cm (18 in.) from the floor.
- **G.** *Jack spring (V jump).* Touch the hands to the toes of the outstretched legs at the top of the jump.
- **H.** *Agility six-count exercise.* (1) Squat; (2) extend the legs back; (3) extend or scoop the legs forward; (4) turn over; (5) return to a squat-rest position and (6) return to the standing position.
- **I.** *Alternate splits (mountain climbing, prone sprinting).* From a front-leaning rest, sprint in place, striving for maximum split.
- **J.** *Reverse situp.* From a supine position, swing the legs over the head and lower to the floor, with and without the knees extended.
- **K.** *Single (crossing the x) and double leg side-to-side swing overs* from a supine position on the floor.

III. Weight Training

Recommended weight-training exercises are drawn from the foundation program for weight training discussed in Chapter 3. The suggestions are basic, minimal, and arranged to exercise large muscle groups alternately. The selection can and should be modified to suit individual needs.

- **A.** Squats.
- **B.** Straight arm pullovers.
- **C.** Leg presses.
- **D.** Bent arm pullovers.
- **E.** Jumping squats with dumbbells.
- **F.** Bench press.
- **G.** Bouncing split jumps.
- **H.** Single and double erect pullunders and forward arm raises.
- **I.** Bent leg sit-ups.
- **J.** Gather exercises are also recommended for the straddle style, while exercises may be selected from the sections relating to torque and rotational requirements of the hip for the flop technique.

IV. Overemphasis Exercises

Overemphasis exercises and drills are valuable for any athlete seeking improvement of sprint and takeoff action. They require overemphasis of specific movements within gross movements. Minimize the attendant, necessary movements, and maintain an erect trunk in all exercises. The exercises are fatiguing and inclined to cause breakdowns and soreness if done too ambitiously when condition is poor. Start gradually with one repetition per set, over 50 m, and advance slowly to two or three repetitions per set, over 75 to 100 m on grass, with a rest-to-work ratio of about 3:1 between repetitions.

- **A.** *High knee lift.* Accelerate from a standing start to about half speed over 30 m, at which point, the knees are lifted with the thigh parallel to the ground or higher if possible. As the knee is lifted, the foreleg is in a normal recovery position, pointing straight down. Avoid the stiff leg lift of the drum major. Drop the foot very slightly in front of the knee, while keeping the trunk perfectly erect. The lift should be accomplished by the hip-flexor muscles and not facilitated by counterbalancing, backward body lean. Carry this action for 50 m and then float out for 30 more m.
- **B.** *Ankle flips.* This is a bounding type of exercise done with ankle extension and toe power while the knees are in a locked position.
- **C.** *Arm action drill.* Stand, and start moving the arms, gradually increasing the tempo. As a result of correct arm action, the athlete should experience the overwhelming feeling to correspondingly move the legs to keep rhythm.
- **D.** *Rapid Cadence drill.* This drill is similar to the high knee lift (A) with the 30-m buildup at 90-percent effort instead of half speed. Leg action should take place as quickly as possible. Again float out for 30 m to complete the exercise.

    E. *Stride length drill.* Overemphasize the support phase of the stride. Do not do this, however, by delaying the takeoff aspect.

    F. *Relaxation drill.* With the usual erect trunk posture, build up over 30 m and run at 90-percent effort for 50 m with the jaw loose, shoulders relaxed, arms moving correctly, with the knees up, and normal leg reach. Again, float out for about 30 m to complete the exercise.

From the moment the drills are introduced, athletes must do them correctly. As condition improves and the number of repeats are increased, attention must be directed to correct technique, in spite of lower and outwardly directed knee lift, sloppy arm action, and reduced stride length caused by fatigue. The drills are not only designed to teach correct running technique but are valuable conditioners as well.

V. Running, Sprinting, and Climbing Activities

A. *Running.* Early-season running in particular may be of the Fartlek variety, composed of easy runs of 400 to 500 m, interspersed with jogging similar distances for recovery, followed by easy sprints up to 200 m in length with commensurate jogging recovery. This running, as well as progressively faster work later on, may include transition or gather phases injected frequently during the run. This is useful for developing the high-speed, low-pelvis approach that is particularly useful for straddle jumping, and it may also find a place in the style of some flop jumpers.

B. *Sprint activities.* Routines selected from Anaerobic-Aerobic Training for Sprinters (Chapter 13) are valuable for high jumpers. Those that are recommended may again be altered for individual needs. Curvilinear, run-flop jumpers may wish to do as much of this as possible around indoor and outdoor turns for transfer to their event.

    1. Pickup sprints.

    2. Hollow sprints.

    3. Interval sprints.

    4. Repetition sprints.

    5. Run ladders.

    6. Acceleration drill.

    7. Shuttle relays.

C. *Climbing activities.* Stadium step work should progress from a few sets over a short distance to several sets over a longer distance. This work is critical in terms of its explosive nature. If the concept is oriented solely for endurance, its value decreases and the possibility of injury increases.

VI. Depth Jumping

Verhoshanski recommends the idea of jumping as high as possible off of a platform adjustable from .3 to 1.14 m (1 to 3 3/4 ft) and landing on the floor to

Figure 10. The depth-jump concept to develop the ability to yield and rebound.

develop the ability to yield and rebound (12). The time-honored practice of slightly stretching muscle to obtain a better contraction strengthens the body for the lower pelvis or flat-run approach of the straddle and the stretch reflex important for the takeoff in any style of jumping. Using eccentric muscle contraction under stress, with a concentric contraction of the same muscles immediately following, provides for application of force over a longer range in a short period of time. This impulse provides the momentum necessary for all jumping. As in the case of running the stadium steps or doing jump squats, little if any additional weight in terms of holding a barbell or dumbbells is used initially, for fear of slowing down reaction and obtaining slow-reacting strength. This training procedure, however valuable, should be introduced and conducted with caution and be closely supervised. The possibility of injury in the novice as well as the experienced jumper is increased with overzealous attempts from high platforms and a large number of attempts.

A. Jump as high as possible off of a 38-to 61-cm (15 to 24 in.) platform onto a cushioned area and emphasize a landing, yielding with both legs. A target placed at a challenging distance above the head may be used to encourage higher jumping (Figure 10). Variations include continuous work, jumping up to and off of a series of boxes of varying height after each landing.

B. Associated exercises, gradually introduced, feature jumping split squats, yielding with both legs, graduating to landing on either foot. Jumping over high and low hurdles is also recommended.

VII. Plyometrics

The stretch reflex is again challenged in this old form of training with a new name previously discussed in Chapter 3. Exercises for the high jump include:

  A. Depth jumps discussed above.
  B. Horizontally oriented depth jump, landing on the takeoff leg, 2.13 to 2.435 m (7 to 8 ft) from a 30- to 45-cm (12 to 18 in.) high takeoff and executing a straddle or flop takeoff into a pit.
  C. Bouncing and bounding, skipping and hopping exercises in an up-down-yield-explode pattern on the level or down an incline are appropriate.
  D. Endurance hopping with natural and double-arm thrust is valuable for flexibility, agility, and the plyometric concept, as well as endurance.

   1. In sucession, up and down.

   2. Straddle style.

   3. Alternate stride style—skipping (alternate two hops on each leg with vertical emphasis).

   4. Hop some distance on one leg, then an equivalent distance on the other.

   5. Full squat-jumps—off the floor, up and down stairs.

SAMPLE WEEKLY PROGRAMS
OFF-SEASON
Precede and conclude each workout with the suggested warm-up and warm-down.

MONDAY—*Weight training. Select exercises from those discussed in the foundation program, alternating upper-extremity and lower-extremity exercises. Follow the suggestions for starting procedures and endurance, power, and strength lifting discussed in Chapter 3.*

TUESDAY—*Running. 3000-m Fartlek of the variety described in the foundation program.*
Depth jumping from a 38- to 61-cm (15 to 24 in.) platform or overemphasis exercises.

WEDNESDAY—*Weight training. Devise a weight-training schedule and log so that different exercises may be alternated to work the same muscle groups. Additional exercises for the body segments are found in Chapter 3. Some athletes and their coaches prefer to work the upper extremities one session and the lower extremities the next.*

THURSDAY—*Sprint activities. Pickup sprints: 6 to 8 × 100 m or 3 to 4 × 200 m at 80-percent effort with frequent injections of low-pelvic, phase running, particularly if the straddle is the preferred method of jumping.*
Climbing activities. Stadium step work. Start with running up the stairs, gradually substituting hopping from the takeoff leg, the free leg, and then alternating the legs during the exercise.

FRIDAY—*High jump for technique 20 to 30 times.*
Weight training. Either continue on the alternating program, or do the Monday/Wednesday routines together with one set for each exercise.

SATURDAY—*Recreative sports and games. Don't forget the warm-up and warm-down!*

Sunday— *Rest.*

EARLY SEASON

Early-season training features a continuation of off-season training. The emphasis, however, is on increasing the loads in lifting, employing the power rather than the strength concept. A reduction of sets and repetitions is necessary. The running aspect of the warm-up and warm-down may be reduced to 800 m with no let up in flexibility-agility exercises or the lightweight lifting warm-up implied. High jumping for technique is pursued more frequently.

MONDAY—*Plyometrics. Full squat jumps, off the floor, up and down stairs. 1 to 2 repetitions of each exercise over 60 m.*
Weight training. Emphasize strength lifting this session.

TUESDAY—*High jump for technique. 15 to 20 times.*
Overemphasis exercises. 1 to 2 repetitions of each exercise over 60 m.

WEDNESDAY—*Sprint activities. Interval sprints, 6 to 8 × 100 m at 90-percent effort.*
Weight training. Emphasize the power concept in this session.

THURSDAY—*High jump for technique. 10 to 12 times.*
Depth jumping. The jumper will have graduated to a higher platform 50 to 75 cm (20 to 30 in.). Land with both feet together, in a split squat and on either foot.

FRIDAY—*Warm-up.*

SATURDAY—*Competition, followed by a weight-training session concentrating on weak lifts.*

SUNDAY—*Rest, recreation activity or cross-country running as needed.*

LATER SEASON

The quantity of training decreases as the season progresses with high-quality work emphasized. Precede and conclude each workout with a warm-up and warm-down.

MONDAY—*High jump for height with the bar 5 to 8 cm (2 to 3 in.) higher than seasonal best, 10 to 12 times.*

Weight training. Emphasize the power concept, work all segments of the body employing 1 to 2 sets.

TUESDAY—*Sprint activities. Repetition sprints, 2 to 3 × 150 followed by 3 to 4 × 75 m, emphasizing transition phase at various points while sprinting if the straddle is the preferred technique.*

Plyometrics. Horizontally oriented depth jump. 6 to 8 times.

WEDNESDAY—*Technique high jumping. 6 to 9 times.*

Climbing activities. Stadium step work, one set of each exercise: running, hopping on takeoff and free leg, alternate legs on final set.

THURSDAY—*Overemphasis exercises. One repetition of each exercise over 80 m.*

15 to 20 minutes of swimming.

FRIDAY—*Warmup.*

SATURDAY—*Competition.*

SUNDAY—*Rest, recreative activity or a cross-country run as needed.*

BIBLIOGRAPHY

1. Bosen, Kenneth O., "Teaching the High Jump," *Modern Athlete and Coach, 6,* No.5A (1968).
2. Cooper, J. M., "Kinesiology of High Jumping," *Track and Field Quarterly Review, 2,* 104 (1972).
3. Dobroth, John, "High Jumping—With Photos," *Track Technique, 27,* (March 1967).
4. Dobroth, John, "Teaching Beginners to High Jump," *Track Technique, 47* (March 1972).
5. Doherty, Ken, "The High Jump, Transition Phase, Skill and Power," *Track and Field Quarterly Review, 4,* 234 (1971).
6. Doherty, Ken, "The High Jump, Transition Phase, Skill and Power," *Track and Field Quarterly Review, 4,* 213 (1972).

7. Fix, G. Elden, "Contributing Variables to High Jumping," *Track and Field Quarterly Review, 1,* 15 (1974).

8. Labescat, Claude, "An Interpretation of Fosbury Technique," *The Jumps: Contemporary Theory, Technique and Training,* edited by Fred Wilt, Track and Field News Press, Los Altos, CA, 1972.

9. Ozolin, N., "Jumps—The Take-Off Mechanism," *Yessis Review of Soviet Physical Education and Sports, 9/4,* 100 (1974).

10. Sharpley, Frank, "Teaching Beginners to High Jump," *Track Technique, 5* (September, 1961).

11. Steiner, Hans, "Teaching the Fosbury Flop," *Die Lehre der Leichtathletic, 29* (1970).

12. Verhoshanski, Yuri, "Are Depth Jumps Useful?", *Yessis Review of Soviet Physical Education and Sports, 3/3* 75 (1968).

13. Verhoshanski, Yuri, "Perspectives in the Improvement of Speed-Strength Preparation of Jumpers," *Yessis Review of Soviet Physical Education and Sports,* 4/2, 28 (1969).

14. Vittori, Carlo, "Should High Jumpers Use the Straddle or the Fosbury Flop?", *The Jumps: Contemporary Theory, Technique and Training,* edited by Fred Wilt, Track and Field News Press, Los Altos, CA. 1972.

15. Wagner, Berny, "The Fosbury Flop High Jump Style," *Track and Field Quarterly Review. 1,* 8 (1974).

16. Wagner, Berny, "The High Jump," *Track and Field Quarterly Review, 1,* 35 (1969).

17. Wilt, Fred, Personal correspondance, April 1976.

Chapter 5

The Long Jump

Essentially the major sequence phases of the long jump are the (1) approach run or transition period; (2) takeoff; and (3) flight in air/landing (Figure 11, frames 1–11 and Figure 12, frames 1–17). The approach run can be broken down further into the run itself and the transmission from approach to takeoff while the takeoff can be subdivided into the foot plant, absorption of impact, and active lifting of the takeoff. To provide for the best possible landing, a variety of forms adapted for each individual's talent may be used for flight in air. Since it is quite difficult to improve the landing without correcting the entire jump including the transmission from approach to takeoff, a smooth landing is usually a good indicator of the quality of the performance that preceded it.

Approach Run (Figure 11, frame 1; Figure 12, frames 1–2)
The run-up of 36.5 to 42.5 m (120 to 140 ft) should emphasize the best sprinting speed coincident with gaining a necessary, vertical component at takeoff. As a result, the run is a compromise, since an all-out sprint would allow little time for a vertical thrust and a recommended 15 to 20 degree takeoff angle from the board.

Figure 11. Jacques Pani of France using the hang technique in the long jump. PR 8.15 m (26 ft, 9 in.). Courtesy of Toni Nett, West Germany.

The present school of thought emphasizes acceleration over the length of the run-up, with its optimum velocity obtained at the moment of takeoff. The cadence should be constant, regardless of conditions requiring proportinate adjustment of stride to assure accuracy at the board. Wilt, however, contends that the final four to five strides of approach should increase in cadence (stride frequency) to preserve run-up momentum (speed) for takeoff (9).

Included in the run-up is a study of the last three strides (transition period) into the board, which require the trunk to be in an upright posture, with the hips lowered on the next to last stride so that body rotation is decreased in either direction in the sagittal plane, and allowing impulse (force × time) to be directed over a greater distance. This stride is slightly longer to execute the lowering of the hips for the gather or transition. The upright trunk allows placement of the slightly flexed takeoff leg ahead of the center of gravity. This action stretches muscles, which contract explosively when the leg is extended at the knee for an active, running takeoff (3). Bosen amplifies the subtle nature of this procedure, indicating that a good jumper does not purposely shorten or lengthen closing strides to the board but assumes a more upright posture, imperceptibly sinking over the nontakeoff leg on the next to last stride. This allows a slight reaching of the takeoff leg and facilitates forward/ upward sprint drive characteristics (1).

Takeoff (Figure 11, frames 1-2; Figure 12, frames 2-4)

At the takeoff, the knee of the free leg is punched forward/upward in unison with natural arm action for effective transfer of momentum along the projection path. The takeoff foot is placed flat on the board and, in spite of the slight checking action on the body of this partially flexed leg, little horizontal velocity is lost (3). Swinging movements of the free leg and arms at takeoff, coordinated with the application of force to the continually upward moving center of gravity of the body, reaches

a crescendo toward the end of the support phase. If the swing is too late, the jumper experiences a loss of power, since the upward force then is insufficient to overcome the downward pull of gravity. In keeping with the emphasis on horizontal velocity and human limitations for applying equal vertical and horizontal force components to the center of gravity, the angle of takeoff should be 15 to 20 degrees for the best trajectory. Under practical circumstances, this ideal angle is a little large and probably not really possible for most jumpers.

Flight

With the calculated flight of the center of gravity set by speed, height, and angle at takeoff, the remaining problems are disposition of the parts of the body about the center of gravity and the landing. The problem of forward rotation in flight acquired at, and invariably present to some degree after, takeoff must be countered to prevent premature dropping of the legs into the pit. Once the jumper is airborne, the path of the center of gravity cannot be altered. Movement by the arms and legs in flight to change the position of the body about the center of gravity assures that one can remain in the flight path as long as possible before touchdown.

There are three methods of negotiating the trajectory of the flight path for the

Figure 12. Arnie Robinson using the hitchkick technique in the long jump. PR 8.35 m (27 ft, 4 3/4 in.). Courtesy of Toni Nett, West Germany.

maintenance of balance attendant to a proper landing: the **sail, hang,** and **hitch kick.** Regardless of the style employed, a striding motion is executed by bringing the hip of the takeoff leg forward after the takeoff, causing the trunk to remain

upright or lean back. At the peak of the trajectory, the jumper prepares for the landing by lifting the legs parallel with the ground above the flight path.

A beginner would profit from an adaptation of the **sail** style, maintaining a split-stride posture with the takeoff leg, bringing it forward just prior to landing. The trunk is kept erect and does not bend forward until it must do so in reaction to an upward movement of both legs. The simple sail style in which the legs are immediately brought up to the chest after takeoff should be avoided, since it encourages too much forward rotation with the legs quickly falling below the trajectory of the center of gravity, which results in an early landing in the pit. As the jumper descends, the trunk rises, the hips shift forward, and the legs correspondingly drop into (and more often below) the flight path. As the feet make contact with the sand, the hips and knees flex, and rotation continues with the help of forward-moving arms, hips, and knees.

The **hang** style discourages premature, forward rotation by assuming an extended posture, or increased moment of inertia, as the body approaches the top of the trajectory (Figure 11, frames 3-10). After takeoff, the forward-swinging, free leg is dropped back to meet the takeoff leg, which moves forward. At the top of the flight path, the knees are slightly flexed, with both legs held together, as the arms move forward over the head. The trunk is inclined backward and begins its forward and downward movement coincident with upward movement of the legs just prior to landing.

Although training procedures for the **hitchkick,** or running in air style, can be laborious and difficult for some candidates to adopt, it offers the best possibility for delaying forward rotation and executing a piking action, which makes a better landing possible (Figure 12, frames 5-15). Coordinated rotation of the arms and legs, simulating running and windmilling in the air, alternately increases and decreases the moment of inertia of the arms and legs by extending and flexing them, which neutralizes the forward rotation the jumper developed at takeoff. After takeoff, the free-swinging leg is moved back for the first "stride" simultaneously with the forward movement of the takeoff leg, which temporarily postpones forward rotation of the body. The takeoff leg continues its forward/upward motion and is joined by the returning free leg for a one-and-a-half stride pattern. Very few athletes can successfully expedite two and a half strides while airborne. The extending legs move above the flight path, with the trunk corresponding in a piking action. If the hinge or fulcrum for this action is in the hip, with the arms held extended, there is a greater possibility for eliminating problems of premature dropping of the legs.

Landing (Figure 11, frames 10-11; Figure 12, frames, 15-17)

The projected pathway of the center of gravity of the body and the possible length of the jump are determined at the precise moment of takeoff by a combination of running speed and takeoff angle. If hitchkick or hang procedures have successfully delayed forward rotation, the only remaining way the athlete can increase the length of the jump is to move the arms and trunk downward, correspondingly moving the now outstretched legs into, and hopefully above, the projected pathway. This movement is a product of agility and concentration, with little abdominal or hip strength required.

Just before landing, the arms continue their downward/backward, clockwise swing, either outside of or between the outstretched legs and, by a transfer of momentum, move the body ahead of the center of gravity's pathway. At the precise moment of touchdown, the knees and hips flex or collapse to decrease the lever arm of the entire body. The arms are now brought forward counterclockwise to encourage forward momentum and forward movement of the center of gravity, now that stabilizing contact with the ground has been established. As the arms return forward and upward, the trunk is raised and, with forward momentum retained, the athlete walks up out of the pit.

TEACHING THE LONG JUMP

Since the long jump is an event emphasizing horizontal velocity with sufficient vertical component from a single-leg takeoff to project an individual in flight with-

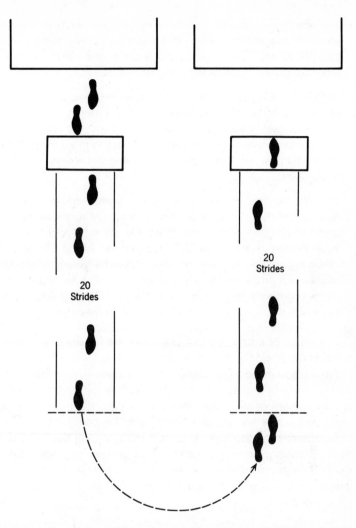

Figure 13. A procedure for establishing the starting position and check marks of a consistent run for the long and triple jump. Start four strides behind the board, and begin the consistent 20-stride sprint pattern from its leading edge, past the instructor at the end of the runway. Turn around, duplicate the starting position, and run, jumping into the pit.

out a premature landing, the following procedure for teaching beginners will start with a short, running approach and strive for basic, step-technique development.

1). Line up all candidates several strides from a generalized takeoff area. Each candidate will run and takeoff from one leg and attempt to "head" a ball suspended 1.52 to 1.83 m (5 to 6 ft) above the ground and 2.13 to 2.44 m (7 to 8 ft) from the point of takeoff.

The dimensions will vary with the size, age, and ability of the candidates. Instruction should be directed to running off the area with the takeoff leg completely extended at push-off, natural, upward, arm action coordinated with this extension, and a dynamic, forward/upward action of the free-swinging leg.

2). Proceed as in step 1, with a string crosspiece set up about 30.5 cm (12 in.) above the pit, midway through the average jumping distance for the group. Keep the takeoff leg back in the extended position, and bring it forward with the free leg right before landing in a pike or jack position. The arms are driven back to move the rest of the body forward as the feet hit the sand. Return the arms forward and upward to get out of the pit without sitting down.

3). To locate check marks and establish a run-up, line up the candidates at the takeoff area and, noting the starting position, (left or right foot forward) have each one run 20 strides in the opposite direction (Figure 13). Station assistants near the end of the run to locate the last stride for each individual (left foot for left starting position, etc.). Turn the candidates around and repeat the routine from the same starting position until the correct position and precise length of run is found for each individual. (Start with the left foot, hit the board with the left foot, etc.). Always include the jumping phase as in step 2, to emphasize the importance of the run that becomes a jump.

This phase of instruction is most important for development of a consistent run; whether the stride shortens or lengthens, the same number of strides must be taken. There is also a need for beginners to either use a mark that is four strides from the start (4 + 20) or into the run (4 + 16) to allow for the shorter strides of acceleration and attainment of the stride pattern for a consistent run. In either case, the length of the first stride and acceleration should be consistent.

As proficiency develops, focus on straightening the trunk during the last three strides (transition period), lengthening the next to last stride, and shortening the final stride to the previous length to develop the concept of a "sprinting gather." Finally, introduce the board and continue the drill, concentrating on accuracy in jumping off the board.

4). As proficiency in the basic phases develops, it may be appropriate to teach either the hitchkick or hang technique to replace the step method originally taught.

Hitchkick

A. Take off as in the step method, keep the legs apart, and land in that position (free leg forward, takeoff leg back).

B. Take off as in the step method, reverse the legs in flight, and land (takeoff leg forward, free leg back).

C. Proceed as in step 2, and bring the free leg forward with the takeoff leg prior

Figure 14. A Reuther board, gymnastic spring board, or inclined plane placed on the takeoff near the landing pit allows the jumper more time in the air to learn and execute the fundamentals of the hitchkick.

to landing. Bosen recommends placing an inclined plane or gymnastic Reuther (spring) board at the takeoff to allow more time in flight for executing movements in the early learning phases (2) (Figure 14).

The Hang
Line up the candidates and follow a procedure similar to the one used in teaching the step technique, emphasizing a hanging-back arch at the top of each jump and the double-leg thrust at landing. The arch should be developed after takeoff, prior to the top of the flight, and held until the peak of the trajectory is reached. To execute the arch, the hips are thrust forward vigorously while the arms and legs, flexed at the knees, move back. The chest is thrust out, the head maintained horizontally, and the arch executed with the pivot or fulcrum in the hips rather than higher up in the small of the back. In the descending half of the flight, the arms, held extended over the head and parallel to the long axis or the sagittal plane of the trunk, are simultaneously swung forward with the corresponding, upward reaction of the legs. As the feet just hit the landing surface, the arms are thrust down and back and returned forward and upward as the jumper flexes the legs at the knee and falls forward.

FOUNDATION TRAINING PROGRAM FOR LONG JUMPERS
Success in the long jump is based primarily on the minimum loss of velocity at takeoff. Most training is designed to help develop maximum, "controlled" acceleration at takeoff from a consistent number of strides over a fixed approach run. The

takeoff requires strength and technique development for obtaining vertical lift without loss of horizontal speed, with the problems of flight and landing requiring less training time.

I. Warm-up and Warm-down

Follow the suggestions for warm-up and warm-down recommended for the high jump (e.g. running, flexibility-agility exercises, and running for warm-down).

II. Weight Training

Follow the suggestions outlined in Chapter 3 for procedures and a more complete list and description of exercises. The following abbreviated listing may be altered to accommodate the needs of each candidate. It is arranged in an alternating order, primarily for the lower body and the trunk, with a minimum of exercises for the upper body.

A. Squats, jumping squats, bouncing split squats.
B. Straight and bent arm pullovers.
C. Forward arm raises, single and double erect pullovers, and pullunders.
D. Heel rise and jumping heel rise.
E. Erect pulldown.
F. Arm swing.
G. Swing and supporting leg exercises, incline extension-flexion leg swing, and gym rings extension-flexion leg swing.
H. Bent and straight leg sit-ups.
I. Split style clean and jerk.
J. Gather exercises, hip press and hip split squat.

III. Jumping or Vertical Lift Exercises

Jumping movements that emulate the movements discussed in teaching the long jump should be expedited on a soft surface and into a jumping pit. The athlete should wear heel cups for prevention of orthopedic injury to the foot while pursuing this work.

A. From a short running start, "head" a ball suspended 1.53 to 1.83 m (5 to 6 ft) above the ground and 2.13 to 2.44 m (7 to 8 ft) from the point of takeoff. Emphasize erect trunk carriage, and never look up at the ball.
B. Proceed as in A, with the addition of emphasis on the forward/upward punch of the free leg. Land in a soft area with the leg still in this position.
C. Jumping runs, in succession. Proceed as in B with or without several "heading" arrangements set up on a level, grass field. Takeoff and swing leg action is accentuated. The legs are kept apart while airborne, with the free leg forward and the takeoff leg back. Land on an extended free leg, take several strides, and repeat.
D. "Free exercise" running. Simulate the running style of a gymnast doing free exercise, emphasizing swinging leg and arm action.
E. Hitchkick and hang drill. Emulate the procedures for the hitchkick and hang discussed on pages 84-5. Use an inclined plane or Reuther board for an

elevated takeoff, allowing more time in flight for expediting the movements. The desired action may also be simulated while hanging onto a high or chinning bar, but this approach lacks the advantage of coordinated arm movement and provides too little transfer to actual experience when there is nothing to hang onto for stabilization of muscular movement.

IV. Plyometrics

The stretch reflex may be stressed and developed by running the length of a short, elevated runway or stage 30 to 53 cm (12 to 21 in.) high. Take off, emphasizing vertical lift, and land 2.5 m (8 ft) away and take off again into a pit for a long-jump landing. Other plyometric drills discussed in the high jump are appropriate, along with box drills of the variety used more exclusively for triple-jump training.

V. Depth Jumping

Depth jumping exercises (chapters 3 and 4) are valuable for the active, give-and-explosion or eccentric-concentric muscle contraction phase of the transition and takeoff of the long jump. Exercise caution and supervise closely for avoidance of injury.

VI. Running, Sprinting, and Climbing Activity

A.   Running. Although cardiovascular endurance is not a factor in the competitive, long-jump event, it is important in being able to sustain practice efficiency and effectiveness. Warm-up runs can help develop the factor, along with the interval-type sprinting and 300-m Fartlek runs injected frequently into off- and early-season workouts.

B.   Sprinting. Essentially, the sprint program emulates that of the high-jump foundation program taken from The Anaerobic-Aerobic Training for Sprinters (chapter 13): pickup, interval, hollow and repetition sprints, acceleration drill, and run ladders. The distance may be longer out of necessity, to help develop the longer run-approach of the long jump. Accelerations are better suited for off- and early-season work over distances of 75 to 300 m on the level, uphill, and downhill.

C.   Climbing activities. Stadium bleacher or stair climbing of a running, hopping, skipping nature, with emphasis on erect trunk and free-leg punch, is valuable training for the swinging and supporting legs. As in the high jump, these activities should be done for power instead of endurance.

VII. Runway Work

Off-season workouts rarely include actual runway or approach work. This activity is better pursued after many weeks of early preparatory conditioning. Off-season running is characterized by accelerating consistently with comfortable, untimed striding. Early-season work requires the same philosophy for about two-thirds the run, with an increase in tempo over the last five to six strides. Under the circumstances, the latter part of the run is a maximum exertion that features consistent stride length with slight lengthening of the next to last stride and a return to normal for the last stride for the transition to takeoff. The takeoff is executed at less than full strength with either a regular landing or a powerful step or run-through.

Later in the season, runway work should emphasize a strong takeoff, using maximum, controlled speed with particular attention directed to the transition period. Keep the trunk erect during this period, and be aware that this *is* the fastest part of the run, in spite of lengthening the next to last stride, with the last one normal in length. Any slowing down to accomplish this results in a weak takeoff, and the practice is wasted. Jarver recommends timing the run, either over its entire length or over the last 10 m (6). Fast, consistent times are an indication of progress. Practice the run under all varieties of weather and runway conditions. The number of strides must always be the same, with the tempo increasing near the end of the run. Slightly lengthening or shortening the run-up, while accelerating, will net dividends in accuracy during competitive circumstances. *Always* finish with a strong takeoff, and again, either complete the jump or follow through with a powerful step or run.

VIII. Pop-Up Jumping

It is difficult to exclude the pop-up type of work, executed with an easy run-up from most workouts. This work, however, represents the bulk of many workouts for some individuals and does not emphasize the transition and active takeoff phases, nor does it recognize the strong accelerating run-up. If the seasoned athlete realizes that the purpose of the pop-up is related to work on flight and landing technique, its inclusion is validated. The chief value of this exercise lies in the practice of landing technique as discussed on page 82.

SAMPLE WEEKLY PROGRAMS
OFF-SEASON
Precede and conclude each workout with the suggested warm-up and warm-down.

MONDAY—*Weight training. Select exercises from those discussed in the foundation program, alternating exercises designed to strengthen specific segments of the body. Follow the suggestions for starting procedures and types of lifting discussed in Chapter 3.*

TUESDAY—*Vertical lift exercises. Jumping runs in succession, 5 × 60 m. Hitchkick and hang drill, 10 to 12 times.*
Running. Sprint activities: pickup sprints, 5 × 165 m, 70-to-80 percent effort.

WEDNESDAY—*Weight training. Either work the upper extremities and trunk Monday and the lower extremities and trunk on Wednesday, or repeat the Monday workout, but with different exercises that work the same muscle groups. Select appropriate exercises from the more complete list in the foundation program for lifting (Chapter 3).*

THURSDAY—*Plyometrics or depth jumping. Depth jumping should be of a less intensive nature at this time (i.e., alternately landing on both feet and on either one). Use low platforms and exercise caution! Plyometrics—bouncing, bounding, and hopping. 5 × 80 m on the level and up and down inclines.*
Running activity. 3000-m Fartlek including 2 × 300 and 4 × 100 m pickup sprints.

FRIDAY—*Running activity. Free exercise running on a gymnastic mat.*
Weight training. Concentrate on swing and supporting leg and gather exercises.

SATURDAY—*Recreative sports and games. Basketball or volleyball.*

SUNDAY—*Rest or a cross-country run as needed.*

EARLY SEASON

Retain weight training twice a week with emphasis on the weak lifts and the swing and support leg exercises. Begin runway and approach work under simulated, competitive circumstances with the sweat clothes off! Too much emphasis cannot be placed on the importance of dedicated attention to runway and transition to takeoff work. Thoughtless practice does little to develop an individual beyond "physical education" condition. Precede and conclude each workout with the suggested warm-up and warm-down. The distance of the running may be reduced with continued emphasis on flexibility-agility exercises and the short lightweight warm-up before lifting weights.

MONDAY—*Running. Sprinting activities, stepdown pickup at 90-percent effort, 300, 200, 165, 100, and 75 m.*
Weight training. Select the weakest lifts and work with the strength concept.
Runway work. 10 to 12 repetitions.

TUESDAY—*Runway work. 10 to 12 repetitions.*
Vertical lift exercises. Hitchkick and hang drill, 10 to 12 repetitions.
Running. Climbing activities. Stadium stair climbing, 5 to 6 repetitions. Running and alternate hopping.

WEDNESDAY—*Depth jumping. Associated exercises, jumping split squats, landing on either foot. 9 to 12 repetitions.*
Weight training. Repeat Monday assignment with the power concept.
Running. 2000-m Fartlek, including 4 × 50 m acceleration drills.

THURSDAY—*Runway work. 10 to 12 repetitions.*
Plyometrics. If a long sturdy bench or platform is available, take a short run off of it, emphasize vertical lift, land about 2.5m (8 ft) from it, and actively take off into a pit. If this is not available, substitute the step drill from the multiple-triple, jump-depth exercises discussed on page 102, chapter 6; 10 to 12 repetitions.

FRIDAY—*Warm-up.*
> *Runway work, 4 to 5 repetitions.*

SATURDAY—*Competition.*

SUNDAY—*Rest, recreative activity, or a cross-country run as needed.*

LATER SEASON

Retain power weight training once a week. Runway work should now emphasize a strong takeoff using maximum controlled velocity for an effective transition phase and active takeoff. Precede and conclude each workout with a warm-up and warm-down.

MONDAY—*Running. Sprint activities, acceleration drill, 5 to 6 × 100 m.*
> *Weight training with the power concept.*

TUESDAY—*Runway work, 10 to 12 repetitions.*
> *Free exercises running on a gymnastic mat.*
> *Depth jumping. This work should now be from a higher platform, 60 to 90 cm (24 to 35 in.) high, landing on each leg alternately, 10 to 12 repetitions. Continue to monitor this exercise closely for avoidance of injury.*

WEDNESDAY—*Plyometrics, bouncing, bounding, skipping, and hopping— 4 × 50 m on the level or uphill.*
> *Running. Climbing activities, stadium step running and hopping, 2 to 3 repetitions—or—*
> *Recreative activity, volleyball, basketball, or swimming.*

THURSDAY—*Runway work, including pop-ups, 6 to 8 repetitions.*

FRIDAY—*Warm-up.*

SATURDAY—*Competition.*

SUNDAY—*Rest or recreative activity.*

BIBLIOGRAPHY

1. Bosen, Kenneth O., "The Long Jump: Hitch-kick Style," *Olympic Track and Field Techniques,* edited by Tom Ecker, Fred Wilt, and Jim Hay, Parker Publishing Co., West Nyack, N.Y., 1974.

2. Bosen, Kenneth., "Teaching the Long Jump," *Modern Athlete and Coach, 6,* No. 4A (1968).

3. Dick, Frank W., "The Biomechanics of the Long Jump," *Track and Field Quarterly Review, 2,* 82 (1974).

4. Farmer, Dixon, "The Long Jump," *Track and Field Quarterly Review, 4,* 234 (1972).

5. Hopper, Bernard J., "The Dropping of the Legs in Long Jumping," *The Jumps: Contemporary Theory, Technique and Training,* edited by Fred Wilt, Track and Field News Press, Los Altos, CA, 1972.

6. Jarver, Jess, "The Most Important Phase in the Long Jump," *Modern Athlete and Coach, 7,* No. 6 (1969).

7. Verhoshanski, Yuri, "The Importance of Swinging Movements at Take-Off," *The Jumps: Contemporary Theory, Technique and Training,* edited by Fred Wilt, Track and Field News Press, Los Altos, CA, 1972.

8. Verhoshanski, Yuri, "The Long Jump and Triple Jump Approach," *The Jumps: Contemporary Theory, Technique and Training,* edited by Fred Wilt, Track and Field News Press, Los Altos, CA, 1972.

9. Wilt, Fred, Personal Correspondance, April, 1976.

Chapter 6

The Triple Jump

With the focal point being the maintenance of horizontal velocity throughout three jumps, this event requires a faster approach to takeoff than the other jumping events. Whether to employ the flat, shallow running approach or the steep jump concept which emphasizes horizontal and vertical components, respectively, seems to have been settled in favor of a compromise that directs attention primarily to a forward jump, with teaching and training emphasizing equal leg strength and power (1). The interruption of summed linear forces by the three jumps decreases the horizontal velocity and presents the greatest problem in the event. The "fast gather" or transition concept necessary in the long-jump approach is either absent or of secondary importance to an increase in cadence over the last four or five strides, emphasizing horizontally oriented acceleration on and off the board.

The decision to teach beginners a natural, single-arm or an unnatural double-arm action, in the hop and step phases, again depends on the characteristics of the candidate. In the double-arm technique, the athlete gathers for successive phases and must concentrate on moving both arms simultaneously during the airborne hop and step. In spite of the last three world records having been set with the double-

Figure 15. Carol Corbu of Rumania demonstrating the "natural" technique of triple jumping. PR 17.12 m (56 ft, 2 in.). Courtesy of Toni Nett, West Germany.

arm approach, the difficulties encountered in maintaining balance and horizontal velocity argue well for teaching the natural method to beginners, introducing the more complicated style later with more gifted candidates. In this section, both styles will be discussed with emphasis placed on the natural method.

The Natural Method (Figure 15, frames 1–18)

Initially, the run, within the limitations of its length (usually as long as the long-jump run), provides for maximum velocity in the last four to five strides to the board. A low-pelvis run or gather at this point used by some outstanding athletes is not recommended, since the emphasis at takeoff for beginners must be forward (Figure 15, frame 1 and Figure 16, frame 1).

The hop, or first jump, emphasizes a forward punch of the takeoff leg, after its fully extended drive off the board, with the thigh held parallel to the runway, allowing the "ground to come up" prior to reaching out, landing on the ball of the foot and "giving" with that leg. Emphasis is directed to an active or action type of landing and subsequent takeoff. A powerful, eccentric contraction arising from the alternate "give'" and extension of the hopping leg, coordinated with normal arm action, supplies the transfer of momentum and continuance of the horizontal component with the vertical thrust of the step (Figure 15, frames 2–8).

The step, perhaps the most important of the three jumps, is enhanced by acquiring a good thigh split during the hop, allowing a maximal range through which to drive the free leg during the step takeoff. Free leg action is similar to that of the takeoff leg in the hop, again waiting for "the ground to come up," while the trunk is held upright. Arm action is an overemphasized, natural sprint style as the lead

Figure 16. The *moving statue* — double arm thrust technique of Victor Saneyev, USSR. PR 17.44 m (57 ft, 2 3/4 in.) Courtesy of Toni Nett, West Germany.

leg reaches forward. Contact is made, with the center of gravity of the jumper over the whiplike supporting leg, which paws back immediately after reaching out (Figure 15, frames 8–14).

The takeoff for the jump is enhanced by the free leg and the transfer of momentum of the arm action. The arms are held up in readiness after the upward/forward punch for the hang style, considered more expeditious at the conclusion of the series, since horizontal velocity has decreased from its initial value. Some highly talented jumpers continue to postpone forward rotation and premature landing by using a hitchkick in the jump.

Moving Statue—Double Arm Thrust Style (Figure 16, frames 1–23)

The hop is initiated with both arms partially flexed in front of the chest, with the intention of bringing them behind the body during the hop. Both arms are then driven forward after the initial running takeoff and returned just prior to reaching out and "giving" with the same leg, which enhances transfer of horizontal momentum with sufficient vertical thrust for the step (Figure 16, frames 1–10).

In the step the arms are returned forward simultaneously with the takeoff, reminiscent of the old double-arm, high-hurdle attack posture. During the flight, the parallel arm action is again returned and forward movement duplicated coincident with action landing and active takeoff for the concluding jump (Figure 16, frames 10–16).

Sanejev has popularized the Russian "moving statue" posture with a pronounced lean of the trunk toward the lead leg during the step, using the action/reaction principle not only to keep the thigh up and maintain forward momentum but also to balance the arm-leg, torque-countertorque occuring in the transverse plane (3). Novices should be careful in adopting this innovation, since Sanejev, in spite of being the recent, former, world-record holder [17.44 m (57 ft., 2 3/4 in.) 1972], displays considerable lateral deviation in the event, moving alternately from one side of the runway to the other, thus decreasing linearly measured distance. In the concluding jump, a forward/upward arm thrust is timed with the final takeoff. The arms, returned during the jump, ideally should be quickly thrust forward again in preparation for the landing (Figure 16, frames 16–23).

TEACHING THE BEGINNER

Taking the beginner through the paces does not involve as sophisticated an approach as the mechanics suggest. A simple step by step approach would feature the following progression (Figure 17):

1). Divide a short runway and pit into several lanes, laying out three transverse/diagonal lines across the lanes at the end of the runway so that the lines (representing each takeoff) are equidistant from each other (2). The lines may be 1.22 to 1.525 m (4 to 5 ft) apart in the right-hand lane, graduating to 2.765 and 3.05 m (9 to 10 ft) apart in the left-hand lane.

2). Place the candidate on the first line in lane 1. Instruct the candidates to jump from line to line in a hop, step, jump sequence, initially using the strongest leg for takeoff. Emphasize the rhythm rather than speed or strength. Encourage an equal time sequence between each jump to either hand clapping or a prerecorded rhythm from a record or tape player. There should be a slight pause in the recording to allow for positioning the next candidate in line.

3). Coaches who wish to start with ratios may decide to lay out the transverse lines with the distance between them arranged in a 35–30–35 percent ratio. The phases of the new world record of 17.89 m (58 ft, 8 1/4 in.) set by Joao Oliveira of Brazil at Mexico City

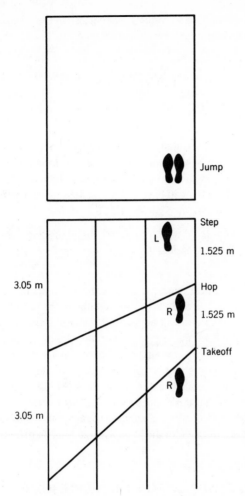

Figure 17. A procedure for progressively teaching the triple jump, emphasizing hop, step, jump rhythm. Place the jumper on the first line in the right-hand lane for a standing triple jump. Progressively move the candidate to subsequent left lanes, introducing a short run duplicating the hop, step, and jump procedure.

in 1975 were 34–30–36 percent [6.08, 5.37, 6.44 m (19 ft, 11 1/2 in.; 17 ft, 7 1/2 in.; 21 ft, 1 1/2 in.)]. The sound sequence is then adapted on a similar ratio with the first subdued to imply a running takeoff and the other two increased in volume for an action /active type of landing and takeoff, emphasizing the forward/upward concept.

4). As the goal is met in the first lane, the candidates graduate to successive lanes, using the same procedures—strength and speed permitting.

5). The coach may elect to delay specific suggestions for step technique or introduce them during the graduation sequence. For the step, emphasize the mechanics of a thigh-hang and the development of a higher long step featuring an erect trunk and naturally synchronized arm/leg action. The eyes should be directed about 30 degrees above the horizontal plane of the head.

6). Because of lack of strength, the point is eventually reached when the takeoff leg fails to demonstrate an action takeoff after an active-sinking landing.

7). As the run is gradually lengthened, with the transverse lines now absent but the rhythm concept retained, the buckle or collapse problem of the landing takeoff leg may again appear. The decision must now be made to either introduce drills to strengthen the legs or to use a controlled velocity approach to allow the jumper time to use the strength he or she has.

8). Arm action has been natural, similar to that used in sprinting. If a coach decides to teach the double-arm style immediately, a simultaneous, parallel, forward arm action should be timed with the takeoff of each jump in the initial phases of the drill. During the flight of each jump, the arms are returned together with the next forward movement timed coincident with the active-sinking landing and the next action takeoff.

9). The final takeoff should be considered as important as the preceding two and not regarded passively. Attention to correct landing with both feet together, arms forward, is important.

10). As in teaching the double-arm thrust, introduction of a hitch leg action in the step may be delayed for the novice, if not avoided. It is suggested that, if the takeoff from the board is indeed horizontally oriented, there will be forward rotation of the whole body. This orientation is continued by the flat trajectory of the hop and the subsequent takeoff for the step. To maintain horizontal velocity, the rotational orientation must be controlled, and the landing leg for the step should be moved forward and then backward with the knee flexed, and then forward again, gradually extending at the knee just prior to touch-down for the jump. Simonyi claims that this "special trick" assures better posture and balance by keeping the flexed legs closer to the center of gravity and simultaneously "activates" the takeoff, leg-extensor muscles for the jump by stretching them before usage (4).

FOUNDATION TRAINING PROGRAM FOR THE TRIPLE JUMP

The triple jump is a strength/speed discipline, the training for which rests on speed, muscle endurance, general and specific body strength, and technique. Most training formats, as well as technique, evolve from the practices of mature, national and international champions. Suggestions for less mature beginners require a modified approach in terms of quality and quantity. Continue the practice of using heel cups while training for this event, as in other jumps.

I. Warm-up and Warm-down

Follow the suggestions discussed previously relating to the high and long jump. During the preseason, this important part of the training session will be longer, with the distance of running decreasing gradually as the season progresses. Always regard this work as important, and consistently include flexibility-agility exercises.

II. Flexibility-Agility Exercises

The major part of a workout, especially during preseason, could be devoted either to these exercises or to the overemphasis drills discussed in the high-jump chapter. As condition and the season develop, they are more valuable in lesser quantity as the concluding part of the warm-up.

III. Weight Training

A weekly preseason training cycle features training for general body strength and endurance. During the competitive season, strength should be alternated with power training, placing stepwise emphasis on specific movements. The suggested exercises are a sampling of a more complete list (See Chapter 3).

A. Squats, jumping squats, bouncing split squats, bouncing split jumps.
B. Torso twist and side bender.
C. Single and double erect pullunders and forward arm raises.
D. Step-up.
E. Bench press.
F. Hanging straight and bent leg lifts.
G. Split style clean and jerk, and snatch.
H. Medicine ball foot push and throw.
I. Bent and straight leg sit-ups.
J. Swinging and supporting leg exercises: include extension/flexion and gym rings extension/flexion swings.
K. Gather exercises: hip press and hip split squat.

IV. Overemphasis Exercises

This work is especially valuable for triple jumpers, enhancing spring technique as well as the great stress incurred in the multiple landings of depth jumping, plyometric exercises, and the triple jump event itself.

V. Running, Sprinting, and Climbing Activities

A. *Running.* Triple jumping requires a more extensive program of quantity running than other jumps. Preseason running assignments should be characterized by cross-country and Fartlek workouts with injections of accelerations featuring short intervals of plyometric concept running, bounding, skipping, and hopping.
B. *Sprinting.* Select routines from the Anaerobic-AerobicTraining for sprinters (Chapter 13). All are recommended and are briefly repeated here: pickup; hollow; interval and repetition sprints; distance-run/pickup; run ladders; acceleration drill; and shuttle relays.
C. *Climbing.* Use the erect trunk, power concept of running, stepping, and hopping up and down stadium steps, bleachers, or stairwells.

VI. Runway and Transition to Takeoff Work

Follow the recommendations discussed in the foundation program for long jumpers, Chapter 5. During the early, competitive season, accelerate over two-thirds of the run and increase the tempo over the last five to six strides into the takeoff, including the low-pelvic phase for the last three strides of the transition, if this approach is used. Later in the season, strive for greater speed, keeping the number of strides consistent. Logically, this will increase the length of the run.

VII. Depth Jumping

Start jumping from an elevation of 30 cm (12 in.) and gradually increase this to 90 or 100 cm (33 to 39 in.) as the season progresses. Land on both feet initially and subsequently introduce variations: jumping split squats and landing on either foot. Follow suggestions from the high-jump foundation program. Exercise caution and supervise this activity closely for avoidance of injury.

VIII. Plyometrics

Bouncing, bounding, skipping, and hopping exercises done on grass, beach sand, or gymnastic mats will stress and develop the stretch reflex important for the approach run and several takeoffs of the triple jump. Do these up and down inclines as well as on the level.

IX. Multiple (Triple Jump) Depth-Plyometric Exercises (Box Drills)

These exercises may be altered in a number of ways by varying the height, placement, and number of risers in a sequence. The adjustable risers should have an adequate base for stability and top-landing area for safety. Use a running start from the floor or a long platform, or a standing start from a riser, landing on or jumping over them, with combinations of stepping, hopping, and jumping (Figure 18).

A. Place several risers in a line for a *step drill.* Starting with a short run, take off with the right leg, clear the riser, land on the left leg, step and takeoff with the right leg again until clearing all the risers, landing in a pit. Repeat with the left leg.
B. Place the risers a shorter distance apart and repeat A with a *hopping drill,* landing and taking off with the same leg.
C. In a similar manner to B, jump on and off the risers, taking off the box and landing with the same leg.
D. From a short run, land on the top of a riser with the right leg and jump into a pit. Repeat with the left leg.

SAMPLE WEEKLY PROGRAMS
OFF-SEASON
Precede each workout with a run of 1200 to 1600 m followed by 30 minutes of flexibility-agility and overemphasis exercises. Conclude the workout with an easy run of 800 m or swimming. On weight training days, precede lifting with a short lightweight warm-up.

Figure 18. Multiple depth-plyometric box drill exercises for the step, hop, and jump phases.
A. Step drill.   Step over the boxes and land in the pit.
B. Hop drill.   Hop over the boxes, alternating takeoff legs with every other box.
C. Hop drill.   Hop on and off the box, landing and taking off with the same leg.
D. Jump drill.   Land on top of the box and take off, landing in the pit.

MONDAY—*Weight training. Select exercises from those suggested in the foundation program, and develop a program to systematically develop all areas of the body.*

TUESDAY—*Running activity. Sprinting, hollow sprints (sprint, jog, sprint, walk—equal increments), 6 to 8 × 75 m at 80-percent effort; 2 sets. Inject low pelvic phases if this approach is to be used by the athlete in the transition period.*

Plyometrics. Hopping exercises. 5 to 6 × 30 m for 2 sets, alternating legs with each repetition (i.e., one rep with the right, the next with the left, etc.).

WEDNESDAY—*Weight training. Either repeat the Monday plan, or develop a routine of selective alternation to avoid monotony. Additional exercises and information regarding lifting concepts are discussed in the foundation program for weight training, Chapter 3.*

THURSDAY—*Running activity. Sprinting—distance-run/pickup sprint—1600 m, sprint 4 × 50 m per 400, jog for rest. 6:15 goal.*

Depth or multiple depth plyometric exercises (box drills). Start from a 30-cm platform if depth jumping. Multiple exercises, 2 × 30 m step drill 2 × 30 m drill, alternate legs.

FRIDAY—*Weight training. One set of exercises emphasizing double arm thrust and swing, and support leg activity.*

Running activity. 2000-m Fartlek including 2 × 300 m and 4 × 50 m at 80-percent effort.

SATURDAY—*Overemphasis exercises or multiple depth-plyometric exercises. Jump on and off boxes, landing and taking off with the same foot. Repeat using the other foot.*

SUNDAY—*Rest, recreative activity, or cross-country run as needed.*

EARLY SEASON

Precede and conclude each workout with a warm-up and warm-down. Reduce the length of the warm-up to 800 m, followed by 20 to 30 minutes of flexibility-agility and overemphasis exercises. Continue weight training twice a week, and increase the height of platforms for depth-jumping activities.

MONDAY—*Running activity. Sprinting, interval sprinting, 5 to 6 × 75 m, 90-percent effort.*

Weight training. Employ the strength concept.

TUESDAY—*Runway work. Run for check-mark accuracy, 5 to 6 repetitions at 95-percent effort. Low pelvic phase for the transition optional with the style of the individual. Follow through with a strong hop and run-through.*

Jump for technique. 6 to 9 times with the validated check marks.

> *Recreative activities. Preferably swimming and diving, featuring sprint-type dives with the back flat to hyperextended, beginning the flutter kick before hitting the water.*

WEDNESDAY—*Weight training. Employ the power concept.*

> *Depth and multiple depth-plyometric exercises (box drills).*
>
> *Depth Jumping. Run the length of a low (30-cm) bench, landing about 2.5 m away, and triple jump into the pit—or—employ more conservative approaches, jumping off of a higher platform (50 cm), executing split squats, or landing on either leg.*
>
> *Multiple depth-plyometric exercises (box drills). step drill, 2 × 40 m. Hopping drill, 2 × 40 m. Pit jump drill, 4 repetitions.*

THURSDAY—*Runway work. 10 to 12 repetitions with technique jumping.*

> *Running activity. Climbing, run and hop stadium stairs, 4 to 6 repetitions.*

FRIDAY—*Warm-up.*

SATURDAY—*Competition.*

SUNDAY—*Rest or recreative activities.*

LATER SEASON

Midseason and final-season training may follow a similar format, varying the elements as need prescribes. Less volume-weight work of improved quality is suggested, with a session that occurs once a week, concentrating on specific strength or power procedures. More emphasis should be placed on runway work and check-mark accuracy to assure the confidence an individual needs to ultimately concentrate on technique while jumping. The background of interval running, and particularly hopping, depth jumping, and riser emphasis should be retained with drills at least once a week. As the season progresses, concentrate on quality instead of quantity work.

Precede and conclude each workout with an adequate warm-up and warm-down. Include power weight training once a week.

MONDAY—*Weight training with particular attention to arm thrust, support and swing leg. Total squat and gather exercises.*

TUESDAY—*Runway work. 10 to 12 repetitions with technique jumping.*

> *Running activity. Run a 2000-m Fartlek including 4 × 100 m (2 at 95-percent effort on the level, 1 at 80 percent downhill, and 1 at 80 percent uphill) and 2 × 300 m at 85 percent.*

WEDNESDAY—*Jumping exercises. (See pages 86-7, Chapter 5.) Jumping runs, in succession, 2 × 60 m. Free exercise running on a gymnastic mat. Reuther board drill, 4 to 5 repetitions.*

THURSDAY—*Runway work for check-mark accuracy. 6 to 8 repeats with an active takeoff and run-through or pop-up type of hop.*

FRIDAY—*Warm-up.*

SATURDAY—*Competition.*

SUNDAY—*Rest or recreative activity.*

BIBLIOGRAPHY

1. Prihoda, L., "Shallow or Steep," *Coaching Review, 4,* No. 1 (1966).
2. Sharpley, Frank, "Teaching Beginners to Triple Jump." *Track Technique, 18* (December 1964).
3. Simmons, Steve, "The Triple Jump," *Track and Field Quarterly Review, 2,* 110 (1972).
4. Simonyi, Gabor, "Triple Jump Technique and Method of Teaching," *The Jumps: Contemporary Theory, Technique, and Training,* edited by Fred Wilt, Track and Field News Press, Los Altos, CA, 1972.
5. Starzynski, Tadeusz, "Triple Jump Training," *Track Technique, 45* (September, 1971).

Chapter 7

The Pole Vault

Perhaps a preliminary item of importance to a discussion of technique is the question of when and how the candidate should learn the event. Flexible pole vaulting requires that the athlete must hold the pole as high as his strength and speed will permit, convert horizontal into vertical energy, and lift the body as high as possible over the handhold and crossbar. Primary considerations are the strength and speed of the candidates and the selection of the vaulting pole.

With the advent of shorter and lighter flexible poles for young vaulters and the more recent prebent implements, manufacturers' guidelines for the weight a pole will tolerate with a given handhold should be carefully considered. In most instances, one pole may suffice for a group of novices who vary little in weight, if the guidelines for handhold and body weight are followed. A heavier person may grip lower, although poles are not generally engineered to accommodate this stress. The novice who selects a pole at less than maximum grip specifications, however, will discover that raising the grip after initial success produces unmanageable flexibility. The same thing will happen as the athlete develops confidence and uses

Figure 19. Tadeusz Slusarski of Poland in the pole vault using the "Eastern" variation wide-hand-hold and high grip. PR 5.62 m (18 ft, 5 1/4 in.). Courtesy of Toni Nett, West Germany.

more speed and strength in the run, plant, and takeoff. Any increase in momentum and leverage applied to the pole will change its operating characteristics.

An inexpensive 8 or 10 foot nonflexible, aluminum pole of small diameter may suffice for beginners, although the technique for nonflexible vaulting requires that one stay close to the pole and employ a scissors-style kick for the turn. Conditioning the novice to this technique may make it difficult to adjust later to flexible-pole technique, which requires that the vaulter stay relatively distant from the pole, with the turn facilitated by the latent torque of the wider grip (5).

The alternatives must be weighed by the coach, but perhaps it is ultimately better to delay instruction until the growth and development of the candidate are commensurate with the stress involved.

. When the coach begins working with a "new" pole vaulter, whether the vaulter is a beginner or a seasoned transfer, it is important to identify and define the terms to be used in communicating. As an example, never employ, "Get your right hand higher at takeoff." Instead say, "Get full extension of the top arm at takeoff." Identification and use of specific terms helps develop intrinsic understanding of the vault by the athlete and prevents misunderstandings between right and left-handed coaches and athletes.

The Pole Carry and Run (Figure 19, [frames 1-17] frame 1)

The ability to hold high on the pole is dependent upon runway speed, a properly timed pole plant, the takeoff position, and the ability to physically shorten the top grip to planting-box distance. With the realization that the planting box is 20 cm (8 in.) deep, nonflexible vaulter, Don Bragg [4.81 m (15 ft, 9 1/2 in.)], employed a top hand grip of 4.215 m (13 ft, 10 in.), lifting his body 80 cm (2 ft, 7 1/2 in.). Andy Steben, an outstanding, flexible pole vaulter [5.08m (16 ft, 8 in.)] of the late 1960's, vaulted 94 cm (3 ft., 1 in.) over his 4.34-m (14 ft, 3 in.) grip (1). The advantage of the flexible pole then, is the ability to hold higher, since the linear distance from the grip to the end of the pole is reduced considerably because of the bend achieved just prior to leaving the takeoff (3). Physical shortening of actual lever length enhances the ability of the pole and vaulter to eventually reach the vertical. Therefore, if athletes grip too high for their speed and strength, the pole will not bend sufficiently, and the pole and vaulter will stall out without reaching a vertical position. A basic formula for the grip height of an accomplished athlete would be twice the height of the athlete plus 61 to 92 cm (2 to 3 ft) (8).

The pole is held palm down with a comfortable spread of 61 to 92 cm (2 to 3 ft) between the top and bottom hands. To allow for maximum velocity during the pole plant and takeoff, the run is negotiated with a minimum of arm action. To reach the desired plant and takeoff points, one to two check marks are advisable, with the length of the run 27.43 to 36.58 m (90 to 120 ft) varying according to the individual's ability (Figure 20). Improved sprint action and balance during the run may be provided by carrying the pole waist high, close to the side of the body, with the tip about head level and directed diagonally across the runway.

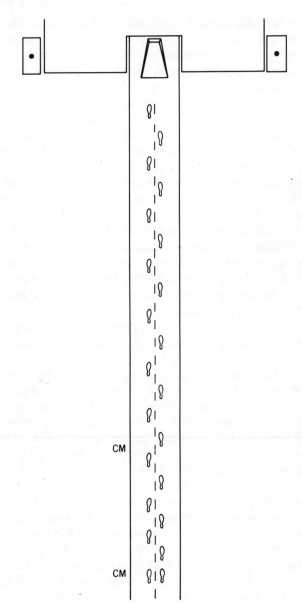

Figure 20. Twenty-stride run-up pattern for the pole vault, with two check marks: the first one at the beginning of the run and the next after six strides.

The Pole Plant and Takeoff (Figure 19, Frames 2-8)

In the last two to three strides of the run, with the elbows directed forward, the pole tip is lowered and allowed to slide into the box. This is accomplished with a curl-press (inverted question mark) or a forward, diagonal movement, which places the pole at right angles to the crosspiece in the center of the runway. With the takeoff foot directly below the space between the top and bottom (lead) grip, the body is fully extended. Soviet and Polish performers have recently popularized an extreme, wide, handhold and high grip with the takeoff directly below a point closer to the bottom (lead) grip. This "Eastern" variation is not particularly new but is said to benefit smaller vaulters who are sufficiently fast and strong. The style requires that the vaulter stay behind the pole for a longer period of time and still be able to emerge from the rock-back into an extension and push-off when the pole straightens out (6).

The powerful, forward-sprinting drive of the free-lead leg, with the wide hand spread providing a differential application of energy, initiates pole bend and converts horizontal energy to vertical energy. If the pole bends, the body cannot stay close to it, and one can keep the body away from the pole by "extending" the top arm and hanging on with the grip, while the lead arm provides relaxed resistance.

One of the principle faults of novice vaulters is to allow the collapse of the lead arm, with the elbow passing the pole, which encourages a premature pull. It is imperative that the beginner realize there will be some give of the lead arm, but that it will and should come back to a more extended position, keeping the body away from the pole during the swing and enhancing pole momentum. The athlete should not plan to bend the pole by pulling with the top arm and pushing with the lead arm. The "extension" of the top arm is accomplished by eccentric contraction of shoulder extensor and elbow flexor muscles, providing a shock-absorber effect (7). The net result of these applications of force produce a top-bottom force couple, the lateral bend of which subsequently allows the body to swing through without hitting the pole while the vaulter's takeoff velocity produces the forward bend (4).

The Swing and Rock-Back (Figure 19, frames 9-13)

The conversion of horizontal to vertical energy initiated in the takeoff is continued by emphasizing the forward drive of the free-lead leg, with the vaulter's center of gravity remaining low relative to the top grip. This has a desirable tendency to slow down the swing of the vaulter while speeding up the progress of the pole (4). Additionally, the longer pendulum of the takeoff, trailing leg begins to drive forward in an attempt to duplicate the free-lead leg's action and position, and the vaulter has the sensation of hanging or being suspended in space.

As the pole begins to reach a condition of maximum bend, the vaulter will bring the legs and hips up, while the arms remain eccentrically extended (stretched), with the shoulder and head under the grip. One should concentrate on driving the knees to the chest. This tuck-back position should be continued, lifting the center of gravity to a position in line with, or slightly beyond, the center of support between the hands. The critical point in the execution of the rock-back is reached as the pole begins to straighten out. The rock-back must be continued at this critical time to maintain the center of mass in line with the center of support and speed up the swing of the vaulter as the pole slows down. If the rock-back is not continued, the vaulter will "flag out" or become perpendicular with the pole. When the pole approaches a straightened, vertical position, the vaulter begins an explosive arm and shoulder pull. The hips continue lifting the extending legs parallel with the pole, pointing the heels to an imaginary target above the crosspiece.

Lifting the Body Over the Grip (Figure 19, frames 14-17)

The pull continues to emphasize the continuous nature of the pull-push, release action with a motion similar to that experienced in paddling a canoe. The unbalanced position of the hands on the pole produces a torque, turning the entire body as it rises toward, past, and above the grip. The lower arm is released only when it is fully extended. The upper arm continues pushing down on the pole and is finally released when it is fully extended. The thumbs of both hands rotate downward and inward at their respective release times to facilitate turning the elbows outward and away from the crossbar. At final release, the chin drops to the chest to aid in keeping the trunk concave relative to the crossbar.

Although the continued path of the center of gravity is of paramount importance, there is the related matter of avoiding the crossbar with the legs, hips, chest and, particularly, the arms.

A few vaulters prefer a jackknife style, where the center of gravity is sometimes outside the body and either in or slightly above the crosspiece. With the trunk and legs both below the bar at a precise moment, it can be appreciated that the body is raised relative to the center of gravity. Timing must be very precise to avoid brushing the crosspiece with the chest or arms. The athlete who uses this technique must delay sweeping the arms upward to avoid pushing the chest down into the crossbar. After the delay, the upward sweep of the arms will push the chest forward, but rotation of the body about a lateral axis through the center of gravity will put it a safe distance from the bar.

Although the center of gravity must be lifted higher in the flyaway styles, they require less precise timing. With the hips and legs in an extended position, the body follows the center of gravity in the modified flyaway where the sensation is one of being parallel to the ground. In the ultimate flyaway style, the arms and trunk are raised with the hips and legs correspondingly reacting upward. The center of gravity must be lifted highest in this technique, but the problem of timing to avoid hitting the crosspiece with limbs is reduced.

The Landing

The vaulter should present the greatest surface area possible to the landing pit. To avoid a back somersault, unless one is desired, a stretched-out position after clearance will slow down any rotation and dissipate the shock of landing.

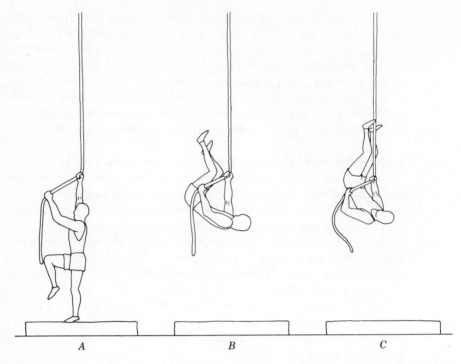

A   *B*   *C*

Figure 21. An exercise for introducing and simulating the feel of the body pendulum in the pole-vault event on a stationary rope.
(A)   Grip the rope above the head, simulating the extended takeoff position.
(B)   Drive the knee of the free leg to the chest, following and duplicating this action with the takeoff leg.
(C)   After a maximum rockback, lift the hips, extend the body upward, and pull. Do not release the grip from the rope, allow the legs to return to the floor. (Please see text pages 114-5 for further information regarding the letter code).

TEACHING THE POLE VAULT

Following are a series of step by step procedures of increasing complexity designed to help beginners learn the pole vault. Each stage demands an escalation of understanding, strength, timing, and agility from the candidate.

1). The pole vault involves a double-pendulum action, with the body pendulum rotating around the grip and the man/pole pendulum rotating around the box. The speed of the two pendulum actions must be coordinated per individual to prevent stalling or coming up short of the crosspiece. If the takeoff-trailing leg is correctly extended, it results in a desirable slow body-fast pole pendulum. The purpose of the following exercise is to introduce and simulate the feel of the body pendulum to the candidate (Figure 21). Place gymnastic pads around the base of a climbing rope.

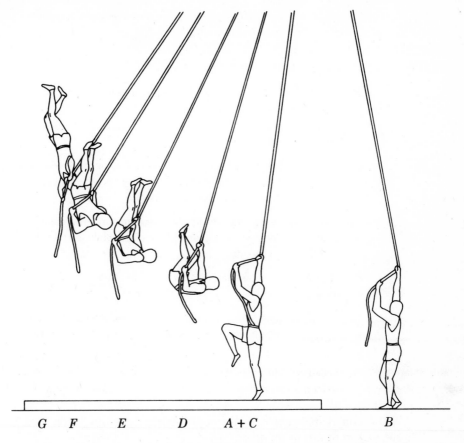

G   F   E   D   A + C   B

Figure 22. A dynamic pendulum exercise on a moving rope simulating the pendulum action of the pole. (*A*) Grip the rope, (*B*) move backward two or three strides and, from a run, take off at (*C*). Swing from (*D*) through (*F*) executing a rockback, emphasizing lead leg action. (*G*) Turn and invert the body, and return to (*A*) without releasing the rope. (Please see text pages 115-6 for further information regarding the letter code.)

    A.   Grip the rope above the head, simulating the extended takeoff position.

    B.   Drive the knee of the free-lead leg to the chest, maintaining a longer lever or pendulum with the takeoff-trail leg. This keeps the vaulter from getting up on the rope or pole too soon, which would reduce pole momentum and encourage a premature pull.

    C.   After a maximum rockback, lift hips, extend the body upward, and pull.

    D.   Do not release the grip from the rope; allow the legs to return to the floor.

2). Once the candidate has mastered the body-pendulum action on the stationary rope, it is time to add a simulation of the pendulum action of the pole on a moving rope. Check the anchoring of the rope to be sure it is secure and safe. Place gymnastic pads along the intended path of the swinging rope (Figure 22).

A. Grip the rope, simulating the extended takeoff position from a location that will be the takeoff point for the exercise.

B. Back up to a starting position, several feet in front of the position described in A, and grip the rope. The distance from the starting point to the takeoff point should be long enough to be negotiated in two or three short, powerful, accelerating strides.

C. Run to the takeoff point described in A, driving the free-lead leg powerfully forward and extending maximally from the takeoff trail leg and foot. The top grip arm should be fully extended upward.

D. As the rope swings and lifts the body forward and upward, initiate the rock-back by driving the free-lead leg toward the chest while the takeoff-trail leg remains slightly more extended.

E. The rock-back is continued as the hips are lifted and extension of the body is initiated.

F. As the rope nears the extent of its swing, the final phase of hip lift and body extension is timed with initiation of the pull by the widely spaced arms.

G. A few degrees of swing and fractions of a second later, the chest has been pulled past the rope, the body inverted as a result of the torque of the widely spaced arms, and an attempt is made to emulate pushing off the rope.

The grip is maintained as the rope begins its return swing, and the legs are allowed to return to the floor.

3). After the rope work has been mastered, it is time to move to the pole-vault facilities. Although it may or may not be advisable to use a crossbar initially, it is important to begin using it as soon as possible. Start the bar low, and work it up rapidly to challenging heights ' (Figure 23).

A. The candidate grips the pole in a takeoff attitude (full extension) at the 1.83 to 2.44 m (6 to 8 ft) level while it is held in the box by the coach.

B. Starting from a standing position, the candidate drives the free-lead leg knee forward as the coach assists by lifting the vaulter, by means of the pole, upward and toward the pit.

C. As the coach pulls the pole forward, the candidate executes the rock-back, hip-lift, pull, turn, and release.

4). When the initial exercise on the pole has been mastered, allow the candidate to run into the takeoff with the pole. The coach may then assist the vaulter/pole system through steps B and C as in the previous exercise.

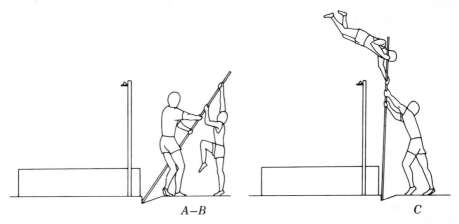

Figure 23. A dynamic stabilization exercise for the pole vault. (*A*) The vaulter grips the pole in a fully extended takeoff position at a grip of 1.83 to 2.44 m (6 to 8 ft). (*B*) With the coach lifting the vaulter/pole forward/upward, the candidate drives the free leg forward. (*C*) Vaulter executes rockback, hip lift, pull, turn, and release with the coach continuing to push the pole forward.

5). As skill and confidence increase, the coach will notice a diminishing need to assist the candidate through the vault.

6). The candidate walks through the planting action from five to six steps out, using a curl-press action in the final one and one-half to three steps, to coordinate the run with the pole plant and takeoff. Repeat over and over again, gradually increasing the length of approach as speed increases. The coach assists the candidate through the vault, as in steps 3, 4, and 5, decreasing assistance as need diminishes.

7). When the candidate is self sufficient, allow him to move the grip above the 1.83- to 2.44-m (6 to 8 ft) level, lengthen the run, and establish check marks.

8). After step 7, when the candidate has established a run and check mark, a "maximum" grip, and a powerful, consistent takeoff, it is appropriate to move him onto a pole with the potential bend when used properly (i.e., one formulated for the candidate's speed, weight, and handhold). Do not allow the candidate to use too light a pole just for the sake of bend.

Correcting Vault Problems

Experienced as well as beginning vaulters may display faults apparent to even the untrained observer. Generally, however, the human eye cannot detect what a home movie camera will reveal when slow motion or slow projection of normal speed films, taken from the front, side, and back of the vaulter are viewed. Many of the problems that occur while the vaulter is off the ground are developed on the runway, particularly before and during the plant and takeoff. Unfortunately, in the next to last stride, the shoulders must be in line with the sagittal plane to plant

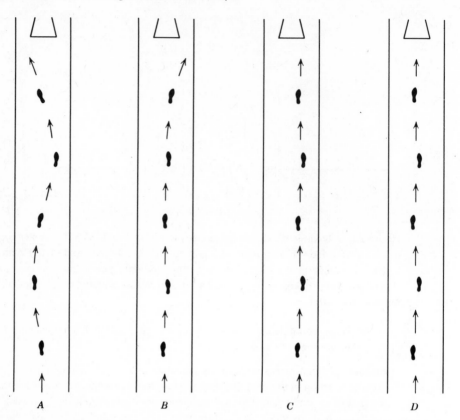

Figure 24. Correct and incorrect runway pole and body alignment as viewed in a transverse plane.

(*A*) Zig-zag run to center of runway causing takeoff to the left.

(*B*) Veer run causing takeoff to the right.

(*C*) Straight-ahead/off-center run resulting in a left torque (counterclockwise spin of the body about the pole).

(*D*) Correct run and takeoff.

the pole. This has a tendency to rotate the hips in the opposite direction, causing the free-lead leg to be pulled across the body. If this is not controlled, the takeoff will be off-balance (2).

1). If the pole or body of the vaulter are not perpendicular with the crossbar, the misalignment can be traced to the run, the takeoff, or the direction of drive of the free-lead knee at takeoff.

   A   The final steps of the run can result in pole and body misalignment if they do not remain in a vertical plane perpendicular to the center of the runway (Figure 24).

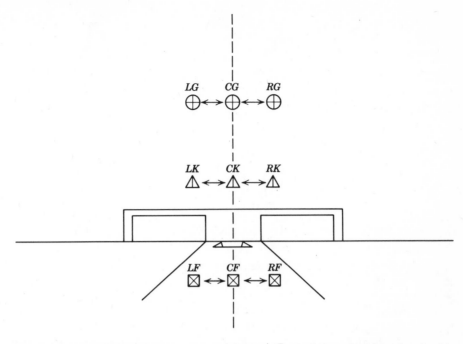

Figure 25. Correct positions (C = center of runway) for (G) top-grip hand, (K) free-lead leg knee, and (F) trail-takeoff foot at take-off as viewed in a frontal plane. Any other position (L = left, R = right) of the three variables will result in 26 possibilities for body/pole misalignment.

B. Takeoff (Figure 25). While the approach steps determine the position and vector of the takeoff step and swing of the free-lead leg, the location of the top-grip hand must also be considered. The elbow of this arm must be fully extended above a centered run and takeoff step to place the grip hand in the correct position.

   Depending on the combination of variables, any takeoff relationship between the top-grip hand, free-lead leg knee, and trail-takeoff foot that deviates from a center of the runway position (CG/CK/CF—center top-grip hand/center, free-lead leg knee/center, trail-takeoff foot) with action directed within a plane that bisects the runway will result in 26 possibilities of body or pole misalignment. Some of the confounding combinations would required unusual agility on the part of the vaulter. Normally such agility, if employed correctly, would spell success. Embarrassing linear vectors (direction of resultant forces) and torque (rotational force) will throw the vaulter in varying degrees to the right or left, with or without adverse spin about the pole.

C. Direction of free-lead knee drive at takeoff (Figure 26). Misalignment of the body relative to the pole may occur when the free-lead leg-knee drive is not straight

A B

Figure 26. Direction of knee drive at takeoff.
(*A*) Correct free (lead) leg drive at takeoff.
(*B*) "Inside" drive of free leg resulting in undesirable torque (turning force or spin) at takeoff.

ahead and within the center plane of the runway. Faulty knee drive is sometimes directed to the "outside," but usually to the "inside" (i.e., across the chest), resulting in undesirable torque at takeoff.

2). If the swing is weak, or the pole rubs against the vaulter, or visible jerk in movement is detected:

A. The takeoff is either too close or too far from the planting box. X marks the ideal takeof spot (Figure 27A and B).

B. The top arm is not extended and free-lead, leg-knee drive is weak (Figure 27C).

If the above items are properly executed, errors that persist relate to faulty movement during the period off the ground.

1). If the vaulter stalls out, recommend:

A. A delay in hip lift or any pulling action and a continuation of the rock-back. Keep the head forward to avoid a righting reflex, and encourage space awareness (Figure 19, frame 11, Figure 28A).

B. Eliminate a mechanical, push-pull action with the arms during and after takeoff, accentuate full extension of the body and free-lead leg-knee drive after takeoff, with continuing knee drive through the hang (Figure 28B).

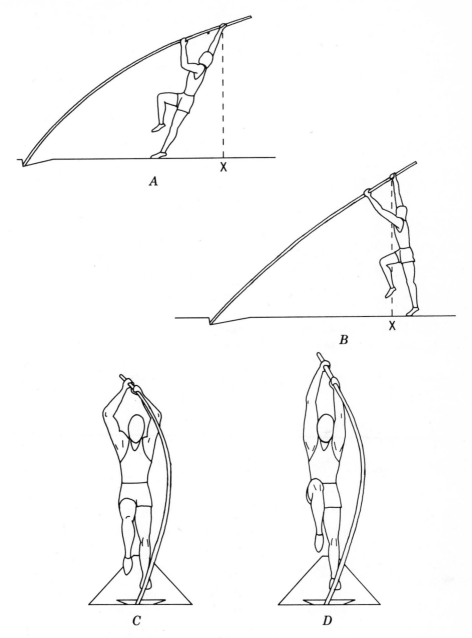

Figure 27. A weak swing, pole rubbing, and jerking tendency may be the result of:
(A) Takeoff too close to planting box.
(B) Takeoff too far from the ideal takeoff position (X); or
(C) Incomplete extension at the elbow and shoulder, with weak knee drive after takeoff.
(D) Correct takeoff alignment.

A   B   2 A

Figure 28. Stalling out may be a result of (A) premature pull and hip lift from the rockback; or (B) using a "push-pull" action at, and after takeoff, which eliminates required full extension of the top grip arm.
(2A) "Flagging out" or hitting the bar with the legs may be due to a premature pull and turn, or hurried hip lift.

2). Continually "flagging out" or hitting the bar with the legs may be eliminated by advising (Figure 28-2A):

A. Continued rock-back and delay of pull with the arms until the hips and legs are at least even with the top grip (stay on the back) and a vigorous forward/upward lead-leg action toward the top of the pole. The swing of the lower body should not be interpreted as the pull (Figure 19, frames 13–14).

B. If this procedure doesn't work, move the standards back and try again.

3). Coming down on the bar or hitting the bar with the hands, arms, or chest may be overcome by (Figure 29):

A. Completing the pull-up while the feet are above the grip, following through as though paddling a canoe.

B. Maintaining contact with the pole, releasing it when vertical with a pushup action.

C. Coordinating arms and legs with style of clearance.

D. Moving standards forward.

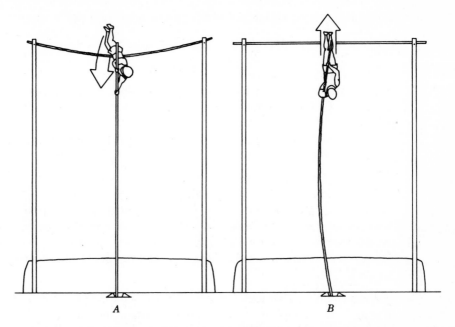

Figure 29. (*A*) Coming down on the bar or hitting the bar with the hands, arms, or chest may be remedied by (*B*) staying on the back throughout the hip lift and pull.

Selecting the Pole

Selection of a pole for the vaulter is the first consideration in initiating training. Factors to be considered in selection of a pole include the functions of growth, strength development, speed, endurance, and gymnastic aptitude. As discussed earlier, manufacturer and dealer are able to provide details regarding the weight for which a pole is designed in relation to the maximum top grip possible on it. As the grip is lowered, the pole will accommodate a heavier candidate, but the bending qualities will be substantially reduced. It is possible that one 3.05– to 3.66-m (10 to 12 ft) pole will suffice for a group of novice vaulters in the early training stages, but later develpment will require the properly engineered pole for each athlete. Whether the coach uses small diameter 2.44– to 3.05-m (8 to 10 ft) and 3.66-m (12 ft) aluminum poles to teach beginners is a consideration to be weighed in view of the budget, along with the possible, confusing consequences in technique as the vaulter graduates to a flexible pole.

Currently available prebent flexible poles provide less shock to muscles at takeoff. They are advertised as performance improvers based on the technicalities of the load-deflection characteristics of columns. A standard pole, however, will function satisfactorily once the athlete has found the position of greatest sag and becomes accustomed to turning this part of the pole away from him while carrying and planting the implement.

FOUNDATION TRAINING PROGRAM FOR THE POLE VAULT

I. Warm-up and Warm-down

Regardless of the geographical area and the attending weather conditions, the off-season aspect of training should feature general running, preferably of a cross-country nature, followed weeks later by sprinting. As the season develops, this running may be reduced in length to allow time for increasing amounts of more specific work. Stretching and calisthenic exercises of the flexibility-agility variety and overemphasis exercises should follow the general running and precede other aspects of practice throughout the season.

II. Flexibility-Agility Exercises

General warm-up running should be followed by flexibility-agility exercises, which include abdominal stretches; hurdlers' spread; shoulder stretching with arm swing in vertical planes; large doses of leg lifts; sit-ups, pushups, hands together, shoulder width, and also wide stance; and pull-ups, normal and behind the head, all cautiously initiated to reduce soreness and the possibility of injury.

III. Weight Training

Weight training is particularly important during the off-season when there is more time for it, to establish the foundation for strength and power. An abbreviated list of the more complete assortment of exercises discussed in Chapter 3 is presented as a basis for a program. Coach and athlete can develop routines to systematically develop important segments of the body, gradually substituting specific, quality, power lifting for general strength and endurance lifting as the season progresses.

A. Squats (25 to 50 percent).
B. Bench press.
C. Jumping squats with dumbbells.
D. Incline bench press.
E. Hanging straight and bent leg lifts (hip and pelvic lifts, respectively).
F. Bent and straight arm pullovers.
G. Military and back presses.
H. Straight and bent-leg, incline sit-ups with trunk twisting.
I. Erect pulldown and bent rowing, or bench-prone pulldowns with a weight machine.
J. Hamstring curls and knee extensions.
K. Reverse incline sit-up (rock-back hip lift).
L. Supine and prone flyaways.
M. A variety of the total lifts (clean and jerk with split, etc.).

IV. Gymnastic, Rope, Trampoline and Tumbling Exercises

Curiously enough, perhaps because of conflicting seasons, somatotyping, difference of interest, or possibly lack of leg speed, divers and gymnasts rarely participate in the pole-vault event, yet pole vaulters benefit from many of their training activities. A variety of gymnastic activities are listed for inclusion in the vaulter's training program.

A. Gymnastic activity.
   1. Rings—front and back uprise, chinning, front and back dislocates, and the kip.
   2. High bar—chinning, kip and chin-up to a front support, pullovers.
   3. Parallel bars—front and back uprise, hand balance, stationary and swinging dips, pushups from a handstand (may be done from the floor against a wall if balance is difficult to maintain on the parallel bars).
B. Rope activity
   1. Climbing without the use of the legs.
   2. Inverted climbing—swing into a rock-back position on a stationary rope, straddle the rope with the legs, and climb.
   3. Swinging.
   4. Vaulting.
C. Trampoline
   There are countless exercises that are of value with varying degrees of difficulty. The following may require intermediate and advanced comprehension but should be learned for their great value to the pole-vault event. Beginning exercises should be reviewed and practiced before trying any of the more sophisticated stunts. Basic bouncing exercises and drops of various kinds are recommended. Routines of these simple exercises can be developed for their flexibility and agility value.
   Advanced exercises:
   1. Somersaults: forward tuck and piked, backward tucked, semitucked, and open back. The back somersaults may be done from a backdrop, over a flexible crossbar for clearance-style work.
   2. Twisting exercises: half and full twists, and various combinations of front and back drops with half twists.
   3. Twisting somersaults: half twist piked forward (Barani), half twist tucked forward, half twist open back, and full twist forward and back somersaults.
D. Tumbling exercises: front and back somersaults, front dive roll, cartwheel, roundoff, and back handspring.
E. Strength exercises on the mat: handstand, knee and foot lift to handstand, bent arm, bent knee press, bent arm, straight leg press, and the straight arm, straight leg press.

V. Overemphasis Exercises
Overemphasis exercises, discussed in detail in Chapter 4, are universally valuable for any track athlete whose event requires leg speed, vertical lift and takeoff ability. They are comprehensive enough for the bulk of early practice sessions but

should be part of the warm-up routine throughout the season. High knee lift, ankle flip, arm action, rapid cadence stride length, and relaxation drills should be undertaken with caution at reduced distances and effort until initial soreness is overcome.

VI. Running, Sprinting, and Climbing Activities
A. Running. Early-season running may be accomplished primarily in the extended warm-up. As condition improves, less general running gives way to sprint activities.
B. Sprint and hurdling activities. All of the sprint routines and drills discussed in Chapter 13 are applicable to the pole vaulter. Pickup sprints and acceleration drills are most valuable initially, complimented later with interval and repetition activity. Low hurdling is also suggested for its versatility, emphasizing controlled velocity and flexibility.
C. Climbing activities. Stadium or stair climbing and hill work, both shallow and steep, are valuable for emphasis on explosiveness, upright posture, and vertical lift.

VII. Depth Jumping and Plyometrics
Essentially pole vaulting requires more horizontally oriented takeoff mechanics than other jumping events, somewhat similar to that of the triple jump. A major criterion for success in the vault is proper use of the pole with a forward/upward takeoff. Running off the ground with a wide grip on even a prebent pole, however, does require a powerful takeoff, and depth jump/plyometric work is invaluable for fast-working musculature. See Chapter 4 for more detailed discussion and exercises.

VIII. Vaulting
A. Technique work is best accomplished with the bar set 15 to 30 cm (6 to 12 in.) below personal best heights, with the understanding that faults do not usually appear until commanding heights are attempted. Working for technique should emphasize overcoming those faults.
B. Pop-up vaulting. Like pop-up jumping, this activity causes problems because it is more applicable to the experienced vaulter than to the novice. Beginners brought up primarily with this kind of work never learn the value of the check mark and the full run for maximal, controlled, velocity work.
C. Vaulting for height. This activity is essential later in the season to verify that technique work has been successful. It is difficult work to do in practice but must be done with utmost seriousness at heights 15 to 30 cm higher than personal bests. Without this kind of work, the athlete can never completely understand what phases of the vault must receive more work and attention.

IX. Recreative Activity
Since the vaulter is perhaps the most versatile of all track athletes and must experience a greater variety of training procedures, boredom is probably a small

factor in training. However, all work and no play has its disadvantages, and recreative activity (volleyball, basketball, flag football, surfing, diving, bicycling) is occasionally warranted.

SAMPLE WEEKLY PROGRAMS
OFF-SEASON
Precede and conclude each workout with the suggested, extended warm-up and a normal warm-down. Always engage in substantial flexibility-agility exercise following the warm-up and preceding the workout.

MONDAY—*Weight training. Alternate upper and lower extremity exercises, lifting for endurance.*
Overemphasis drills—3 sets each.
Swim four to six lengths of pool at medium pace.

TUESDAY—*Use normal rather than extended warm-up.*
Selected gymnastic, rope, and tumbling exercises followed by 3 to 6 km of cross-country Fartlek.

WEDNESDAY—*Sprint work with the pole (i.e., 40 to 50 m carrying the pole).*
Trampoline work.
Weight training, strength concept, alternating upper and lower extremity exercises.

THURSDAY—*Sprint activities, 6 to 8 × 100 m or 12 to 16 × 50m.*
Overemphasis drills, 1 set each.
Depth jumping.

FRIDAY—*Technique vaulting, 15 to 25 jumps.*
Stair climbing.
Weight training, endurance concept, alternating upper and lower body exercises.

SATURDAY—*Recreative activities with warm up and warm down.*

SUNDAY—*Rest or recreative activities.*

EARLY SEASON
Reduce the extended warm-ups to "normal" warm-ups (800 m). Gradually shift from strength and endurance weight lifting to the power concept. Vaulting should be mostly for technique with some height work.

MONDAY—*Vault for height, 10 to 15 jumps.*
Overemphasis drills.
Weight lifting, strength concept, alternating upper and lower body segments.

TUESDAY—*Selected gymnastic, rope, tumbling, and trampoline work.*
Cross-country style Fartlek, 3 to 6 km—Or—
Sprint activities as needed.

WEDNESDAY—*Technique vaulting, 20 to 30 jumps.*
Weight training, power lifting.

THURSDAY—*Technique vaulting, 8 to 12 jumps.*
Trampoline work.
Selected moderate (i.e., quality, not quantity) work on weak areas as needed. (gymnastics, sprints, etc.).
FRIDAY—*Warm-up.*
SATURDAY—*Competition, followed by weight training for weak areas or Fartlek cross-country.*
SUNDAY—*Rest, recreative activity, or light workout as needed.*

LATER SEASON
Emphasize quality work. Vault for height more than technique. Power weight lifting takes precedence over other types.

MONDAY—*Jump 10 to 15 times for height.*
Overemphasis drills, 1 set each.
Weight training, power concept, 3 sets.
TUESDAY—*Overemphasis drills, 1 set.*
Sprint work.
Horizontal plyometrics.
WEDNESDAY—*Jumping for height.*
Weight training, power concept, 1 set.
Moderate trampoline activity.
THURSDAY—*Gymnastic and tumbling activities.*
Overemphasis drills.
FRIDAY—*Warm-up.*
SATURDAY—*Competition.*
SUNDAY—*Rest, warm-up, recreative activity, or light workout as needed.*

BIBLIOGRAPHY

1. Boudreaux, John P., "A Comparison of Selected Factors in Fiberglass and Pre-Fiberglass Pole Vaulters," Unpublished MS thesis, Louisiana State University, 1969.
2. Elliott, Geoff, "The Pole Vault," *Olympic Track and Field Techniques,* edited by Tom Ecker, Fred Wilt, and Jim Hay, Parker Publishing Co., West Nyack, N.Y., 1974.
3. Ganslen, Richard V., "Developments in Pole Vaulting," *The Jumps: Contemporary Theory, Technique and Training,* edited by Fred Wilt, Track and Field News Press, Los Altos, CA, 1972.

4. Hay, Jim, "Fundamental Mechanics of Jumping," *Olympic Track And Field Techniques,* edited by Tom Ecker, Fred Wilt, and Jim Hay, Parker Publishing Co., West Nyack N.Y., 1974.
5. Jeitner, Gerhard, "Pole Vault Technique," *Track Technique, 28* (June 1967).
6. Lohre, Guenther, "Wide Pole Grip—World Round Up," *Track Technique, 62,* (June 1967).
7. Steben, Ralph E., "A Cinematographic Study of Selective Factors in the Pole Vault," Unpublished PhD dissertation, University of Utah, 1968.
8. Wilt, Fred, Personal Correspondance, April, 1976.

section three

Coaching the Field Events (Throws)

Each Chapter of this subdivision is organized to correspond with the description found on page 51.

Chapter 8

The Shot Put

Sequence curves of the path of a shot, before release, reveal a phase when the horizontal component of the momentum gained from the start to the center of the ring must be skillfully integrated with the more vertical component of the put. This transition represents one of the most difficult phases of the event and must be executed rhythmically to assure that all available potential is released to obtain acceleration of the shot at an optimal release angle of about 41 degrees.

All hesitations, detours, and curves of the path of the shot should be eliminated, or reduced to a minimum, for an optimal summation of forces in the desired direction. A systematic analysis of the phases of the event, to discuss the importance of the principles involved for successful putting, will be identified as the: (1) start; (2) glide; (3) drive (weight lift); and (4) release and follow-through (Figure 30, frames 1-17).

The Start (Figure 30, frames 1-4)
Initially, it is important to establish a position in analyzing mechanics of the shot-put event. The time-honored, *T* position and the more recent Feuerbach

Figure 30. George Woods in the shot put. PR 22.01 m (72 ft, 2 3/4 in.). Courtesy of Toni Nett, West Germany.

inspired torqued position at the *start* will be discarded in favor of more efficient technique. The *T* position features considerable gyration in terms of lifting the free arm above the head and, with a dip of the trunk, lifting the lead leg until a body posture is assumed that resembles the letter *T*. This position is of little value in putting the shot.

Feuerbach contends that he initiates a swing movement in the direction of the putting arm by a combination of trunk flexion and twisting, with the putting elbow oriented in the same direction. He holds this uncomfortable position throughout the glide (shift) to obtain torque for the delivery. However, once he breaks contact with the ground, with the power foot in the glide, this "advantage" will be lost because of loss of stabilization and what we know about the law of action and reaction. If, for some reason not known to science, this twist is not lost, the effect would be to take the shot off the line of desired projection.

Figure 31. The DDR ''short-long'' technique of Hans Peter Gies. PR 21.31 m (69 ft, 11 in.). Courtesy of Toni Nett, West Germany.

A more simplified, efficient start begins with the back facing the throwing sector. The shot is pressed against the base of the neck, with the forearm and elbow of the putting arm held high. Avoiding unnecessary gyrations, the free arm is held in a comfortable position below the head. To keep the trunk from rising too high during the glide, look at the toe of the power foot. A dip is executed with flexion of the power knee and the trunk, in order to assume the lowest anticipated position of the body during the event. With the center of gravity of the body well over the thigh, the shot is positioned directly above the power foot. The free arm continues

to hang freely, opposite the power knee. An explosive contraction of the power leg, coordinated with the downward-directed reach of the lead leg for the board, supplies thrust for the glide.

The Glide (Shift) (Figure 30, frames 5-9)

The putter drives off the toe and through the heel of the power foot, while the lead leg reaches forward and down, toward a point slightly off-center of the toe board. Although very difficult to do, the low position of the trunk during the glide should be maintained by quickly flexing the power leg, bringing it under the trunk without straightening up. Throughout the glide, the relaxed, free arm is held downward and back, as though it were a dangling rope, to help keep the back facing the sector.

A torqued posture, popularized by the expression "crossing the X" should now be developed at the moment of grounding in the latter phases of the glide and should be maintained to pretense the trunk muscles preceding delivery. Ideally, the shoulders are approximately at right angles to the axis of the hips, which should be parallel with the linear direction of the put. At the instant of grounding, the drive begins from the stronger and slower muscles near the body's center of gravity and then through the power leg, with its foot now approximately at right angles to the direction of linear activity (3).

Figure 32. The glide of the East German "short-long" shot put technique.

East German putters (Figure 31, frames 1-15), by adopting a short-long rhythm, say they are increasing the range of the putting action itself by substituting a shorter glide. By eliminating the "T" position, they drop into a squat with the weight behind the power foot, swing the lead leg toward the toeboard, and execute a glide that places the power foot 15 to 31 cm (6 to 12 in.) *behind* the center of the circle. The lead leg grounds near the toeboard, offset from its center by 15 to 31 cm. This permits a longer application of force on the shot during the putting action.

Putters using this style never seem to lift body weight over the lead leg, get little impulse on lift from it in delivery, and often put with both feet off the platform. Wilt contends that elimination of the "T" position and overhead free arm action at the start is good for all putters, but he dislikes the wide stance during the lift phase (10).

East German technique might be considered a super standing put, which attempts to eliminate the poor 30- to 40-percent transfer of speed to the shot developed during the glide to the actual putting action. Joachem Spenke, its author, and others do not recommend the technique for beginners, since its use requires superior coordination and great leg and back strength (7, 9) (Figure 32).

The Drive (Weight Lift) (Figure 30, frames 10-14)

WEIGHT LIFT.   (frames 10-12) The most important part of this phase relates to the velocity imparted to the shot before the arm strike begins. The position at the end of the glide should be similar to that at the start. With weight beginning to shift from the power foot to both feet, torque of the upper torso developed in the shift should be maintained, with the pelvis now at a greater angle with the shoulders. The power foot is inclined about 60 degrees with its heel and the tip of the lead foot touching a straight-line path parallel with the throw and bisecting the ring. From this semiopen hip position, with the back still facing the throwing sector, the initial lift comes from the lower body. Drive from the medially rotating power leg should lift the power hip. The putting shoulder is correspondingly lifted without

Figure 33. The rigid left arm to keep shoulders "closed" and pretensed slightly "open" hips concept (after Peter Tschiene). This produces an uncomfortable but profitable torqued "cross the X" position for the start, glide, and initiation of the arm strike.

unduly lowering the lead, retaining the closed-shoulder position. Rotation of the pelvis, followed by the shoulders, allows the hips to lead the shoulders in the put, while driving the flexed free arm back assures correct timing of the arm strike and linear delivery of the shot along the path across the ring. In the explosive action, release of torque accompanies a thrust that will ultimately lift and extend the entire body. The pattern of movement suggests rhythmical pushing, driving upward and forward with the turn quickly following (1).

The Hungarian coach, Koltai, correctly states that any torque developed at the start cannot be maintained during the glide, so it should be created at the end of that phase, immediately prior to the weight shift (6). Peter Lay, British National coach, agrees and comments that rotation at the rear of the circle is not necessary for torsion at the putting stance, although he admits that some putters appear to do it very well (6).

Peter Tschiene of West Germany recommends a rigid, free arm to keep the shoulders closed, while a pretensed power hip places the pelvis and legs in a slight "foot in the bucket" position, which produces an uncomfortable, but profitable, "crossing the X" torque position (8) (Figure 33).

THE DELIVERY.   (Figure 30, frames 13-14) With both shoulders and the putting elbow held high, the arm strike of the put is coordinated by initially pushing from the trunk through the power leg, followed by unwinding the trunk. Rotation should be completed with both feet pointing in the direction of the put for added leg power and lift. As the trunk and chest move forward and up for the lift component, the arm strike passes the head, and the action/reaction emphasis changes quickly but smoothly from the power to the lead leg. The free arm, flexed at the elbow, is probably unconsciously (but desirably) driven back to create greater rotational speed, pulling the head out of the way of the shot, driving the putting shoulder ahead and slightly above the free shoulder.

By "Wilt's Law" of shot, discus, and javelin, the arm does not strike in the delivery action until all weight is off the power leg (10). This advice, however, is not intended to encourage a late arm strike. The movement starts early enough to take advantage of a percussion-point principle in which the ground reaction passes from the power to the lead leg. According to Wilt, the power leg first breaks contact with the circle, the chest turns to the front, body weight moves over the front leg, and only then does the arm "strike."

Release and Follow-Through (Figure 30, frames 15-17)

The ultimate lift position having been executed with the power hip preceding the putting shoulder, the velocity of the shot is augmented by the explosive, inwardly rotated putting action of the arm strike. As the shot put leaves the hand with a final powerful snap of the wrist and fingers, the power foot is just off the platform, while the lead leg is thoroughly posted, pushing forward through the toeboard. The movement resembles placing an object on a shelf, above and beyond the reach of the putter. The entire body is completely stretched, with both feet leaving the platform precisely after the instant of release, as though the putter were going to follow the trajectory of the shot. Ideally, the slightly bent lead leg should extend at the instant the shot is above it. To extend sooner will drive the shot backward to some extent.

A reverse is executed to avoid fouling by rotationally bringing the putting arm around the opposite hip as the body is lowered for stability or by lowering both arms along the outside of the legs to obtain reverse thrust from the toe board as the power leg is flexed to lower the center of gravity. The final flick of the wrist, hand, and fingers in conjunction with the reverse, while the lead toe is still in contact with the toe board and platform, is instrumental in an action/reaction impulse and also helps the putter retain balance and avoid fouling.

TEACHING THE SHOT PUT TO BEGINNERS

Whether to break the event into its component parts and teach the standing put first, followed by the start, glide, and weight shift, depends on interpretation of motor-learning theories. Although much can be said in defense of either the whole or the part method described here, the teacher must realize that the standing put is essentially a different event and, while valuable for introductory purposes, it should be quickly followed and integrated with the full putting action. Its chief value in later phases of development is with training work involving heavier implements [6 to 9 kg (13 to 20 lbs)].

1). Most candidates will place the shot on the base of the fingers and thumb, without allowing the ball to rest in the palm of the hand. There are minor variations of the grip, and athletes will find adaptations as they progress.

2). Cradle the shot against the neck and jaw with the elbow pointing directly behind, away, and slightly below the implement.

3. A beginner may learn to put from a standing position, with special emphasis on action/reaction or ground reaction, essential in a throwing event that features a substantial weight.

4). With the back facing the throwing sector, the candidate's lead leg will be slightly flexed at the knee and placed just to the left of the center of the toe board.

5). Initially, the free arm is either held pointing downward toward the platform or is held slightly flexed at the elbow and in the plane of the shoulders.

6). The center of gravity will be concentrated over the power leg, which is flexed at the hip and the knee.

7). Rotating thrust of the power leg lifts the hip and shoulder first, followed by complete hip and then shoulder rotation. Torque is released by explosively bringing the trunk up, forward, and around, without beginning to extend the putting arm. The hip should lead the motion, with the entire body beginning to stretch out in the direction of the release.

8). The chest is thrust upward and forward, as the putting shoulder begins to move ahead of the free shoulder.

9). Without dropping the free shoulder, tip the head toward it (i.e., attempt to keep the shoulders square without the position of the head interfering with the push of the shot off the base of the neck).

10). The free arm will now be flexed at the elbow and held close to the side of the body.

11). Coordinate the arm strike by initially pushing through the power leg while unwinding the trunk. As the trunk moves forward and up for the lift, the arm strike will pass the head, and ground reaction will change smoothly to the lead leg.

12). With some velocity imparted to the shot before the arm strike, inertia of the shot will be overcome, and the arm strike should now add additional velocity to the implement.

13). Direct the shot with a snap or slap of the wrist, hand, and fingers to a point beyond the outstretched reach of the putting hand. The sensation is one of following the implement with the entire body.

14). The angle of release will not be the optimum 45 degrees discussed in some basic kinesiology texts. This applies only to a missile that starts and returns to the same horizontal plane and requires that vertical and horizontal force components be equal. It is sufficient to say that, since speed improves slowly with diligent work on the event over the years, the greater the height of release, the less is the optimum angle. Most champion putters deliver at about 42 degrees.

15). Immediately after the moment of release, both feet may momentarily leave the platform, with the entire body stretched out in the direction of release.

16). At this time the emphasis may be placed on obtaining all available force from the

Figure 34. "Rocking," allowing the center of mass to get ahead of the back leg, and "opening up" or losing the "crossing the X" or torqued position during the glide results in this ineffective putting posture for the delivery.

power leg by omitting the reverse. If the reverse is taught, caution must be exercised to avoid introducing it too early in the delivery. The weight shift must pass from the power leg, to both legs, and finally to the lead leg, with the reverse delayed until a precise moment after the shot is released. Full benefit of an effective follow-through, using the reverse, must be realized at this moment and not after the shot is well on its way. The reverse may be executed by reversing the legs, placing the power leg in the toe board, swinging the lead leg behind the body and the putting arm around the opposite hip, and rotating away from the toe board or by lowering both arms along the outside of both flexed legs while lowering the body.

17). As these essentials are mastered—learning to summate and add on forces in sequence at the right time—the putter graduates to the back of the ring for the development of the start and glide.

18). The initial stance resembles the one discussed for the beginning of the standing put. This relative "crossing the X" posture must be reestablished at the completion of the glide. If this is not done, the candidate will be guilty of "opening up" and losing the quarter turn, or 90 degrees, which allows more impulse (force x time) to be applied to the implement (Figure 34).

19). The center of mass has to be ahead of the power leg to enable the putter to move, but the leg must catch up and pass the center of mass before it lands in the center of the ring. "Rocking" or allowing the center of mass to get too far ahead of the power leg in the delivery position must be avoided or advantage of the weight shift will be lost (Figure 34).

20). To maintain correct orientation during the straight-drive glide across the ring, look at a point near the power toe.

21). Movement of the putter across the ring is started from the crouched position, with raising and lowering the lead leg to gain momentum followed by pushing off through the power leg. This action ressembles a kick followed by an explosive drive from the power leg.

22). Push off the toe, over the foot, and finally through the heel of the power foot. The hop should be as low and long as the position and strength permit.

23). As Dyson explains, the putter must feel this activity emanating from the pelvis through the body like the ripples that flow outward from a pebble thrown into a pond (3).

24). Synthesis of the glide with the weight shift and delivery represents the most difficult part of the event. Emphasize retention of the start posture of the upper body at the end of the glide. The shoulders are at a right angle with the path across the ring, while the hips approach a right angle with the shoulders, producing the torqued position.

25). The weight shift proceeds from the power leg, to both legs, and finally to the lead leg as the delivery is executed.

26). The concepts developed in the standing put are synthesized with the start and glide for effective weight shift, delivery, and follow-through.

TRAINING FOR THE SHOT PUT

Preparation for the shot put requires a combination of flexibility, speed, and strength training. The event requires a discretely timed summation of forces from the start to the final flick of the wrist. A torque feature increases the distance over which inertia of the implement is overcome, developing velocity and acceleration prior to that added by a properly timed arm strike.

Preseason training is the time for establishing a broad base for strength, speed, and flexibility. A novice will require some time to determine starting loads for strength and power-weight training, as well as advice regarding the technique of lifting. Speed training for explosiveness, drills for development of technique, and gymnastic work for torque suppleness are also included.

Success in the shot put depends, to a major extent, on the mass of the putter. The velocity imparted to this mass by available strength applied over a short period of time requires that the majority of it be muscle. In spite of the importance of mass, if the putter is overweight, the excess weight must be shed to assure that thrust will be optimum for the circumstances. If a 136-kg (300 1b) man with naturally acquired weight-training strength can push against the ground with 181.5 kg of force, subsequently and immediately receiving 181.5 kg back, this will allow 45.5 kg left to be used for pushing the shot!

Geoffrey Capes, the talented 1.98-m, 140-kg (6 ft, 6 in., 309 1b) British shotputter, commented before the 1976 Olympics that his bulk was natural and that tests (administered prior to the games) "will separate the men from the boys,—and the genuine athletes from the blown-up athletes" (5). He was referring to the illegal practice of ingesting steroids for alleged increases in muscle-producing bulk. Capes did place in the games, while others who were previously superior to him fell far below their personal bests. The question remains—are steroids really bulk producing, and do they correspondingly produce strength commensurate with the smaller frame? Will the bulk they produce be retained as muscle or fatty tissue when steroids can not be ingested for fear of detection by a test?

FOUNDATION TRAINING PROGRAM FOR THE SHOT PUT

Weight training procedures (Chapter 3), running prescriptions (Chapter 13), and flexibility-agility exercises (Chapter 3) are treated generally here. Specialized work dealing with isokinetics and the concept of the pretensed hip and the rigid, free arm are described in detail. Sample workouts for various parts of the season are then developed with reference to these activities, The precise makeup of other practice sessions is left up to the imagination and needs of the individual.

I. Warm-up and Warm-down

Every practice session should begin with a warm-up. General conditioning by means of cross-country type running may occur before and early in the season for weight control and general toughening up. When useless weight has been shed, this emphasis on warm-up may be reduced. In subsequent workouts, easy running should precede general stretching with flexibility-agility exercises followed by several easy accelerations of 40 to 50 meters. Preceding the weight-training sessions, a lightweight warm-up is additionally suggested. Each practice should be concluded with an easy run or swimming for warm-down.

II. Flexibility-Agility Exercises

Contrary to common opinion, the weight-events athlete either is or needs proficiency in this component of physical fitness. The fact that the athlete is massive is not enough. Strength, power, explosive speed, and the coordination to put it all together from a 2.13-m (7 ft) ring requires unusual flexibility and agility. All of the exercises suggested in Chapter 4 are applicable: high kick; hurdler's spread; wrestler's bridge; floor touch; trunk flexion and extension; jack spring; six-count exercise; alternate splits; reverse sit-up; and leg swingovers. Running should always precede this work, just as flexibility-agility should always precede sprinting.

III. Weight Training

Exercises to work the trunk and extremities of the body for power and strength may be arranged in alternate sequence and either be repeated every session or further arranged into routines and alternated session by session, eventually repeating the routine. A "must" listing is described with additional exercises and procedures regarding starting and concepts described in Chapter 3.

A. Squats (25, 50 percent, and full).
B. Incline bench press.
C. Heel rises.
D. Snatch with squat clean.
E. Twisting incline, bent knee sit-ups.
F. Clean and jerk with squat clean.
G. Lateral raises.
H. High pull-up.
I. Step-up exercise.
J. Torso twist.
K. Hang cleans.
L. Wrist curls.

IV. Running, Sprinting, and Climbing Activities

A. *Running* has been referred to in the warm-up procedures.
B. *Sprinting activities.* Activities described in Chapter 13, particularly pickups, accelerations, interval, and repetition work over short distances are most appropriate. The shot putter does not need endurance work or 100-m dash capability. Sprinting long distances is unnecessary, and any games that feature short bursts of speed may be substituted occasionally for variety. Speed work over distances from 40 to 60 m should become more intensive as the conditioning period progresses.
C. *Climbing activities.* The weight-training, step-up exercise may be complimented with stadium or stair climbing without weights. The exercise should be conducted explosively over short distances.

V. Depth Jump—Plyometric Exercises

The standard bouncing, bounding, hopping exercises over short distances are initially appropriate for stressing the stretch-reflex apparatus utilizing fast eccentric-concentric principles.

Low Platform Drill. As condition improves, the putter can glide from a low platform, first without and then with the shot, landing on the takeoff or supporting leg with a yielding motion and then executing the lift and delivery.

Pendulum drill. The upper extremities may be exercised by swinging a suspended, overweight implement into the hand, returning it forward explosively after yielding (recoiling) from a standing position.

Supine Drill-Gravity Catch From a release point above the putter, lying supine on a bench, carefully direct and drop an overweight shot. The shot is caught with an eccentric yielding action and explosively returned upward. Some retrieval procedures will need to be rehearsed to assure that the practice will be safe.

VI. Special Technique Drills

The following technique-flexibility drills help to integrate the event with strength training and speed by requiring work that emphasizes lateral flexion, torque position, and the leg drive of the start, glide, and weight transfer.

A.   Isokinetic exercises suggested by Ivan Dobrovloski, USSR, include the following (2).

1.   Assume the start position in the ring with the shot held in both hands above the head. Drive off the power leg, to the glide position, hesitate for about 2 seconds in the stretched, torque position and, with both arms, throw the shot over the head in the direction of the sector.

2.   With both legs together in the center of the ring and the back facing the toe board, hold the shot where it is normally positioned, but with both hands. With the trunk in an extreme, lateral flexion to the right, hesitate for 2 seconds and then explosively drive the lead leg into the board, lift the power hip, and follow with an inward rotation of the power knee and hip to deliver the shot.

3.   Using a buddy system, hold the putter down in the start position for 2 seconds, and let go for the completion of the put.

4.   An Exergene or Isokinetic Minigym may be connected to the putting forearm. Hold for 2 seconds, and execute the put dynamically with a challenging preset load on the device.

5.   From a start position with a wide base, push a loaded barbell forward/ upward with the putting arm as though it were a shot, while the other end is held down close to the free shoulder with the free hand.

B.   Tension drills. Peter Tschiene, advocate of the "pretensed" hip and the rigid, free-arm concept recommends a series of exercises for development of the essentials of this theory as it relates to the weight shift and delivery from the torqued position. In these exercises, the back of the shoulders and trunk are facing the sector. The hips are parallel with the direction of the put (8).

1.   Without using an arm strike and without (and later with) a shot, push off the power leg from the delivery position emphasizing lift of the power hip without rotation of the trunk and shoulders. The power knee will point in the direction of the put at the completion of the exercise.

2.   Do the same exercise while emphasizing the rigid, free arm held downward and close to the power knee.

3.   Drive from a start position, execute the glide, landing with the shoulders at right angles to the path across the ring, while the hips are parallel with this line. (Pretensed hip).

4.   The desired hip-axis/shoulder-axis orientation can be expedited alternately while hopping up and down (i.e., turn the hips to the open position and back again, keeping the shoulders closed while pushing with the free arm against a wall (Figure 35). A buddy system can also

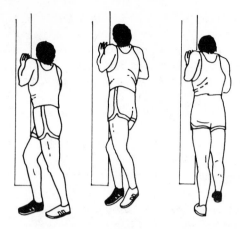

Figure 35. A pretensed hip drill for the shot put. Either brace the free arm against a wall or post, or link hands with a partner, alternating hopping in place, repeatedly torquing and untorquing the hip-shoulder orientation. Always keep the bilateral shoulder axis "closed" to the direction of an imagined put.

be used to alternately hold the shoulders in position by linking free hands.

5. Repeat exercise 4 while moving forward with each two-legged hop.
6. Overemphasis glide—hop on the power leg and kick with the lead, striving for distance to the delivery postion.
7. Restricting the glide, repeat exercise 6, with and without the delivery.
8. The entire sequence with maximum glide from a low starting position.

VII. Heavy Implements

An old training method that uses 6- to 9-kg (13 to 20 lb) shots has recently been resurrected as a training procedure. Although fundamentally valuable for beginners from a standing-put position, it is valuable for the more advanced athlete as a guide for weight training (see page 166-7). Heavy-implement training may be introduced into the program regularly or periodically on nonweight training days.

VIII. Recreative Activity

Rapidly moving ball games are recommended, (e.g., basketball, handball, paddleball, and flutter-board kicking in the pool).

SAMPLE WEEKLY PROGRAMS
OFF-SEASON
Precede and conclude each practice session with the recommended warm-up and warm-down. The quantity of general running is increased during this part of the season. The majority of work will feature weight training alternated with general conditioning, speed, flexibility, and technique development.

MONDAY—*Depth jump-plyometrics. Bounce in place, 5 × 20 seconds.*
Bounding and hopping, 5 × 40 m.
Weight training.

TUESDAY—*Running activities, 10 × 40 m accelerations, finishing with 80-percent effort.*
Isokinetic exercises 1, 2, and 4. 20 repetitions each.
Climbing activities, 10 × 20 m stair climbing.
WEDNESDAY—*Depth jump-plyometrics. Pendulum drill, 10 repetitions.*
Weight training.
THURSDAY—*Running activities, 10 × 50 m interval sprints at 80-percent effort.*
Tension drill, exercises 1, 2, 3, and 4. 10 repetitions each.
Recreative activity. Handball.
FRIDAY—*Putting. 20 standing puts with overweight shots.*
Weight training.
SATURDAY—*Isokinetic exercises 3, 4, and 5. 10 repetitions each.*
Tension drill exercises 5, 6, 7, and 8.
SUNDAY—*General running of the steady or Fartlek variety for 2 to 3 km or recreative activity.*

EARLY SEASON

At this time the pyramid of training should feature continued strength and power weight training, 90-percent efforts; continued technique drills; and more putting. Start and conclude each session with recommended warm-up and warm-down procedures. General running may be reduced in length.

MONDAY—*Isokinetic exercises 2, 3, and 4. 12 repetitions each.*
Weight training.
TUESDAY—*Putting. 30 to 40 serious gliding puts. 10 to 20 standing puts with overweight shots.*
WEDNESDAY—*Putting. 20 to 25 serious gliding puts.*
Weight training, power concept.
THURSDAY—*Depth jump-plyometrics. Pendulum drill, 10 repetitions. Low platform guide drill, 10 repetitions.*
Tension drill exercises 5, 6, 7, and 8. 6 to 8 repetitions each.
Weight training. One set of power concept exercises.
FRIDAY—*Warm-up.*
SATURDAY—*Competition.*
SUNDAY—*Rest, general running, or recreative activity.*

LATER SEASON

There should be at least one strength and one power workout a week to retain strength and explosiveness. The frequency of putting sessions will decrease with work on technique and speed continuing. Warm-up and warm-down for each session.

MONDAY—*Depth jump-plyometrics. Pendulum drill, 20 repetitions.*
Special technique drills, isokinetics, and tension exercises as needed.
Putting. 30 to 40 serious gliding puts.
Sprint activities. 6 to 8 × 60 m accelerations or pickup sprints at full effort.
TUESDAY—*Weight training.*
WEDNESDAY—*Putting. 15 to 20 gliding puts.*
Depth jump-plyometrics. Low platform drill, 10 repetitions.
THURSDAY—*Sprint activities. 4 to 5 × 60 m interval sprints at full effort.*
Weight training, power concept, 1 to 2 sets.
FRIDAY—*Warm-up.*
SATURDAY—*Competition.*
SUNDAY—*Recreative activity (handball, basketball, paddleball, cycling, swimming) or rest.*

ROTATIONAL SHOT PUT STYLE (Figure 36, Frames 1–12)

The personal success of Brian Oldfield and Aleksandr Barishnikov, using the whirl, twist, or rotating, discus-style spin in the shot put, necessitates an assessment of the technique, with the reminder that Josef Malek, a former Czechosolvakian hammer throw record holder used the innovation as early as 1960 to improve his personal shot-put record. The recent 22.86-m (75 ft) performance by Brian Oldfield (a professional athlete whose livelihood is dependent not only on winning consistently with excellent performances but also on innovation and showmanship) enhanced by Barishnikov's new amateur world record of 22 m (72 ft, 2 1/4 in.), will certainly lead to much experimentation among novice and experienced shot putters.

The term, rotating "discus style" spin, may lead some financially hard-pressed college track coaches to think about recruiting a discus thrower who can also put the shot. In the past ten years of sophisticated specialization, the two events have been considered somewhat incompatible. A well-meaning kinesiologist, not thoroughly acquainted with the rules, will suggest a discus-style spin with the shot brought to the neck just before the arm strike. Whatever thoughts are nurtured and can legally be put into action, the adoption of the new technique will undoubtedly parallel that of the flop in the high jump and require learning a different motor movement for the action phase of the event.

The linear style of pre-O'Brien putters was plagued by the problem of obtaining a good putting position at the completion of the glide. Fonville and Fuchs, both extremely fast athletes, introduced variations to overcome this problem by unorthodox progression across the ring and lengthening the shot path by leaning far over the back of the circle, respectively. The problem of hesitation still remained after O'Brien introduced the back to the throwing sector (step-back "glide") con-

Figure 36. The rotational shot put technique of Alexsander Barishnikov, USSR. PR 22 m (72 ft, 2 1/4 in.). Courtesy of Toni Nett, West Germany.

cept, which, like Fuchs' contribution, sought to increase the time that force could be applied to the implement.

Emphasis on pretorqued positions and East German inspired, short-glide procedures represent more recent attempts to improve impulse and transfer of momentum. The rotary method represents a combination of the latter two principles,— it attempts to increase the impulse- and delivery-phase times if the first spin does not take up any more than half of the circle. The problem of hesitation may still be present if the first turn is too fast and the second poorly executed. Continued impulse may be difficult to obtain during the second unilateral support phase, since there is a tendency to lose control of the shot with its stationary inertia overcome.

Present procedures for the rotary method call for a discus- style stance at the rear of the circle (9). A rotation of the trunk to the right is followed by a spin to the left, pivoting on the toe of the lead foot. The power leg is driven, sprinter style, through the midportion of the spin to facilitate linear progression across the ring. The free arm is held extended and parallel to the platform, increasing force but decreasing

rotary velocity, compensating for the putting arm pressing the shot against the shoulder and neck in reaction to increased, centrifugal force. This in turn keeps the trunk behind the hips and has a desirable pretensing effect on throwing muscles of the upper torso.

It is vital that the power foot land quickly in line with the proposed put for the second pivot, thus suggesting a position similar to the one initially assumed. To reduce hesitation, the free arm is now brought in to increase rotation about the polar or inertial axis, and the pretension of putting muscles is unleashed the instant the lead foot is placed near the center of the toe board. The explosion and release is comparable to that of other techniques, and the follow-through is probably more easily facilitated with a continuation of rotary movement (Figure 37).

The method may be better suited for the smaller athlete although Barishnikov [1.98 m, 125 kg (6 ft, 6 in., 276 1b)], third in the 1976 Olympic Games, managed to adjust the inertial-axis problem (the amount of body mass outside of the polar axis of the body). The principle problem is to be in a good throwing position while rotating through the lift, delivery, and follow-through—hence the erratic performances to date. Although there is no possible modification of the implement in this event, development of superefforts by future shot putters may be similar to the phenomenal efforts of the new generation of flop high jumpers who have added a new "style" to an old event.

TEACHING THE ROTATIONAL SHOT PUT STYLE
Teaching the rotation technique would synthesize, with some modification, the first and second spins of a discus throw with the delivery phase of the shot put. The shot is put, rather than slung like a discus, which necessitates a different position for the arm; and the circle is smaller, requiring tight spins that will not consume any more than half the circle, which leaves room for the delivery phase.

1). Proceed with items 1 through 6, as outlined in "Teaching the Shot Put to Beginners" on pages 140-1.

Figure 37. The rotational progression of the "discus"-style shot put.

2). If the circle were divided into quadrants, the putter would be standing, with the feet about shoulder width apart, on the left half of the back, right sector.

3). While in a squat position with the trunk erect, rotate the trunk to the right with the shot pressed up against the base of the neck.

4). Accelerating slowly, transfer weight from the right to the left leg while in the squat position, and pivot about the toe of the left foot, driving the flexed, right leg forward. The free arm is held out, parallel with the platform, to assist in slowing down the spin, and the right leg is held close to the left to facilitate its quick return to the platform.

5). Continue the spin, pressing the shot into the neck to counter centrifugal force, bringing the free arm in to speed up rotation from the grounded right leg.

6). Essentially the procedure from this point approximates what is covered specifically in items 7 through 16, pages 141-2, with the large muscle groups of the thighs, hip, trunk, and shoulders making their contribution, decelerating, and then transferring momentum to the putting arm and the shot.

TRAINING
Training for the rotational shot put would eliminate work designed to develop the glide and emphasize exercises and drills for putting from the power or torqued position. Development of the shot-put spin would be similar to technique work for the discus described on pages 166-7 with the arm in position for a put. Step B of discus technique, page 167 would emphasize shot put instead of discus hip rotation.

BIBLIOGRAPHY

1. Delavan, Phil, "Techniques of Putting the Shot" *Track and Field Quarterly Review, 4, 211 (1973).*

2. Dobrovloski, Ivan, "Specific Shot Put Exercises" *The Throws: Contemporary Theory, Technique and Training,* edited by Fred Wilt, Track and Field News Press, Los Altos, CA, 1974.

3. Dyson, Geoffrey H.G., *The Mechanics of Athletics,* Sixth Edition, University of London Press, London, 1973.

4. Grigalka, Otto, "Fundamental Shot Put Technique" *Track Technique, 49 (September 1972).*

5. Jares, Joe, "A Long Shot Right on Target," *Sports Illustrated, 44,* No. 4 (1976).

6. Lay, Peter, "A Rebuttal to Koltai's Biomechanical Ideas," *Athletics Coach, 7,* No 1 (1973).

7. Spenke, Joachem, "Problems of Technique and Training in the Shot Put," Speech, International Track and Field Coaches Congress, Madrid, Spain, 1973.

8. Tschiene, Peter, "Perfection of Shot Put Technique," *Modern Athlete and Coach, 5,* No. 5 (1967).

9. Ward, Paul, "A Review of Modern Shot Put Technique," *Track and Field Quarterly Review, 1,* 11 (1975).

10. Wilt, Fred, Personal correspondance, April, 1976.

Chapter 9

The Discus

"Slinging" the discus for maximum distance involves skillful integration of a number of mechanical factors, culminating in maximum release speed at an optimum angle several feet above the platform (10). Basically, the linear or tangent-release speed depends on the relationship between rotational velocity of the discus thrower and the length of his or her power arm. In conventional one and three-quarter turn discus technique, the development of implement acceleration by rotational and translational movements of the athlete for about 1 second necessitates correct use of body force in applying power over the longest pathway possible. The following description is for a right-handed individual.

Stance-Start (Figure 38, [frames 1–15] frames 1–4)

Although footwork will vary, to direct force over the longest pathway, the candidate should start with a comfortable stance—(feet slightly wider than the hips) the back facing the sector—with the left foot placed on a line bisecting the throwing sector. After one or two preliminary swings, the hips and shoulders are maximally rotated to the right. At the far end of the swing, the discus should be behind the

Figure 38. The discus throw by Jay Silvester, USA. PR 70.38 m (230 ft, 11 in.). Courtesy of Toni Nett, West Germany.

right hip with the slinging arm held straight. A lateral axis through the shoulders will reveal a greater torqued position relative to a similar axis through the hips.

As in the shot put, any pretensed position will be modified or lost when progressing from double through single support and airborne phases of the event, but the

relationship between the shoulders and the hips should be retained as much as possible. The thrower will always lose and regain the "trail" of the throwing arm in small degrees relative to the hip axis. This is no cause for alarm, and no effort should be expended to "force" the arm back. The restraining effect of the finger tips will allow centrifugal force to maintain the discus in secure position throughout the circular pathway.

Start-First Turn (Figure 38, frames 5–9)

From a one-quarter squat position with an erect trunk, the turn is started with the legs moving body weight to the left but not across the circle. As the center of gravity of the body moves from its position over the right leg toward the left, the right leg is whipped into the turn in a knee-leading sprint action, initiating the movement across the ring while pivoting on the ball of the left foot. Failure to precisely time this action causes the hips to start the turn and destroys the relationship between the throwing arm, the shoulders, and the hips.

Initially the right leg is held a comfortable distance away from the left, increasing its moment of inertia and assuring a gradual acceleration of the body by keeping it away from the vertical axis of rotation. At the same time, movement of the right knee counter-clockwise will assure that the right power arm will reciprocate in a clockwise sense by the law of action/reaction and remain well behind the right hip.

As the pivot continues, the right knee (driving across the ring) is now brought in closer to the axis of rotation, which, by decreasing the moment of inertia of the body, increases angular velocity. This causes the thrower's body to spin more rapidly as he or she drives across the circle with a typical sprinter's lean. The important concept here is to relate progression in discus throwing with sprinting from a standing start. The function of the legs is to initiate the spin to the left and then across the ring, gradually accelerating the movement. Some coaches advise a mechanical lean and high, right-knee action when the shoulders are parallel with the intended direction of the throw (2, 7). This may be good advice, but it is important to remember that it is the acceleration that produces the lean.

Airborne Phase (Figure 38, frames 9–10)

During the airborne, low-jump phase, the pivot foot leaves the platform and body weight is directed forward rather than obliquely to the left, avoiding any shortening of the overall path of the discus and the application of force to it. The discus is held well behind the right hip, as far from the axis of rotation as possible, thus maintaining an increased moment of inertia of the shoulders and slower rotational velocity of the upper torso. Correspondingly, the left leg is held close to the right, which conserves the hip-shoulder axis, torque-countertorque relationship by maintaining a decreased moment of inertia of the legs for their corresponding greater rotational velocity.

Second Turn (Figure 38, frames 11–13)

The ball of the right foot will ground in the center of the ring and turn left as far as possible. With the original throwing arm-shoulder-hip axes positions regained, the pivot is continued with the center of gravity over the slightly flexed right leg. The outstretched free arm leads into the turn at shoulder height, but wraps across the chest as the right foot grounds at the center of the circle, helping to keep the shoulders back and countering centrifugal force in the process.

The discus is behind the right hip and at or approaching the lowest point of its circular pathway. There are contrasting styles of discus carriage at this stage of the throw. Al Oerter carried the discus "on the hip" while John Powell carries his much higher and distant from the axis of rotation, correspondingly slowing down the turn. The most important task, in this phase, is to continue pivoting to bring the left leg down as soon as possible, on or slightly to the left of the line bisecting the ring. Failure to do so will place the lead foot "in the bucket" and result in loss of torque and acceleration (3, 4, 8, 11). The pivot action itself produces considerable friction and contributes to the problem of maintaining acceleration. Grounding the left foot quickly lessens the loss of acceleration, providing better stabilization and ground reaction. Coincident with placing the left leg correctly, the drive for the throw begins with inward rotation of the right knee, while the pivoting action continues.

Delivery (Figure 38, frames 14–17)

The delivery is accomplished by extending both legs and the trunk, with the hips preceding the shoulders in a rotary forward/upward movement. The original torque is released by contracting the well-stretched trunk muscles, thus effecting a transfer of weight and rotary momentum against the "posted" left leg. This is followed by the whiplike, slinging action of the extended throwing arm at the completion of the lift action, with the discus held in a more parallel attitude with the intended direction of the throw. It should be emphasized at this point that the "arm strike" is not completed until weight is off the rear leg, the chest turned to the front, and body weight over the front leg.

Impluse for the throw is transferred from the power to the lead leg, as the discus is pulled from its low to higher release point. Technically, at least the tip of the front foot should still be grounded at the final moment of release to obtain ground reaction. Because of the small mass of the implement, however, some athletes gain more release speed from the conversion of angular to linear momentum with the feet off the platform than they might gain in action/reaction with one or both feet grounded.

Release of the discus occurs at a tangent to the circular path of the implement. The angle of release will be governed by wind conditions, varying from about 30 degrees for a headwind to 40 degrees for a tailwind. Control of the plane of the discus, in relation to the flight path and wind conditions, can be effected by the thumb and wrist to obtain a constant, small angle with the horizontal and thus assure the discus will either land flat or on its back edge (Figure 39). To prevent fouling and to provide an uninterrupted flow of force, a spinning or shot put type of follow-through is executed in completing the throw.

TEACHING THE DISCUS THROW

Teaching this dangerous and complicated event can be simplified by first introducing the concepts of a standing throw, and following with instruction in the weight shift, the first turn, and finally the whole movement of the event. The goal to throw for maximum distance should be postponed until basic mechanical re-

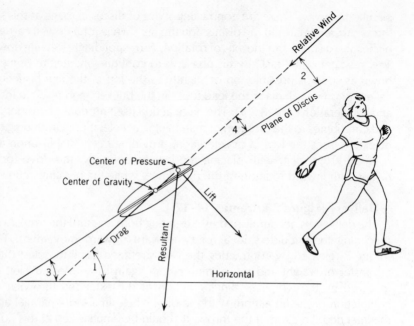

Figure 39. When a missile is inclined at an angle to the wind, the resultant of the forces exerted upon it is resolved into lift and drag components. Controllable variables in the release of the discus are:

(1). Angle of release—the angle between the flight path of the center of gravity immediately after release and the horizontal.

(2). Angle of attack—the angle between the plane of the discus and the relative wind, which is negative in this case (preferential for good throwing) and becomes positive shortly after release, directing lift upward while maintaining satisfactory lift and drag ratios.

(3). Attitude angle—the angle the central plane of the discus is inclined to the horizontal at the instant of release.

(4). Angle of incidence—the angle between the flight path and the plane of the discus. James G. Hay, *The Biomechanics of Sports Techniques,* (C) 1973. Adapted by permission of Prentice-Hall, Inc. Englewood Cliffs, NJ.

quirements are satisfied and control in the release of the implement in the desired direction is mastered, thus reducing the element of danger to other members of the group. A number of athletic suppliers stock inexpensive junior discuses for small hands, but an enterprising and budget minded coach can improvise with discuses of standard or varying diameter and weight made in the school workshop (9).

Although a stepwise procedure will be outlined, this does not imply that the whole event need be taught in a discrete series of individual maneuvers. Technical considerations include: control of the implement, position, balance, transfer of weight linearly and rotationally, and the elements of release.

British National AAA Coach, Wilf Paish, recommends spreading out a group of beginners in an outside turn lane of the track. Each candidate, with a minimum of instruction, takes a turn, stepping up into an inner lane, throwing to the center of the infield, and returning to the outside lane (9). After several initial attempts with the entire group, if the coach has senior team members who know the procedure, smaller groups can be set up at variouus other locations with the coach visiting each group for supervision.

The following procedure is now recommended for instruction.

1). Place the left hand under the discus to prevent it from dropping and the right hand on top of it, with the fingers comfortably spread and the finger tips curled over the edge. Demonstrate the importance of spinning the discus off the index finger, imparting a clockwise spin in the desired tangent direction. To emphasize the tangency of the event, a weighted tin can with a string attached can be whirled over the head and released, followed by a demonstration with the discus. With the instructor facing the group, each candidate is called up to take a turn with a standing throw in which no attention is directed to foot work. Have several discuses available and a retriever to quickly return them.

2). Demonstrate the back to the sector approach. Assume a well-balanced, comfortable, one-quarter squat stance, with the left leg dropped back, straddling a line on the ground representing one that would bisect the ring into right and left halves (Figure 40). Take several preliminary swings with the shoulders in a horizontal plane and the left hand supporting the discus. Draw the discus back and keep the eyes on the horizon with the body weight over the right knee and foot. Begin the throw by pivoting on *both* feet, transferring weight from the right toward the left leg. A sensation of rotating and lifting with the hips and legs should be experienced. The extended, slinging arm is brought through, with the chest and eyes directed above the horizontal. The discus is released parallel with the line on the ground. Insist that the feet *remain* in their relative positions, in spite of the twisted feeling the candidates experience while releasing the discus.

3). An alternative step may be substituted or used after step 2 (Figure 41). Again assume the back to sector position, but place the outside of the right and the instep of the left foot on a previously drawn line. This stance will be poorly balanced in a lateral sense but will result in a comfortable position when the pivot and release are completed.

4). A further option involves facing the sector with the feet straddling the line (Figure 42). Rotate the hips and shoulders to the right as far as possible. Hold this position momentarily to emphasize required posture, and throw the discus, emphasizing weight transfer, untorquing, ballistic (slinging) arm movement, and release. Any one of the procedures (or all of them) may be used, depending on the coach's philosophy of instruction. The candidates may initially experience some difficulty in hanging onto the discus but will soon learn to take advantage of centrifugal force and the position of the fingertips over the edge of the implement.

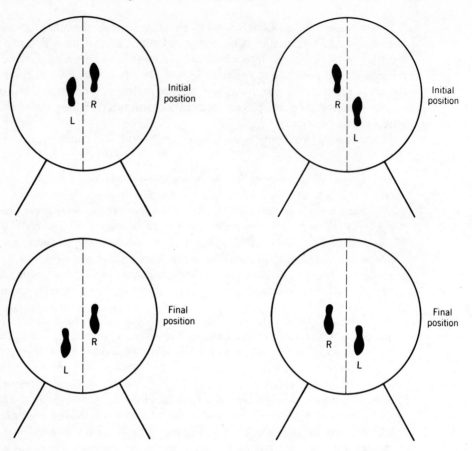

Figure 40. A comfortable initial to uncomfortable final position for progressively learning the pivot without moving the feet.

Figure 41. An uncomfortable initial to comfortable final position for progressively learning the pivot without moving the feet.

5). When the desired fundamentals have been mastered, the candidates may synthesize the weight shift with the first and second turn. This involves merging step 2, with the feet about shoulder width apart, through a running turn with step 4. The candidate should begin step 2 by directing body weight by means of the legs to the left, delaying movement of the right leg in sprint action across the ring until body weight is over the left foot (Figure 43). Repeated experimentation with the right leg is necessary until the right foot naturally falls on the line at the end of the running phase. This will automatically help subsequent placement of the left foot to the left of the line in the final turn. Initial attempts may display improper alignment of the trunk and head, but repeated efforts that concentrate solely on trunk alignment over the back leg will gradually evolve.

6). When proficiency in these events has been mastered, the reverse (either spinning or

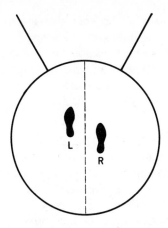

Figure 42. Foot placement for a standing throw facing the sector. Swing body to the right without moving the feet, emphasize return of hip and arm sling prior to release.

of the shot-put variety) may be introduced for a follow-through to avoid fouling and to provide for a better transfer of momentum to the discus.

7). Instruction pertaining to the desirable angle of release, as well as the guiding control of the thumb and wrist to convey the concepts of dealing with an aerodynamic implement affected by prevailing wind conditions, can be introduced at appropriate intervals anywhere in the basic steps. It is probably sufficient to advise a lesser angle of release when throwing into the wind and a higher angle when throwing with the wind, while the plane of the discus is maintained slightly above the horizontal.

The athlete should understand the relationship between the flight path of the center of gravity of the discus and the horizontal (angle of release), and the plane of the discus and the horizontal (attitude angle). For best results the plane of the

Figure 43. A discus drill emphasizing transfer of weight from right to left, pivot, and drive straight ahead with sprint-style lean because of linear acceleration in direction of throw.

discus should be slightly below the flight path of the center of gravity of the implement at release. This should produce a desirable, negative angle of attack, which becomes positive later in the flight, assuring a favorable lift component and a flat landing (Figure 39). Additional stability in flight can be enhanced by use of a "hollow" discus, with mass concentrated near the circumference, increasing the moment of inertia characteristics that produce a stable spin.

FOUNDATION TRAINING PROGRAM FOR THE DISCUS

The ground work for a successful season is set up in the months before competition, with an ambitious strength program for the upper and lower body that evolves into a continued, quality-strength program for the legs and a power-oriented program for the upper body. Speed, flexibility, and technique work are the other important aspects of the program. Speed training may be accomplished with a percentage system similar to that employed for the shot put. Generous portions of time should also be spent on flexibility-agility and technique to develop the torque position while transferring linear and angular momentum and accelerating under conditions of equilibrium.

I. Warm-up and Warm-down

As in the shot put, great quantities of running are unnecessary, but warm-ups prior to the season should begin with cross-country type running and Fartlek, followed by a generous number of flexibility-agility exercises that are always expedited before completing the warm-up, with several short, accelerating sprints at reduced effort. As the season progresses, the length of the beginning run may be reduced to 800 to 1000 m, but it is still the first order of business for the serious athlete. A short warm-down run or swim should follow even the most tiring practice sessions to hasten the elimination of fatigue metabolites. On weight training days, include a lightweight warm-up routine before lifting.

II. Flexibility-Agility Exercises

Use the exercises discussed in Chapter 4 for a serious, rapidly expedited 15 to 20 minutes of flexibility-agility work. This activity is sufficiently important to warrant daily attention and be incorporated into the athlete's warm-up procedure.

III. Weight Training

The following abbreviated assortment of exercises are taken from a more complete listing and discussion of lifting concepts and procedures in Chapter 3. In this instance the lifts are divided into three categories: leg exercises using the strength concept; repetitions with lesser loads for torque and rotational requirements of the hip and trunk; and speed-oriented type of power training for the arms, shoulders, and wrists. Exercises from each group may be assembled into routines and repeated, or emphasis may be placed on a different category each weight lifting day.

    A.   Exercises for the legs (strength concept).

      1. Squats (25 to 50 percent).
      2. Split and squat-style clean and jerk.
      3. Leg press.
      4. Split and squat-style snatch.
      5. Heel rise.

  B. Exercises for torque and rotational requirements of the hip and trunk.
      1. Leg lifter.
      2. Single and double leg swing.
      3. Bench single leg swing.
      4. Upright hip rotation.
      5. Squat hip rotation.

  C. Exercises for the arms, shoulders, and wrists (power concept).
      1. Bench press.
      2. Supine and prone flyaway.
      3. Back press.
      4. Military press.
      5. Wrist curls.
      6. Wrist abduction (radial wrist flexion) exercise. Resistance may be applied to the index finger for emphasis of the necessary counterclockwise release of the discus. This may be done by flipping an overweight discus, a barbell plate, or by applying tension isometrically.

IV. Running, Sprinting, and Climbing Activities

A. *Running activity.* Warm-up running is adequate to meet training needs for the event.

B. *Sprinting activity.* Short sprinting of the pickup, acceleration, interval, and repetition variety is necessary to emphasize the sprint-style pivot of this event. Although some champions keep the free leg extended during the pivot (displaying little high knee lift), the support leg must still drive (while pivoting) in a manner somewhat similar to the sprinter driving from the blocks.

C. *Climbing Activity.* Short bursts of running up stadium steps accomplish the same thing as the sprint drills but add the factor of gravity for increased resistance.

V. Depth Jump-Plyometric Activities

This not so new application of the old stretch-reflex principle is actually seen in some of the exercises already mentioned. The torso-twist, weight-training exercise is an example, although the emphasis is incorrect for the discus. Instead, substitute those recommended in the weight-training section above: upright and squat hip rotation where the twist emphasis comes from the hip rotators, instead of the torso as it should in the discus.

A low platform drill, similar to the one used for the shot put is also recommended. Spin off of a low platform, land with yielding, and throw the discus.

A pendulum drill comparable to the one discussed for the shot put may be used with a 40- to 60-kg (20 to 30 lb) plate or discus suspended on a swivel instead of the 40- to 80-kg (20 to 40 lb) shot. If the backward swing of such a vertical arrangement is reversed with a standing throw, retrieving problems can occur, because the weight will not only oscillate as a simple pendulum, but also circularly (i.e., it might circle around and hit the thrower in the head!). This can be controlled to some extent by hanging a net or stringing a rope up to the side to catch the pendulum. An assistant can recover the assembly and swing it back for another throw.

An adaptation of the shot-put pendulum drill may be attempted. Weld a plate or other object resembling an overweight discus to a lever. Pivot the lever on a tipped table or platform at the release height of the athlete. On a signal, an assistant can push the lever toward the athlete, who catches it with a yielding action and explosively returns it for repeated efforts.

Perhaps a simpler way of doing this is to throw overweight discuses. If a Jay Sylvester pumping action is emulated several times before the throw, the stretch-reflex mechanisms will be activated, and the desired eccentric-concentric contractions will occur.

VI. Technique Work and Overweight Implements

Possibly the best training for the discus is to throw it. Several discuses of varying weight may be used to provide a specific type of weight training. Although some coaches are erroneously fearful that use of under weight and overweight implements will develop timing problems if one practices with several combinations, including the normal weight implement, this procedure can serve as a guide to strength training (i.e., if more progress is demonstrated with the light implements, emphasis should be placed on strength-oriented lifting). Conversely, more progress with heavy discuses warrants directing attention to speed or power-oriented weight training).

A. Back of the ring drills (Figure 43).
    1. First without, and then later with the discus, practice the first turn, directing body weight from over the right leg toward the left, pivoting when the body weight is over the left leg, emphasizing movement of the center of gravity to the left and then forward, rather than diagonally, into a "bucket" position (3, 4, 8, 11).
       (a) Slow down the speed when going into the first turn to avoid movement of the right foot in too wide and slow an arc during the turn (i.e., do not pivot excessively fast on the left foot at the rear of the circle).
       (b) When the turn is started, all body weight must be above the left foot if stepping into the "bucket" is to be avoided in the front half of the circle when in the delivery position.
    2. When this is mastered, synthesize the running-rotation airborne phase,

quickly returning the right foot to the line that bisects the ring. Any lean in this phase should develop as a cause and not an effect of acceleration, since a voluntary, mechanical lean will destroy the concept of acceleration.

B.   Front of the ring drill.

The second turn may be practiced separately in the front half of the circle while facing the back of the ring. Assume the hip-shoulder torque position, and untorque during the pivot, upward/forward with the legs first, followed by the hips, torso, shoulders and then the arm strike. It is particularly important to ground the left foot close to the bisecting line.

C.   Implement drill (throwing—standing or spin).

Finally, synthesize A, B, and C with implements of varying weight, and introduce either the spinning or shot put style follow-through.

VII. Tumbling and Trampoline Activities

There are countless exercises with varying degrees of difficulty that are of value. Beginning exercises should be reviewed and practiced before trying any of the more sophisticated stunts. Basic bouncing exercises and drops of various kinds are recommended. Routines can be developed for their flexibility and agility value.

VIII. Recreative Activity

Recreative activity is recommended occasionally during all phases of the season to allow a break from the tedium of training and conditioning and to derive benefit from the flexibility-agility, coordination of related motion experience, and relaxation aspects of ball and racquet games, dancing, swimming, and cycling.

SAMPLE WEEKLY PROGRAMS
OFF-SEASON
Precede and conclude each workout with the recommended warm-up and warm-down.

MONDAY—*Technique work. Back of the ring drill exercise, 1a and 1b without a discus.*

Weight training. Either concentrate on the leg and torque routines, emphasizing the strength concept with leg exercises, or develop routines working all parts of body, (e.g., leg, strength; torque and rotational exercises for the hip and torso; and power exercises for the upper extremities).

TUESDAY—*Depth jumping-plyometrics*

Upright and squat hip rotation with a barbell, 5 to 8 repetitions for 6 sets.

Sprint activities. Acceleration sprints, 6 to 8 × 40 m finishing with 80-percent effort.

Recreative activity. Handball or paddleball.

WEDNESDAY—*Technique work. Back of the ring drill, exercise 2 without a discus.*

Weight training. Repeat weight training with a different set of exercises designed to work the same muscle groups. A stereotyped approach is not necessary, since there are sufficient exercises to alternate and still work the same muscle groups.

THURSDAY—*Depth jumping-plyometrics. Depth jump from a low platform to a mat.*

Sprint activities. Interval sprints, 6 to 8 × 40 m at 80-percent effort, 2 sets.

Technique work. Implement drill with overweight implement from a standing throw position.

FRIDAY—*Cross-country workout. 5 to 10 km (3 to 6 miles) with intermittent rests involving calisthenics and stretching.*

Tumbling and trampoline work. Select exercises from those discussed in the pole-vault chapter (e.g., tumbling-cartwheel, roundoff, front and back somersaults, back dive half twist). Trampoline—twisting exercises and somersaults: swivel hips, barrel roll, half twisting piked and tucked forward somersaults.

Weight training.

SATURDAY—*Technique work, done with a regulation discus. Back of the ring drills, exercises 1 and 2. Front of the ring drill. Implement drill (throwing from a spin) 40 to 50 repetitions.*

SUNDAY—*Rest, recreative activity, or easy cross-country running.*

EARLY SEASON

Precede and conclude each workout with the suggested warm-up and warm-down.

MONDAY—*Throwing, with standard and variable weight implements, 50 repetitions.*

Sprinting activities. Pickup sprints, 6 to 8 × 50 m, 2 sets.

TUESDAY—*Weight training, of all extremities and the trunk, strength concept.*

WEDNESDAY—*Depth jumping-plyometrics. Low platform drill, 6 to 8 repetitions, 2 sets. Pendulum, lever, or pumping action drill with overweight implement, 10 to 12 repetitions.*

Tumbling and trampoline work. See Friday, off-season.

Sprint activities, repetition sprints, 6 to 8 × 60 m at 90-percent effort.

THURSDAY—*Weight training, repeat the Tuesday routine with the power concept.*

FRIDAY—*Throwing, 10 to 12 easy throws.*
SATURDAY—*Competition.*
SUNDAY—*Rest, recreative activity, weight training, or running as needed.*

LATER SEASON
Continue warm-up and warm-down procedures.

MONDAY—*Throwing, 15 to 20 hard throws.*
Weight training, strength-oriented training for the legs;
power-speed training for the arms and trunk.
TUESDAY—*Depth jumping-plyometrics. Upright and squat hip rotation with*
barbell, 10 to 12 repetitions, 2 sets. Platform drill, 10 to 12
repetitions.
Sprint activities, acceleration sprints, 5 to 6 × 60 m, 2 sets at
full effort.
WEDNESDAY—*Repeat Monday workout, using different lifts for the*
weight-training session.
THURSDAY—*Sprint activities, acceleration sprints, 5 to 6 × 60 m.*
FRIDAY—*Warm-up.*
SATURDAY—*Competition.*
SUNDAY—*Rest, recreative activity, weight training or running as needed.*

BIBLIOGRAPHY

1. Dyson, Geoffrey H.G., *The Mechanics of Athletics,* Sixth Edition, University of London Press, London, 1973.
2. Editors, "Development of Discus Technique," *Modern Athlete and Coach, 5,* No. 5 (1972).
3. Endemann, Friedhelm, "Another Look at Discus Throwing," *Athletics Coach, 7,* No. 2 (1973).
4. Gemer, George V., "Munich—Observations and Comments on the Discus," *Track Technique, 53* (September 1973).
5. Hay, James G., *The Biomechanics of Sports Technique,* Prentice-Hall, Englewood Cliffs, 1973.
6. Ivanova, L., "New Strength Approach for Discus Throwers," *Track Technique, 50* (December, 1972).
7. Morris, Frank, "Simplifying Discus Technique," *Track Technique, 51* (March 1973).
8. Paish, Wilf, "Fundamentals of Discus Throwing," *Athletics Coach, 6,* No. 4 (1972).

9. Paish, Wilf, "Teaching the Discus Throw," *Athletics Coach, 4,* No. 1 (1970).

10. Ward, Paul, "Discus Slinging," *Track and Field Quarterly Review, 2,* 35 (1973).

11. Wyler, R. M., "A Fresh Look at Discus Throw Technique," *Athletics Coach, 6,* No. 4 (1972).

Chapter 10

The Javelin Throw

The most important mechanical principles for javelin technique interrelate the linear velocity of the man/implement during the run with the transfer of energy from one body part to another, while applying force through a bow-string and torqued body position to the javelin. If the aerodynamic rating of the javelin is appropriate for the athlete's ability, this combination of forces and velocities applied at an optimum release angle, partially determined by wind conditions, should produce desired results.

Although the evolution of the event is probably prehistoric, "modern" rules have allowed only one improvisation that is responsible for improved distance—the Dick Held aerodynamic implement. The discus-oriented, "soapy hand," slinging technique, inspired by Spaniard Miguael Salcedo, was quickly outlawed by international rulemakers, leaving the classical European technique intact.

Javelin scholars may debate aerodynamic principles, the relative merits of keeping the hips at right angles or parallel to the delivery line during the crossover or transition stage, and the merits of a lower center of gravity through the last long step, but the essential task of imparting maximum velocity to the implement re-

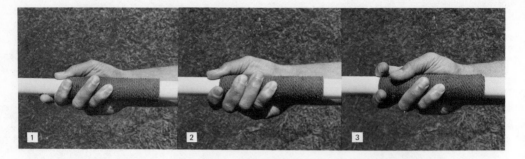

Figure 44. A variety of methods for gripping the javelin: (1) Finnish, (2) American, (3) Fork.

mains (2, 5, 8, 13). Argument over the merit of heavy, strength-oriented weight training versus the use of light, iron shots or 1.35 to 1.8-kg (3 to 4 lb) stubbies as part of the conditioning program is probably more controversial than the debate over technique (6, 11, 12, 13).

The Grip

The correct grip will be a matter of choice. The important item is contact of the upward-oriented heel of the palm with the javelin cord to control the point and the use of the fingers to aim the implement and impart a clockwise stablizing spin at release. The Finnish grip, favored by many, places the strong, second (middle) finger and thumb behind the whipcord for release, with the remaining fingers used for aim, balance, and control. A variation grip features the thumb and first finger behind the cord for release with the remaining fingers on the cord. A third style positions the flexed first and second fingers on the shaft behind the edge of the binding in a V or fork orientation, with the thumb and remaining fingers on the cord supplying necessary control (Figure 44).

The Carry

Regardless of individual angular variations, the over-the-shoulder carry (in a plane with the direction of the throw) is standard and allows for a more unrestricted run than the older, under-the-shoulder style. The throwing arm is flexed, elbow pointing to the front, the javelin held horizontally over the shoulder with the palm directed upward and forward.

Check marks

The length of the total run will vary per individual from 18.29 to 30.48 m (60 to 100 ft). Check marks are used at the start of the run and at the beginning of the withdrawal-transition phase, 9.145 to 12.19 m (30 to 40 ft) from the arc (Figure 45). The athlete must have confidence in the check marks to assure an accelerating run up and to eliminate fouling. The second check mark will vary individually, depending on the length and number of hops, bounds, and crossovers used in the

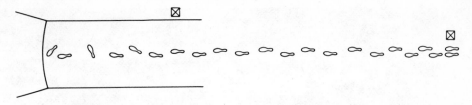

Figure 45. A 20-stride run for the javelin with the second and last check mark placed for a seven-step, six-stride withdrawal-transition, using two crossover strides.

transition phase prior to the throwing stride. Novice throwers must develop a conditioned response to the procedure of directing all activity forward while accelerating and throwing, since forces in other directions and the use of too many animated strides detract from forward acceleration. Directing activity straight ahead in the withdrawal-transition phase recognizes the necessity of angular steps, particularly in the final crossover stride, to facilitate layback and the diagonal torque mechanics required for a good throw. The objective is to achieve the throwing position with the best velocity possible.

The remaining discussion assumes a seven-step, six-stride, withdrawal-transition procedure for a right-handed thrower using two crossovers. With the right power foot hitting the last check mark, the withdrawal of the javelin occurs during the second stride (first crossover) and is completed just prior to the third. The last "crossover" occurs during the fourth stride, with the fifth and sixth strides expedited for the throw and follow-through. A time-sequence rhythm is suggested with the lines representing relative time intervals, the numbers representing steps, and Roman numerals the strides:

I	II	III	IV	V	VI	Stride
	L		L		L	
R		R		R		R
1	2	3	4	5	6	7 Step

The Run (Figure 46, [frames 1–20] frames 1–3)

The run begins in a relaxed, gradually accelerating manner and progresses to a fast, controlled approach preceding the withdrawal and transition phases (no attempt is made to artificially lean or lengthen the stride, since this will occur naturally through the act of acceleration). Although all available effort should be made to increase the release speed of the implement, the fluidity of movement from phase to phase with speed that can be handled will most effectively produce and use the summation of forces.

The Withdrawal and Transition Phases (Figure 46, frames 1–7)

As the right foot hits the check mark (step 1), which is set about 9.145 to 12.19 m (30 to 40 ft) from the arc, the javelin is withdrawn without turning the palm to the outside. Whether the javelin is brought forward first or immediately pulled

Figure 46. A classic example of Finnish torque technique by Hannu Siitonen, Finland. PR 93.90 m (308 ft, 1 in.). Courtesy of Toni Nett, West Germany.

back, the movement should be expedited in a plane parallel and within the direction of the throw and completed before the left foot lands, before the third stride. There will be a natural turn of the shoulder axis to the right and, while the hip axis may have a tendency to follow, this movement should be avoided to retain a torqued position, opposite to the one assumed in shot-put orientation, while continuing forward acceleration. The retention of a torqued position, subject to the same problems as in the shot and discus, is gradually lost when progressing from

Figure 47. The "reverse crossing the X" initiated during the "crossover" and retained through the throwing stride. The hips are at right angles to the shoulders. The shoulders are parallel with the direction of the throw.

double through single support and airborne phases. The reverse "crossing the X" procedure should be initiated with every effort directed to retaining it through the remainder of the six-stride count. The hips should be at right angles to the shoulders, and the shoulders should be oriented in or parallel with the direction of the throw (Figure 47). The left free arm is held partially flexed across the chest during this maneuver.

The torqued position, as uncomfortable as it may be, should be retained without reduction of speed or loss of control of the javelin point. The stretch on trunk muscles induced by this position can be used to advantage a split second later in forceful contraction. Body-implement acceleration is retained within the six-stride pattern, while the body's center of gravity is lowered in a settle, somewhat similar to the transition phase advised for the straddle high jumper. The trunk is inclined backward to produce a posture that resembles a drawn bow (3). Mechanically, this posture and the torqued position expedited at controllable linear velocity will integrate rotary and linear motion, permitting the application of force to the javelin over the greatest possible distance.

The Last Crossover (Figure 46, frames 8-17)

With some world-class athletes, the majority of the drawn-bow lean back occurs during a final crossover step that resembles a natural running stride. Some throwers think of this as a bounding stride but, regardless of the interpretation, it should be as long as feasible and preferably accelerated with emphasis placed on landing actively. To prevent reduction of forward velocity, the right power foot is quickly grounded before the left foot drives in to the post position for the throwing stride.

The length and height of the cross-step is an item of debate among coaches and athletes. Some favor a long, high step, arguing that it will place the left post leg farther forward. This action, in turn, depends on the amount of backward lean achieved in the final crossover stride, which has a tendency to shorten the step. Others favor the shorter step, with lower knee action, to assure acceleration.

The Throwing Stride (Figure 46, frames 17-20)

Shannon feels that American javelin throwers generally have not mastered the ability to maintain the velocity of the run into the crossover and throwing stride (6). Indeed, there is much to accomplish in a split second, while in an unusual posture, to get set for the throw. Tucker, of the U.S. Coast Guard Academy, has studied Finnish throwers and describes their stride as one in which the right foot lands an instant before the left, the pull beginning instantly with a drive off the right leg. The "square" hips rotate forward and down from their slightly open position, while the left post leg is grounded heel first (10).

Initially and correctly, there will be a small degree of flexion at the post knee to maintain forward movement. Prematurely posting the lead leg to increase velocity of the upper part of the body by "hinged moment" principle would only retard forward motion and reduce body lift just prior to release of the javelin. Nevertheless, the leg still has to check some motion. The chest begins to turn forward, and the center of gravity of the body, with the throwing arm above it, moves over the left post foot. The post leg then straightens to impart explosive lift to the javelin (14).

As the body rapidly moves over this leg, the shoulders turn, the chest is pushed forward, and the lead arm is thrust down in an extended position. Finally, leading with the elbow, the flexible, relaxed throwing arm, palm up, is literally whipped over the shoulder, the head turns away, and the javelin is released from the highest position possible above the shoulder. Throughout this phase, javelin/man alignment, largely determined by the location of the javelin tip, must be linearly perfect for accurate, powerful delivery. The picture during the cross-step and delivery stride is of a twisted, drawn bow or torqued horseshoe, the upper portion of which is parallel with the throw and at right angles to the lower portion. This unnatural position is retained during the throwing stride. As the bow's forward progress stops, unwinds, and functions like a whip, its great, centrifugal force projects the missile on a tangent or straight-line course to the arc.

Dynamics of Release (Figure 48)

As with the discus, to obtain a maximal flight distance there are a number of angles that must be controlled by the athlete prior to the actual moment of release. Ability, prevailing wind condition, and the rated, aerodynamic-distance capabilities of the implement also play major roles. Although this might be mind-boggling, the essentials will be defined and suggestions made for practical application.

1). *Angle of release* is the projected angle of the flight of the implement's center of gravity with the horizontal (ground level) at the moment of release.

2). The *angle of attack,* with its vertex at the center of pressure, is between the plane of the javelin and the relative wind. This angle determines the amount of lift and drag the

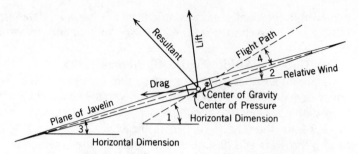

Figure 48. Angular dynamics of javelin release. The angles that can be controlled in varying degree prior to and at the moment of release as governed by ability, prevailing wind conditions, and the aerodynamic "rating" of the javelin are: (1) the **angle of release** determined largely by the layback position of the body and shoulder mechanics in the transition and delivery phase; (2) the **angle of attack,** a relationship between wind conditions and the plane of the javelin resulting in a temporary center of pressure and lift and drag components to the resultant force (positive here since the plane of the javelin is above the relative wind); (3) **the attitude angle,** governed largely by position of the javelin in relation to the forearm, wrist, palm, and activity of the fingers, as is (4) **the angle of incidence** (negative in this case because the plane of the javelin is below the projected path of the center of gravity of the javelin). Based on Juris Terauds, "Research Studies with the Javelin," paper presented at the NCAA National Championships, Austin, Texas, June 6, 1974.

implement will encounter, and the relative wind can be correspondingly reduced or increased if a tail or head wind is encountered respectively. In quiet air, relative wind will be equal and directly opposite the flight path of the implement's center of gravity.

The *center of pressure* is a temporary point where all the lift and drag forces and the relative wind acting on the javelin produce a resultant. The center of pressure will move from just ahead of the center of gravity at release to behind it when coming down in an average good throw.

Fundamentally, the posture of the athlete and mechanics of the shoulder before and during the release determine the angle of release. The angle of attack, the attitude angle, and the angle of incidence are determined by wind conditions, activity of the index finger, and the position of the wrist, forearm, and the palm of the hand at release (particularly if the Finnish grip is employed).

3). The *attitude angle* is between the plane of the javelin and the horizontal.

4). An *angle of incidence* will be negative if the plane of the javelin is below the flight path of the center of gravity.

5). Correspondingly, the *angle of incidence* will be positive if the plane of the javelin is above the flight path of the center of gravity.

To further simplify this approach, Juris Terauds recommends the following suggestions gleaned from research studies with current, aerodynamic implements (9).

1). The *angle of release* for the majority of implements is between 20 and 30 degrees. This may be convenient for the shorter athlete, who is accustomed to placing the tail of the implement dangerously close to the ground prior to release.

2). As the potential for improved velocity of release increases, the angle of release should be systematically reduced by degree.

3). The angle of release should be lowered by degree when encountering a head wind and correspondingly increased when experiencing a tail wind.

4). It may be expected that the typical, slow, clockwise, stablizing spin imparted on the javelin by a right-handed thrower will direct the implement to the left. This, in itself probably does not add or subtract distance from the throw but actually increases the flight to a limited extent when aided by a right-hand quartering wind. All of these conditions are reversed for the left-handed thrower.

5). Within limits, decrease the angle of release if the angle of attack is positive. Correspondingly, increase it if the angle of attack is negative. In other words, decrease the release angle if the plane of the javelin is slightly above the flight path of the center of gravity, and increase it if the plane is below the flight path.

In summary, it is probably best to keep the angle of release relatively low to encourage speed at release. The plane of the javelin should be just below the pathway of the center of gravity with the pressure point quite close to, and slightly ahead of, the center of gravity. The simplest approach is to keep the angle of release at the recommended 20 to 30 degrees, directing the shaft of the javelin in the same pathway as the center of gravity of the implement.

The Recovery
The recovery or follow-through is facilitated by bringing the power leg through naturally, immediately after the release, and flexing it at the knee to further absorb any remaining forward speed.

TEACHING THE JAVELIN
Immediately a spectrum of problems concerning javelin instruction, ranging from the use of an individual or group approach through availability of implements to the complicated nature and danger of the event becomes apparent. If time is of little consequence, an individual approach would be logical and, although this is probably the most common method applied to those who gravitate to the event, it may not uncover latent talent in other athletes. A group walk-through method will be

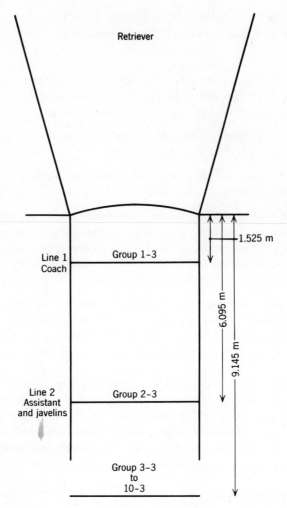

Figure 49. A plan for teaching the javelin throw to a large class of beginners. Phase 1, assemble groups of three at line 3. Send them a group at a time to line 2 for javelins and instruction, then individually to line 1 for a standing throw. Phase 2, assemble at line 3 and expedite a walk-through throw from line 2, for each individual. Phase 3, execute a running throw from line 3.

discussed on the premise that a simple approach to technique with a limited amount of equipment can uncover, as well as stimulate, individuals safely in a certain amount of instructional time.

Assuming that the instructor is working with a 40-minute period gym class of 30 people and has three javelins available, the following procedure is suggested (Figure 49).

1). Mark off a javelin-throwing area on level, closely mowed ground in accordance with the plans outlined in the rule book [(i.e., 4 m (13 ft, 1 1/2 in.) wide, the foul line in the shape of an arc with a radius of 8 m (26 ft, 3 in.)]. The depth of the run-up lane need not exceed 9.145 m (30 ft) for preliminary work and should be marked with lines perpendicular to the lane at 1.525, 6.095, and 9.145 m (5, 20, and 30 ft) from the foul line.

2). The first item of instruction should relate to the grip. Although three methods are most commonly used, the Finnish grip described in the previous section may be introduced initially, with modifications possible later on.

3). The class, divided into 10 groups of three each, is lined up behind the 9.145-m throwing line. One group at a time advances to the 6.095-m line where the javelins are located, and an assistant checks each individual's grip before sending them, one at a time, to the 1.525-m line.

4). The coach double-checks the grip and palm-up over-the-shoulder carry position and instructs the candidate to post the lead leg about 91.5 cm (3 ft) ahead of the back leg, to withdraw the javelin, lean back, and throw it over the right shoulder at a 20 to 30 degree release angle. As this candidate goes to the back of the line, the second member of the first three-person group takes his or her turn, etc. When all three javelins have been thrown, an assistant in the landing area quickly retrieves and returns the implements. Expedited quickly, it may be possible for each class member to throw at least once and possibly twice during the period.

5). Since the class is familiar with the routine, the procedure may be repeated on the second day with each person getting in three or four throws. Emphasis may be placed on square hips, driving the right leg forward before untorquing the shoulder, driving the chest forward/upward, and finally using the elbow-leading throwing arm in a whiplike action.

6). In the third session, a short walk-through approach is introduced. With the class assembled in a semicircle behind the throwing area, the instructor can discuss and demonstrate the routine, counting out each step vocally, while walking through it. He or she stands in the initial position discussed in step 4, with the right foot on the 6.095-m mark and the left foot back about 61 cm (2 ft); withdraws the javelin during the second (this may be a cross-step) and third strides; crosses over on the fourth, emphasizing a straight-ahead, bounding stride; posts the left leg on the fifth stride; throws and completes with the sixth stride follow-through.

With the groups assembled as in step 3, but at the 9.145-m line with the assistant, one individual at a time from each subgroup goes to the 6.095-m line, walks through the routine, throws the javelin, and returns to the back of the line. Again, there may be time for each member of the class to throw the javelin once or twice during the period.

7). The fourth session repeats the procedure of the third, using a slow running approach and initiating the six-stride pattern from the 9.145-m line. Each class member should be able to do this three or four times during the period. Emphasis should be placed on control of the point of the javelin, proper release angle, and the elements of straight-ahead foot alignment throughout the sequence.

With this instruction as an introduction, further refinement is accomplished through individual instruction in after-school sessions with those who demonstrate interest and aptitude. If the supply of javelins is a critical problem, weighted tennis balls filled with sand or lead shot and wrapped with training tape can be substituted. Candidates can practice the technique and step routine, releasing the ball into a wall or throwing for distance on a field. As basic technique is mastered, specifically concentrate on the controlled-velocity concept of the approach run for the development of linear momentum, a smooth transfer of force through the withdrawal-transition phase, and an adequate post-leg position for the whiplike throw.

The four "A's" of Nick Kovalakides may be added as an appropriate epilogue: alignment, accuracy, acceleration, and explosion (2). The implement must be aligned with the direction of power and thrown accurately to an imaginary target above the horizon, while acceleration achieved through a controlled run culminates in an explosive throw and release.

FOUNDATION TRAINING PROGRAM FOR THE JAVELIN THROW

Generally, training theories for the javelin range from the strength-power philosophy to a concept based exclusively on power. All experts agree on the year-round pyramidal system, with the Germans and Finns also placing a good deal of reliance on the idea that the best training for javelin throwers is throwing. Tucker, in describing Finnish training, points out that American concepts are based on strength-weight training as being the key to speed increases, whereas the Finns acknowledge the javelin's light weight and stress the importance of other motor parameters in a throwing program that employs a progressive, deresistance weight-training idea (9, 11, 12, 13). Speed, power, and agility are emphasized, because it is the speed of the total body delivery and not the brute strength of the throwing arm that counts. On the other hand, Fred Luke, an acknowledged premier American thrower, uses a combination program including heavy weight-training exercises that accentuate the importance of the controlled approach and torqued position with lateral flexion of the trunk in the transition phase for an effective release (6).

Frequently American javelinists are involved in other activities, particularly on the high-school level, which seems to preclude the specific year-round training theory. The training suggestions in this section, however, will describe a program with sample workout routines based on the year-round concept.

I. Warm-up and Warm-down
Procedures similar to those suggested for other throwing and jumping events are

recommended. More time should be spent on preliminary running in warm-up, particularly during the off-season, because the event requires elements of endurance and speed to sustain repeated run approaches of 18 to 30 m (60 to 100 ft) in length. The withdrawal and transition phases, as well as the crossover and throwing stride, require unusual flexibility and agility, calling for a sound program of warm-up activities to emphasize and develop these performance traits.

Prior to the season, precede each practice session with 800 to 1500 m of easy running, followed by 20 to 30 minutes of flexibility-agility exercises and the overemphasis exercises used by jumpers and sprinters (Chapters 4 and 13). Conclude each practice session with 800 m of easy running. The length of warm-up running may be reduced to 800 m during the season. On weight training days, include a light weight warm-up prior to lifting.

II. Flexibility-Agility Exercises
Exercises of the variety used by jumpers and sprinters (Chapter 4) and vaulters (Chapter 7) are appropriate.

III. Overemphasis Exercises
The importance of running and sprint technique in the javelin event requires work in this area. Chapter 4 contains a descriptive listing of appropriate activity.

IV. Weight Training
During the off-season, weight training is best obtained with the following exercises. A more complete listing with suggestions for concepts and procedures is found in Chapter 3. After finding starting weights, many sets and fewer repetitions per set with heavy weights produce the best strength development. This concept is gradually replaced with power lifting as the season progresses.
  A. For leg development:
     1. Squat and split-style snatch.
     2. Squats (50, 66, and 75 percent).
     3. Bent leg dead lift.
     4. Heel rise.
     5. Gather (sinking) exercises: hip press and hip split squat.
  B. For abdominal development:
     1. Side bender (lateral raises).
     2. Side bender from a javelin throwing position.
     3. Torso twist while in a standing cross-over and in a post position with the hips square.
     4. Back hyperextension.
     5. Bent leg sit-up from an incline and level bench with legs and hips stabilized and the back hyperextended over the edge.
  C. For wrist, arm, and shoulder development:
     1. Bent and straight arm pullovers.
     2. French curl.

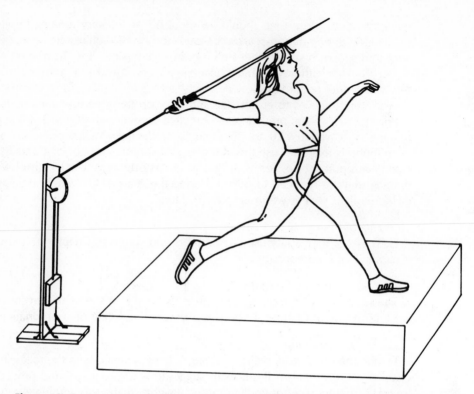

Figure 50. Device training for the javelin. From a post position with the upper torso at right angles to the hips, pull the handle through, emphasizing right hip drive and untorquing of the torso. This drill may also be done with a sawed off javelin attached to the rope, an Exergenie, or with a "stubby" thrown into a mat, retrieved with the left hand and continually repeated.

    3.   Wrist adduction (ulnar wrist flexion).
    4.   Wrist pronation.
    5.   Wrist curls.

V. Special Device Training
A.   Pulley work (Figure 50). Saw off a javelin behind the grip, attach an eyebolt, and secure to the pulley rope of a latissimus dorsi machine or wall weights. Simulate pulling the javelin through while in the post position, emphasizing trunk untorquing and driving the right hip forward from a square hip position. Exercise dynamically forward and return slowly (emphasizing eccentric contraction of the same muscles).
B.   Isokinetic exercising. Similar to the above exercise using an Exer-Genie or Mini-Gym device. Exert isometrically until dialed resistance is overcome before pulling through isotonically.

Special care must be applied in both of these exercises to utilize loads that make a power concept possible, with emphasis on employing a flail-like, elbow-first, high-over-the-shoulder release. Be sure the rope is low enough in A and B to emulate a 20 to 30 degree angle of release movement.

C. Ball or stubby throwing. With 1- to 2-kg (2 to 4 lb) shots, repeatedly emulate the withdrawal-transition phase and throw into a net or mat, retrieving the shot with the left hand. Tucker has advised that a 10- to 20-cm (4 to 8 in.) stubby (a machined shaft with the heft of a javelin) be substituted, thus allowing the required palm-up position with appropriate grip (10).

D. Net throwing. A javelin, fitted with flanges in front of the grip, can be thrown into a net 9.145 to 12.19 m (30 to 40 ft) from the point of release. The flanges will prevent the implement from traveling any further and provide an excellent way to emphasize the technique of throwing the implement in close quarters.

VI. Practice Throwing and Drills

Although throwing in practice is rarely expedited with the same zeal as in competitive efforts, it must be done with contest conditions in mind. Obviously, some hard throwing to stimulate stress and progressively develop technique must be done, yet caution should be exercised. There are a number of substitute procedures that not only maintain interest but also emphasize elements of technique. From the last check mark, which is five or six throwing strides from release, expedite the following drills:

A. Palm-up drill. Run through the last check mark with the palm up, pulling through with the elbow high at release.

B. Straight-ahead rhythm. Run through the last check mark rhythmically, emphasizing straight-ahead or linear progression.

C. Angle drill. Run through the last check mark, emphasizing control of the angle of release by means of body lean and shoulder flexion. Adjust attitude angle by directing attention to activity of the palm and index finger in particular. Keep these angles similar by releasing between 20 to 30 degrees and throwing completely through the point of the javelin.

D. Lay-back, hip-snap drill. Run through the last check mark, emphasizing backward lean by advancing the right leg well in front of the body whether using crossover or normal running strides, and snap the left foot down quickly. This should help the thrower avoid hip drift and maintain the torqued position of the trunk, which is then unleased in delivery.

VII. Running, Sprinting, and Climbing Activities

A. Running. Aerobic (endurance) requirements are met with daily warm-up and warm-down running.

B. Sprinting. A percentage speed-training program, similar to the one used by other field-event candidates; concentrates on repeat-accelerative efforts over 30 to 50 m. All anaerobic-aerobic sprint activities listed and described for sprinters (Chapter 13) are appropriate. The run can be finished with crossovers and bounds that emulate the transition phase. Low pelvic running, accomplished by slightly extending the sprint stride and not by bending the knees should be practiced to imitate the gather position in the transition and early delivery phases.

C.   Climbing. Short power running and hopping bursts up flights of stairs are recommended for the high-knee lift necessary for the run and crossover strides.

VIII. Depth Jumping-Plyometrics

Depth jumping from gradually raised platforms over the length of the season, box drills commonly used by triple jumpers, and several plyometric exercises are valuable for the transition and low-pelvic phase of the javelin event. Plyometric exercises for the legs may be the relatively simple bouncing, bounding, and hopping drills on the grass. For the trunk and upper extremities, they may be the net or mat throwing drill, expedited by swinging the hand weight down and back first and then over the shoulder for the throw, to obtain a stretch-reflex effect (under-over exercise).

IX. Tumbling, Floor Exercise, and Trampoline Activities

In general, gymnastic exercises of all varieties are recommended for flexibility and developing the feeling of rhythm. Tumbling activities help develop basic body control, floor exercises require flexibility, agility, and strength in a continuous pattern, and trampoline work contributes to the feeling of uncoiling from gathered positions.

IX. Recreative Activity

Remember that training is a monotonous chore at times and needs to be interspersed with activities that feature running, flexibility, coordination, and agility. Basketball, volleyball, handball, and swimming are recommended. Of course, since there is always the chance that an ankle may be turned in some of these activities, the choice is elective.

SAMPLE WEEKLY PROGRAM
OFF-SEASON
Precede and conclude each workout with the recommended warm-up and warm-down.

MONDAY—*Weight training. Construct several routines from the recommended exercises or the more complete list in Chapter 3, and plan to alternate them for successive sessions, employing the strength concept.*
Tumbling, floor exercise, and trampoline activities. Concentrate

initially on simple tumbling exercises (e.g., forward rolls: dive, straddle, tucked; backward rolls: pike, straddle, and back; inverted exercises: cartwheel, round-off, front and back somersaults).

TUESDAY—*Special device training. Pulley or isokinetic exercises with resistance at 7 kg.*

Running, sprinting, and climbing activities, interval sprints, 5 to 6 × 50 m. 3 sets at 80-percent effort.

WEDNESDAY—*Weight training. Repeat the Monday program with the second routine.*

Tumbling, floor exercise, and trampoline activities. Concentrate on basic floor exercises—Agility: scissor kick, straddle-jump toe touch, straddle and straight-leg rolls, skipping. Balance: vee sit, splits, front and back walkovers. Strength: handstands, (knee and foot lift), press exercises—bent arm, bent knee; bent arm, straight leg; straight arm, straight leg; hollow back.

THURSDAY—*Special device training. Ball or stubby throwing; 1 1/2 to 2-kg weight, 30 repetitions. Emphasize forward/down movement of "square" hips, as a relaxed arm is brought through in flail-like movement directly over the shoulder, above a posted lead leg.*

Running, sprinting, and climbing activities. Sprint acceleration sprints with crossovers and and bounding, 6 to 8 × 50 m, 4 sets at 80-percent effort.

FRIDAY—*Weight training. Either introduce the third routine, or repeat the Monday one, including gather exercises (hip press and split squat).*

Recreative activity. Basketball, paddleball or handball.

SATURDAY—*Special device training. Net throwing, with a flanged javelin and short approach. 30 repetitions.*

Depth jumping-plyometrics. 6 to 8 × 50 m, 4 sets, bounding, skipping, hopping, and crossovers.

SUNDAY—*Rest, recreative activity, or easy cross-country running as needed.*

EARLY SEASON

Early-season work features a greater emphasis on actual throwing with continuance of ball throwing, specific check-mark running and pantomime throwing, depth jumping, and one or two abbreviated strength and power weight-training sessions. Again, precede and conclude each workout with a warm-up and warm-down.

MONDAY—*Weight training. Employ the power concept.*
Special device training. Ball or stubby throwing, 1 1/2-kg
weight, 4 sets, 10 repetitions.
Tumbling, floor exercise, and trampoline activities. Concentrate
on trampoline activities discussed in Chapter 7.
TUESDAY—*Throwing, from a short run, 30 to 50 repetitions.*
Running, sprinting and climbing activities. Sprinting, pick up
sprinting, 6 to 8 × 60 m at 90-percent effort.
Depth jumping-plyometrics. Depth jumping from a low platform,
10 repetitions. Plyometrics, 6 to 8 × 60 m, bounding,
skipping, hopping, and crossovers.
WEDNESDAY—*Special device training. Pulley or isokinetic exercising with*
resistance set at 5 kg, 10 repetitions, 5 sets.
Tumbling, floor exercise, and trampoline activities. Concentrate
on floor exercises and tumbling activities.
Weight training. 1 to 2 sets with the power concept.
THURSDAY—*Throwing with 75- to 90-percent effort from a complete run*
(run at full effort), 10 repetitions, 2 sets.
FRIDAY—*Running, sprinting, and climbing activities. Sprinting, acceleration*
sprints, 6 to 8 × 60 m, finishing at 90-percent effort.
SATURDAY—*Competition.*
SUNDAY—*Rest, recreative activity, or running as needed.*

LATER SEASON
Weight training is continued one session per week. The power/speed emphasis in weight work is preferred to maximum concepts at this time. With a greater frequency of meets and the increasing importance of many of them, more attention is directed to a combination of check-mark accuracy and the required technique in throwing and actual throwing practice. Follow previously suggested warm-up and warm-down procedures.

MONDAY—*Special device training. Ball or stubby throwing, 1- to 1 1/2-kg*
weight, 2 sets, 10 repetitions.
Depth jumping-plyometrics. Depth jumping from a higher
platform than used previously. (The platform should be
adjustable and raised gradually throughout the training
season). 5 repetitions, 3 sets.
Plyometrics—Under-over exercise with 5 kg weight, 5
repetitions, 5 sets.
TUESDAY—*Throwing from a complete run, 6 repetitions, 5 sets.*
Tumbling, floor exercise, and trampoline activities. Concentrate
on the trampoline activities.
WEDNESDAY—*Running, sprinting, and climbing activities. Climbing, sprint stair*
steps, 5 × 10 m, 2 sets.
Throwing from a complete run, 6 repetitions, 3 sets.

THURSDAY—*Running, sprinting and climbing activities. Running, sprinting, run through the check marks with a soft javelin release, 20 to 30 repetitions.*
Recreative activity. Handball or paddle ball.
FRIDAY—*Warm-up, including a few check-mark run-throughs pantomiming the release.*
SATURDAY—*Competition.*
SUNDAY—*Weight training with the power concept.*

BIBLIOGRAPHY

1. Harnes, Edward, "Javelin Technique," *Leichtathletic, 22, 23* (1973).
2. Kovalakides, Nick, "Four A's of Javelin Throwing," *Track and Field Quarterly Review, 2,* 14 (1970).
3. Markov, D., "Javelin Technique," *Track Technique, 19* (March 1965).
4. Paish, Wilf, "Javelin Throwing for Youngsters," *Modern Athlete and Coach, 9,* No. 4 (1971).
5. Schenk, Hans, "A Disagreement with Harnes' Theories," *Leichtathletik, 23* (1973).
6. Shannon, Ken, and Fred Luke, "Javelin Analysis," *Track and Field Quarterly Review, 1,* 34 (1973).
7. Stirzaker, Brett, "European Javelin Observations," *Modern Athlete and Coach, 11,* No. 2,3 (1973).
8. Terauds, Juris, "The Competition Javelin," *The Throws, Contemporary Theory, Technique and Training,* edited by Fred Wilt, Track and Field News Press, Los Altos, CA, 1974.
9. Terauds, Juris, "Research Studies with the Javelin," paper presented at the NCAA National Championships, Austin, Texas, June 6, 1974.
10. Tucker, Ed, "The Evolution of the Stubby," *Track and Field Quarterly Review, 4,* 246 (1973).
11. Tucker, Ed, "The Finnish Method of Training for the Javelin," *Track and Field Quarterly Review, 4,* 6 (1969).
12. Tucker, Ed, "The Javelin a la Finland," *Track Technique, 41* (September 1970).
13. Tucker, Ed, "The Javelin-Finnish Style," *Track and Field Quarterly Review, 3,* 61 (1969).
14. Wilt, Fred, and Dick Held, "Form Study of Hannu Siitonen," *Scholastic Coach, 45,* No. 9 (1976).

Chapter 11

The Hammer Throw

Although most high-school and college programs do not include the hammer throw, this fascinating event is popular in some regions. Considered a complicated event, teaching progression in the hammer throw, however, is a matter of what and how much is introduced at a time, with the candidate actually throwing the implement from the beginning of instruction (Figure 51, frames 1–29).

A studied approach of the event reveals its rotational nature—moving the tilted axis of the thrower/hammer system across the ring. This system is subject to the outward pulling effect of centrifugal force, countered by an inward, centripetal force that must be exerted by the thrower. Any increase in rotational speed is always accompanied by a greater increase in centrifugal force. Centripetal force cannot be effected without contact with the platform, which necessitates alternate single- and double-support phases while rotating, with increases in hammer velocity that occur primarily during the double-support phases. The tilted polar or vertical axis of the thrower/hammer system must vascillate to some extent as the result of these changing systems but, with the relatively narrow base of support in either position, most oscillation must become evident at the top of the "cone" near the head (Figure 52).

Figure 51. Valentin Dmitrijenko, USSR, in the hammer throw. PR 77.58 m (254 ft, 6 in.). Courtesy of Toni Nett, West Germany.

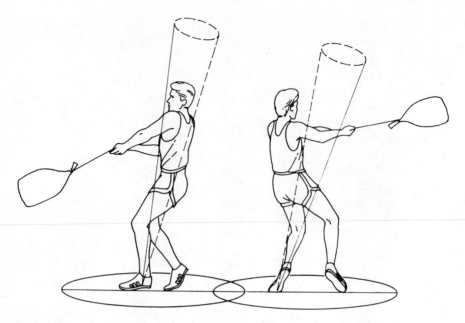

Figure 52. A chalkline footwork drill for the hammer emphasizing repeated left-face, 180-degree spinning and grounding on a line bisecting the ring. The cone represents the correctly placed vertical axis, which demonstrates some oscillation, particularly evident during single-support phases.

Superior hammer throwers display little of this action, however, indicating that the vertical axis of the system must stay close to one of the legs and oscillate little as progress is made across the ring (5). Irv Black reports that East German and Soviet throwers consider this axis to be correctly placed near the right foot rather than the left, in spite of the pivoting that must occur on the left foot in counterclockwise spinning (1).

Continued examination of the event reveals that the law of action-reaction pertains not only to the centripetal-centrifugal force couple but also to related aspects in the vertical direction. Dyson describes this phenomenon as the equal and opposite force of the center of gravity system down, and ground reaction up, through the legs (3). A skilled thrower will sit and hang momentarily, and probably instinctively, as the hammer travels downward during what is known as the double-support phase when both feet are in contact with the platform. This movement increases the moment arm or horizontal distance between the couple, maintaining equilibrium and adding speed to the hammer as it begins to go down, and countering the centripetal-centrifugal forces at the same time.

When the hammer is "horizontal" with the ground, it is accelerated by moving the common, vertical axis to the left, always leading with the legs and hips, developing torque between the hips and shoulders. By pushing down or pressing with the legs, further acceleration can be added as the ball travels upward. We get a picture of hip- and leg-oriented spinning across the ring, with the trunk and shoulders fixed in the direction of relaxed-extended arms, systematically speeding up the hammer as the thrower moves by sitting down, or dropping the body weight, just prior to the ball going down, pivoting and standing more upright and pushing with the legs just prior to the ball going up.

A final principle emerging in this brief examination of the event relates to the effective radius from the common axis maintained by the relaxed arms. Any effort to "muscle" the hammer by flexing the arms and shortening the radius will speed up the spin but make it difficult or impossible to control, reducing the tangent or linear velocity imparted to the ball at release by a loss of momentum. The greatest tangent velocity always occurs when both the rotational velocity and the effective radius are maximal (4). In this event, momentum is the product of the mass of the athlete/hammer system × radius × rotational velocity.

An optimum acceleration curve of approximately 170 degrees would occur from about the 4 o'clock to the 11 o'clock positions counterclockwise during the double-support phases of each spin. Since the shoulders, hips, and feet are all parallel with each other at the 12 o'clock position, and no further acceleration is possible, early lift of the right leg, single support on the left, and an early landing of the right foot are recommended to more easily regain the torqued position (7). This proper acceleration is followed by a powerful release of the hammer on the last spin, by lifting and pulling it into orbit over the left shoulder with the entire body hyperextended to slightly reduce the distance of the hammer head from the common vertical axis (radius) to increase centripetal force and rotational velocity. Provided there is no loss of momentum, this action, executed through a release angle of almost 45 degrees, imparts an increase in linear-tangent velocity to the hammerhead.

TEACHING THE HAMMER THROW

Teaching the hammer throw is a matter of progressionally getting the candidates to swing the hammer about their body with each arm, and then both arms, allowing them to experience the transfer of momentum and centripetal-centrifugal force-counterforce (6). For a right-handed thrower, the half turn is introduced next, with a left-face maneuver directing the hammer up and then slamming it into the ground. This maneuver is followed by a complete turn in which the athlete learns how to bring the right leg around to the left, followed by the hammer, which is then lifted through the vertical by the legs and released with the arms straight. The two-or-three spin is learned next, after weeks of working with the basic spin and the drills that help the athlete practice movement across the ring, which involves developing and maintaining body torque, striving for a low center of gravity with the shoulders forward and the arms extended and relaxed for the most effective radius possible.

1). Some progressions start with a 5.44- to 7.257-kg (12 to 16 1b) shot equipped with a triangular handle resemblant of the implement used in a 16- to 25.5-kg (35 to 56 1b) weight throw. In other instances, improvised equipment may be fashioned out of bags containing inner tube cuttings or sand, with a 91.5-cm (3 ft) cord and triangular handle attached; heavy link chain with cord and handle; or shots of various weights, bored and fitted with a spindle, wire, and handle (9).

2). Safety precautions are essential. All spectators should withdraw from the area, although an experienced instructor can safely stand to the right of the candidate where the hammer will be at the low point of its circular path.

3). Swing drill.—with the left hand in a palm-up position, grasp the handle between the second and third finger joints. The knees are slightly flexed, feet parallel and almost shoulder width, the trunk in an upright position, and the eyes directed to the horizontal. Swing the implement about the body without moving the feet.

4). Repeat step 3 with the right arm and the palm down.

5). Without crossing the thumbs, place the right hand over the left, and swing with both arms. Wind the hammer around the head, and release it into the ground at its low point to discontinue the drill. The right-handed candidate will soon realize that the high point of the swing will be to his left and the low point to his right. A countering action will naturally occur with the hips and legs moving to the right when the ball is to the left, and to the left when the ball is to the right.

In steps 3, 4, and 5, the hands must be kept close to the head when the hammer is behind the candidate and the arms in an extended-relaxed condition at all other times to maintain the longest radius possible. Tension in the elbow is an indication of pulling with the arms and should be discouraged. Countering action by the hips and legs should be a natural outcome, with the suggestion that it should resemble a golf swing-type action with the knees slightly flexed (i.e., shift the hips in the opposite direction of the hammer) (1). Let the upper body stretch in the direction of the hammer with the arms relaxed.

6). Left face drill.—repeat step 5 with a left face, executed by pivoting on the left heel and the ball of the right foot. Some coaches will elect to teach this manuever first without the hammer. Here, it is important to keep the right leg close to the left, pushing with the right leg without lifting the right foot off the platform. Take two preliminary swings, execute the left face, lead the hammer with the hips as it comes off its low point, with the left arm across the chest just under the chin. Guide the hammer off its low point with the arms extended, leading with the hips and pressing with the legs. As the hammer continues upward over the left shoulder, release it with the legs extended, the back hyperextended, and the eyes directed upward. Make no attempt, at this time, to actively pull the hammer with the arms, since this will only upset the balance of the conservation of rotational momentum and reduce the tangent velocity of the implement.

7). Two- and three-turn drill.—once step 6 has been mastered, ask the thrower to attempt two turns and a release, followed by three turns and a release. A balance-winding drill, which requires the athlete to take preliminary swings, turn, and take more swings can be introduced before this step. As the procedure is repeated while advancing across the ring, the thrower is familiarized with rotational equilibrium requirements relative to the high and low points of the hammer. A pyramid, or up-and-down-the-ladder drill, emphasizing relaxed arm extension and leading the hammer with the hips requires gradually increasing acceleration in three spins with deceleration in three more. Repeat several times.

8). Chalkline drill.—Wilt discusses an excellent drill for footwork,which can be done anywhere in a 2.13-m (7 ft) chalked ring with a bisecting mark (9) (Figure 52). Practice the left-face manuever, turn 180 degrees, continue the pivot another 180 degrees on the ball of the left foot while the right becomes airborne, and ground the right foot when it is once again parallel with the left. Continue with the drill, blindfolded, until it becomes a conditioned reaction. In this way, with the left foot always on the chalkline, normal progression can be made across the circle, emphasizing the close proximity of the right leg and the fact that 2.13 m provides sufficient room for the three turns. Repeat this drill with the hammer or a sandbag. Always "lean" toward the hammer with shrugged shoulders and extended-relaxed arms, and the hips counter with the knees slightly flexed.

9). Bosen points out that there are three paramount problems in hammer throwing: (1) movement across the circle and hammer pull; (2) developing and maintaining body torque; and (3) changes in hammer velocity with changes in its radius from the common axis (2).

Keeping the left arm across the chest during the single-support phase seems to be the key to number 1, giving the appearance of hanging away from the hammer prior to double support. Getting maximally ahead of the hammer during the first turn instead of in the successive turns, helps to develop and maintain the proper torque position (i.e., the hip axis precedes the shoulder axis while hanging onto the hammer). Hammer velocity in relation to the radius is best attained by sitting down more and leaning back less. The upper torso maintains a vertical axis of rotation, from the left foot through the right shoulder, that passes forward of the center of gravity of the body.

10). With the actual point of release about 1.525 m (5 ft) above the ground, the angle of release is about 42 degrees. This comes close to the ideal 45-degree angle for an object that leaves and returns to the same horizontal level at the end of its trajectory.

Some important points to consider as tips for better throwing would include:

1). As indicated on page 195, the radius of the hammer is shortened to a small degree in the delivery because the thrower does exert some pulling effort. This is desirable and changes the circular direction of the path of the hammer by application of centripetal force (pulling in), speeding it up in the process just prior to release.

2). As the thrower progresses across the circle, it is advisable to keep the right knee higher than the left one to facilitate an easier transition to pivoting on the left foot. This changes the slightly oscillating axis of rotation from the left (where friction would make it difficult to spin) to the right, making it easier to continue to pivot. It also keeps the legs far enough apart so that, in the delivery, there will be a reasonable base from which to initiate the pull of the delivery and "shorten" the radius as described above (10).

3). The thrower must "lead" the hammer, but never "drag" it. Dragging implies that the right arm is undesirably bent in the last half of each turn.

4). One of the great problems of hammer throwing is either turning too much or too little. Turning more than 180 degrees on the left heel is caused by allowing the hammer to get too far ahead of the thrower. Dragging the hammer is caused by the right-arm flexion mentioned above and turning less than 180 degrees on the left heel.

In conclusion, the following advice may be given to throwers familiar with the basic elements: obtain hammer velocity in the preliminary swings; spin tight; pull with the hips, not the shoulders and arms; and guide the hammer up for release, with the rotational axis tilting away from the implement while extending the legs and hyperextending the back and neck.

Gradual acceleration is facilitated and balance is enhanced by maintaining the body weight over the pivoting leg, leading the hammer with the hips and legs with no concerted effort to pull the hammer in. The secret of good hammer throwing is to utilize balance, torque, and a long radius to guide rather than muscle the hammer into an approximate 45-degree release.

FOUNDATION TRAINING PROGRAM FOR THE HAMMER THROW

Training for this event not only requires coping with the centrifugal nature of the event through stepwise procedures and drills for torque and counterforce orientation but it also necessitates strength training of the legs and hips to accomodate this approach. The additional need to maintain a long hammer radius while accelerating rotationally demands strength sufficient to control the implement through most of the event with pulling strength needed for the release phase.

I. Warm-up and Warm-down
These requirements and their procedures have been discussed previously in the chapters dealing with field events. Do not neglect them!

II. Flexibility-Agility Exercises
Procedures for these requirements are discussed in other field-event chapters. Do not neglect them!

III. Weight Training
The following abbreviated list of exercises, supplemented by those found in Chapter 3, are recommended for hammer-event strength and power training.

Generally, strength workouts may be undertaken two or three times a week with muscle groups that require it, particularly the legs. Power-training concepts should be reserved for the arms and shoulders. An alternating timetable can be worked out by coach and athlete, varying the program to assure recovery, variety, and emphasis for specificity. The program should be continued during the competitive season with a 48-hour recovery before important competition.

A. Hip, knee, and ankle exercises.
1. Squats.
2. Leg press.
3. Dead weight lifts.
B. Exercises for torque and rotational requirements of the hip.
1. Single leg swingover.
2. Bench single leg swingover.
C. Torso or trunk exercises.
1. Bent and straight leg sit-ups with trunk twisting.
2. Back hyperextension.
3. Hang cleans.
4. Torso twist.
D. Total exercises.
1. High pull-up.
2. Snatch, squat, and split style.
3. Cleans, split, and squat style.
4. Power dips.
E. Shoulder, arm, and wrist exercises.
1. Back press.
2. Shoulder shrugs.
3. Conventional and reverse wrist curls.
4. Wrist adduction and abduction.

IV. Running, Sprinting, and Climbing Activities

Although the hammer does not require the running rotation airborne phase of the discus, it does require rapid footwork and sprint endurance, particularly for practice-throwing sessions. Sets of short sprints with numerous repetitions and adequate recovery, alternated with longer sprints and fewer repetitions are advised. Programs can be similar to those discussed for the discus and shot.

V. Hammer Drills

Footwork and the art of leading the hammer can be enhanced by using the drills discussed in the teaching section. Varied weights and short-handled hammers can be progressionally used to learn balance, torque, and the control aspects of leading with relaxed-extended arms. Although there is no substitute for actual throwing, spinning without the weight on a chalkline can naturalize the unusual left-face, ball-heel rotation procedure. The balance or winding drill and ladder or pyramid drill are beneficial for establishing equilibrium under acceleration and the ability to lead with relaxed arms.

VI. Tumbling, Floor Exercises, and Trampoline Activities
As discussed in Chapters 7 and 10, these activities are valuable for rhythm, flexibility, and agility.

VII. Depth Jumping-Plyometrics
Activities suggested for the javelin (Chapter 10) are valuable for the hammer and for an additional weight-throw exercise in which a 16- or 25.5-kg (35 to 56 lb) weight is swung to and fro several times and released with a checking motion over the release shoulder.

VIII. Varied Resistance Throwing
Throwing hammers of various weights on a step-down basis (heavy to subcompetition weight) is a valuable specific power weight-training method. This practice is particularly valuable on a concentrated basis during the off- and early seasons with reduced quantity applications during the later season. The heavier implements develop torso and shoulder musculature, while slightly lighter hammer work develops turning speed.

SAMPLE WEEKLY PROGRAMS
OFF-SEASON
Precede and conclude each workout with a warm-up and warm-down.

MONDAY—*If the work must be done indoors, use a hand weight of 4 1/2 to 9 kg (10 to 20 lb) in this session.*
Preliminary swing drill, releasing weight at low point onto a gym mat.
Left-face drill, releasing weight at low point. 2- and 3- turn drill with short handle hammer or hand weight, releasing at low point.
Running, sprinting, and climbing activities. Pickup acceleration, interval sprints are appropriate, 5 × 40 m, three sets at 80-percent effort.
TUESDAY—*Weight training. Select exercises from the abbreviated listing in this chapter supplemented with exercises found in Chapter 3. Organize this material into routines, and follow the suggestions regarding strength concepts for the lower extremities and power concepts for the upper extremities. During recoveries, practice the chalkline drill.*
WEDNESDAY—*Repeat the drills described for Monday.*
Recreative activity, basketball, handball, paddleball, etc.
THURSDAY—*Weight training. Second Routine.*

FRIDAY—*Varied resistance throwing, if at all possible. Winter weather need not be a deterrent. The ring can be cleaned off, and the hammer does not make as great an indentation in frozen ground as the shot.*
If this is impossible, substitute depth jump-plyometric exercises, including the weight throw.
SATURDAY—*Weight training. Third routine, or repeat Tuesday routine.*
SUNDAY—*Cross-country running or recreative activity.*

EARLY SEASON

MONDAY—*Varied resistance throwing, 40 to 50 hard throws.*
Tumbling, floor exercise, and trampoline activities.
TUESDAY—*Weight training, strength concept.*
WEDNESDAY—*Chalkline, winding, and pyramid drills.*
Throwing, 20 to 30 hard throws.
Running, sprinting, and climbing activities. Sprinting, 6 × 50 m pickup, acceleration, interval, or repetition sprints, 3 sets at 90-percent effort.
THURSDAY—*Weight training, power concept.*
FRIDAY—*Throwing, 10 easy throws.*
SATURDAY—*Competition.*
SUNDAY—*Cross-country running, weight training, or recreative activity.*

LATER SEASON

MONDAY—*Varied resistance throwing, 30 to 40 hard throws.*
Tumbling, floor exercise, and trampoline activities.
TUESDAY—*Weight training, strength and power for legs and arms, respectively.*
WEDNESDAY—*Chalkline, winding, and pyramid drills.*
Throwing, 10 to 20 hard throws.
Recreative activity. Handball.
THURSDAY—*Running, sprinting, and climbing activities. Climbing, 6 × 10 m stair climbing.*
Depth jumping—plyometrics, including weight throw.
FRIDAY—*Warm-up.*
SATURDAY—*Competition.*
SUNDAY—*Rest or recreative activity.*

BIBLIOGRAPHY

1. Black, Irving, "Russian and German Techniques on Hammer Throwing," *Track and Field Quarterly Review, 4,* 204 (1974).
2. Bosen, Ken O., "Some Problems in Hammer Throwing," *Track and Field Quarterly Review, 4,* 239 (1973).
3. Dyson, Geoffrey H.G., *The Mechanics of Athletics.* Sixth Edition, University of London Press, London, 1973.
4. Hay, James G., *The Biomechanics of Sports Techniques,* Prentice Hall, Englewood Cliffs, 1973.
5. Jabs, Rolf-Gunter, "Analyzing the 1972 Hammer," *Track Technique, 52* (June 1973).
6. Kintisch, Irv, "Teaching the Hammer Throw," *Track and Field Quarterly Review, 3,* 11 (1970).
7. Samozvetov, Anatoliy, "The Acceleration of the Hammer," *Modern Athlete and Coach, 11,* no. 2 (1973).
8. Scoles, Gordon, "Pulling Strength for Hammer Throwers," *Track and Field Quarterly Review, 4,* 243 (1973).
9. Wilt, Fred, "Hammer Teaching Progressions," *Track and Field Quarterly Review, 2,* 24 (1970).
10. Wilt, Fred, Personal Correspondance, April, 1976.

section four

Coaching the Running Events

Chapter 12

Basic Science for Teaching Running Events

Sophisticated and popular literature that describes conditioning and training schedules for running events can be found in great abundance. These workout patterns, to be applied completely or partially by the coach and athlete, are often advocated by outstanding runners. Occasionally, some relationship will be made between the schedule and the science of physiology of exercise in terms of anaerobic/aerobic ratio requirements of the event (see Chapter 3). Generally, the importance of biomechanics and neuromuscular factors found in this section will be missing from such discussions.

For the most part, all people walk and run with a basic motor pattern established by some kind of central nervous system programming; but it is rare, even in the case of identical twins, to observe individuals run with precisely the same form. Running should be "quiet" and relaxed, with the understanding that if one walks with stalking, bounding, or leaping movements, the run will reflect the same characteristics. Although it is probably unnecessary to teach an athlete who runs naturally how to run correctly, running is not exclusively a natural skill. Instruction

Figure 53. The running stride of Peter Snell, New Zealand. PR 1:44.3, 3:37.6. Courtesy of Toni Nett, West Germany.

occurring early in life, with emphasis on correction of faults, can be of value (1, 2, 5, 6).

Learning to run involves molding the nervous system by practicing the technique of running. The coach should realize that each individual varies physiologically in many respects, with strength being only one factor. Anatomically, the disposition of the muscle/joint/lever system, governed by the build and posture of the individual, represents another set of variables. Psychologically, attitude and personality also govern running style and may be the final determinant of whether an individual will be a suitable candidate for competitive experience.

Phases of the Stride (Figure 53, Frames 1–14)

Since all running is made up of support-driving and recovery phases including an airborne interval, it is important to understand the relationship of body lean to phases of the running stride. In the following discussion, one should recognize that, regardless of the speed of constant-velocity running, the position of the trunk should be upright. Lean—as recognized by the disposition of the body when the

knees of both legs are together at midstride—is absent. Foot strike occurs from slightly ahead of the center of gravity in slower running to immediately below it while sprinting. Body lean is apparent only during acceleration, when it is the result of the acceleration and is not consciously induced.

The support-driving phase of a stride is subdivided into periods of foot-strike, midsupport, and takeoff, while the recovery phase consists of periods of follow-through, forward swing, and foot descent. Each leg goes through a cycle, which starts with the support phase when the foot strikes the ground, driving from a leading to a trailing position. The same foot leaves the ground from the trailing position for the forward recovery phase, advancing to a leading position, ready for another foot strike and support phase. This occurs simultaneously (in reciprocal fashion) with the other leg, converting the runner into a projectile that is fired into a flat, airborne trajectory, first by the right and then by the left leg and foot. Arm action is in opposition to leg activity, with the *right* arm in a forward position when the *left* leg is forward.

SUPPORT-DRIVING PHASE (Figure 53, frames 1–3, left leg; frames 7–10, right leg) Forward motion should not be momentarily arrested by overstriding at the foot strike. Ideally, there should be a pawing motion, with the foot slightly ahead of the center of gravity, moving backward at the same or greater speed than that of the body moving forward. Forward motion is maintained at midsupport, with the body passing over a lever/strut system of the lower back-pelvis-hip-knee-ankle complex. This lever/strut system demonstrates a slight "give" or flexion of the joints to smooth out the vertical and horizontal path of the center of gravity, and it extends during the takeoff, with power coming from the large muscles of the trunk and hip, radiating to the faster but weaker muscles of more distant parts of the body. Just as overstriding can disturb dynamic balance and act as a brake, it can contribute to poor mechanics at takeoff and place undue strain on the lower back-pelvic unit of the complex lever/strut system (7, 8).

Foot placement is generally in a straight line, with the weight borne by the ball and the outside of the foot. The importance of forward balance in sprinting will require toeing straight ahead, while slower distance running requires a slight toeing out of the foot to control lateral balance. At midsupport, as the body passes over the foot, the heel makes contact with the track. Attempting to run exclusively on the toes is mechanically inefficient (quite difficult to do) and disastrous to the physical condition of the legs. Weight then shifts to the inside as the foot turns out, slightly coincident with the "give" of the ankle, to prevent vertical oscillation and to mechanically help other parts of the lever system move faster. At takeoff, muscles that were slightly stretched when the lever system eccentrically "gave" during midsupport, contract to better advantage as the levers are extended (plyometric principle). The ankle extends and, with the toes providing a split-second balance function, ground contact is broken by driving off the inside front edge of the foot.

RECOVERY PHASE.   (Figure 53, frames 1-7, 10-14, right leg; frames 3-14, left leg) During the follow-through, the foot leaves the ground with the strut/lever system in maximal extension, conveniently stretching muscles to improve the contraction that will begin the limb's forward movement. The foot slows down and the powerful muscles of the lower spine, pelvis, and hip initiate the forward movement. With the body airborne as the hip swings forward, the knee is passively flexed to shorten the limb and help it rotate forward faster. When the limb reaches a point just behind the center of gravity, the opposite leg is beginning to make contact with the track. This period of support, along with the continuing forward movement of the recovery leg, provides stability in the lateral plane and momentum and ground reaction to assist forward progression of the runner. Dynamic inertia continues until the recovery leg is as far forward as it is going to go without any conscious effort to extend it. The sequence is continued as the supporting leg leaves the ground with the runner again completely airborne. When the thigh of the recovery leg is at its highest point, the knee begins to extend, and the foot swings forward, initiating the stretch of the muscles that will extend the strut/lever system during the support phase. As the foot makes contact with the ground, the knee is slightly flexed, a position which stretches the muscles that will again contract and facilitate the support phase.

Stride Length and Frequency

Speed is a function of stride length and the number of strides per second. Both factors increase from slower to faster running, with frequency determined by an inherited sense of rhythm, which is subject to conditioning if it is initiated early in life. Generally speed improves when an increase in one factor is not accomplished at the expense of the other. In novices, sprinting speed is best improved by developing strength and the mechanical aspects of the support phase. Attempting to alter cadence is questionable, except in hurdling where it is largely accomplished by better hurdle clearance.

Length of stride is governed by speed, angle, and height of projection of the runner's center of gravity. If forward progress is further computed in terms of vertical and horizontal components of force created during the support phase, it may be appreciated that the angle of projection with the horizontal will vary with the amount of acceleration of the runner. In the starting phases of sprinting, acceleration causes a forward lean. This is made possible by an increased horizontal component of force and its lever arm from the center of gravity (torque) that counterbalances the oppositely rotating effect of vertical torque. If the runner artificially leans or decreases the angle of projection with the horizontal, without adequate force supplied during the takeoff period of the support phase, the existing greater vertical torque would cause a loss of balance (Figure 54). In slower running, this angle increases as the horizontal component decreases, and the runner assumes a more upright position.

Stride frequency, governed by the speed of running, determines the amount of time the athlete is in contact with the ground and in the air. The faster the run, the greater amount of time the runner is in the air, which decreases the amount of time available to obtain thrust while in contact with the ground. Increased frequency is accompanied by some slight increase in length of stride, even in the short-striding distance runner. Any effort to increase gait by this method over a projected period of time, is mechanically inefficient and physiologically tiring, since the increase in speed takes away an inordinate amount of energy from the available supply. Even the strongest sprinter would find it difficult to improve on speed by increasing cadence. The time spent on the ground would be too short to allow the recovery leg to complete its excursion before it is needed to support and move the body again (8).

Reciprocal and Constant Rotations

Track fans of the 1940s may remember the hip-swing style of Herb McKinley, the fantastic Jamacian quarter-miler who ran for Boston College and the University

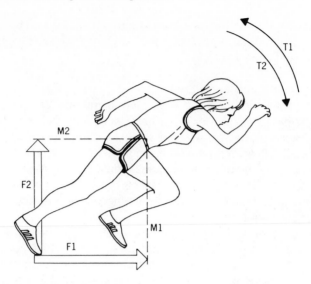

Figure 54. The relation of turning force (T) to linear force (F) in the dynamic balance of the sprint start. The horizontal force ($F1$) times the moment (lever) arm ($M1$) must equal corresponding vertical counterparts ($F2 \times M2$) if turning force (Torque $T1$) is to equal $T2$ and assure dynamic balance. Based on G. H. G. Dyson, *The Mechanics of Athletics*. University of London Press, London, 1973.

of Illinois. With little competition, McKinley ran consistently in the low :46's and performed like a finely tuned violin, using a fluid ground-gaining stride featuring what some kinesiologists call alternate transverse pelvic girdle rotation. The style, indigenous to McKinley and other relatively tall runners, helped increase stride length proportionate with adjustment of cadence, but it is not suggested as a panacea for all 400-meter runners. However, scientifically, the rotations and counterrotations that occur simultaneously in the three cardinal planes of a runner are interesting.

The transverse phenomena referred to above suggest that the trunk of a runner will rotate about a vertical axis oppositely to the direction of the pelvis as the recovery leg swings forward. This motion alternates as the recovery leg becomes the supporting leg and represents a conservation of body momentum designed to coordinate activity in this plane about its perpendicular axis.

In the frontal plane, as one looks at a runner approach head-on, one detects a slight movement of the trunk toward the upward-moving, recovery leg about an anterior-posterior axis that is perpendicular to this plane. The hip of the supporting leg holds up the recovery leg in this dimension, as though it were a cantilever bridge, and this may be a sound argument for strong, gluteal muscles to help prevent a yawing type of gait.

While looking at a runner from the side in the sagittal plane, the noticeable rotations are represented by a simultaneous, clockwise rotation of the centers of gravity of the leg on one side of the body and the arm on the other. This movement is constant and does not require to-and-fro, action-reaction, counterbalancing movements.

Using the same principles discussed earlier relating horizontal and vertical components of force to lean and acceleration, Hopper points out that there are tendencies to rotate the body backward in the sagittal plane when the foot lands slightly in front of the center of gravity at foot strike; forward as the body passes over the foot; and backward once again as the foot leaves the ground at takeoff (4). This rotation is in compliance with a small, vertical, force component that becomes larger as the body passes over the foot and diminishes again at takeoff, suggesting that stride length and cadence should be kept natural to prevent backward lean, both at the beginning and the end of each foot strike.

Transfer of Angular Momentum of the Arms, Shoulders, and Legs

Transfer of momentum has been experienced by anyone in an abruptly braked automobile that is checked in its forward progress. Although the example is related to linear activity, the principle is also true for angular (rotational) activity. In recovery leg activity, momentum is transferred to the lower leg as the thigh or hip move forward. The lower leg flexes at the knee in this transfer, which conveniently reduces the length of the entire lower limb, decreasing its moment of inertia. This makes it easier for anterior hip and abdominal muscles to increase forward and upward velocity of the limb. Near the end of forward recovery, as eccentric contraction or stretching of the posterior hip muscles decelerate the thigh or hip in preparation for reversal of direction, momentum is again transferred to the lower limb, causing the knee to extend in preparation for foot strike.

Just as the thigh and lower leg exhibit transfer, so do the arms and shoulders. Like the legs, the arms and shoulders are not necessarily limited in their ability to move back and forth by the neuromuscular system, but they obtain much of their oscillating, rotary velocity from the length of the appendage while it is swinging through a given range of movement. This, in concert with the plane the arm action is in or the planes it cuts across, helps reverse rotations in the pelvic area that would embarrass the runner if left unattended.

Forward arm and shoulder movement in the sagittal plane coincides and coordinates with forward recovery of the hip and leg on the opposite side of the body. In the transverse plane, the action of the hip and leg tends to rotate the body in one direction about a vertical axis, while arm and shoulder action counter this activity. Additionally, by reaction, forward/upward arm action will drive the same shoulder back, as the opposite shoulder is driven forward from its arm, moving backward/upward. This occurs within the overall movement of the arm-shoulder-trunk rotation in one direction, as the pelvis-hips rotate in the opposite direction.

Lateral balance is controlled in the frontal plane either by keeping the arms close to or some distance away from the sides of the body or by running wide with the legs apart—an alternative that detracts considerably from good, forward progress.

Since sprinters cannot take the time to overcome the twisting inertia of the trunk, they keep their arm action almost square or parallel. The shoulders are held steady, and the greater distance of the arms from the vertical axis, plus partial extending of the backward swinging arm, helps maintain balance in several dimensions. Depending on the skill of the athlete, momentum is transferred quickly and smoothly. Distance runners, requiring more equitable expenditure of energy, employ a more comfortable across-the-chest arm carriage, with varying degrees of shoulder twist, to meet the slower paced requirements of balance and transfer of momentum.

GENERAL PRINCIPLES OF TEACHING RUNNING

Some coaches (and physical education instructors) question whether a natural act, learned pragmatically in early childhood, can be altered to any great extent and, if blessed with good physical material, are apt to look over the candidates and trim the squad with the team cut. If not endowed in this manner, the remaining alternative is to teach character—or running! It is logical, of course, that the longer undesirable habits or conditioned-reaction patterns are practiced, the more difficult it becomes to recondition them into more desirable modes of experience. It is interesting, however, that professional football and baseball clubs frequently employ running coaches to improve the form, technique, and understanding of physically mature superathletes. Either money is spent in a vain cause, or managers and coaches of these organizations understand and recognize the relationship of instruction with improved performance, even at this level! Dintiman admits that "running is a fundamental movement," but adds that "efficient form is far from a natural act" and requires special attention at all competitive levels to eliminate faulty habits as early as possible through continuous awareness of correct form and practice with the intent to improve (1).

This concept is applicable not only to athletic events but to all human activity that employs conscious and unconscious thought processes. If it were not so, we would be wasting our time teaching perceptual motor skills! If there is value in knowing about and relating biomechanics to running, learning, and applying knowledge in the physical education arena and distinquishing between "good" and "poor" coaches based on premises other than personality, a recommended procedure for learning how to run may take this simple form.

Learning Drill

1). Assemble and seat the students in either the gym or athletic field bleachers.

2). Discuss the upper and lower appendage movement and body posture of a master runner, who is running in a circle in front of the group. Discuss the differences of form for short and long sprints, middle distance and distance running, again using the demonstrated services of a master runner.

3). Call the students from the stands, and arrange them in a circle with the master runner at the head. Following the leader, they run in a circle around the coach. Four to six additional master runners run concentrically inside or outside the circle, alongside any assigned three to four novices. Initially the pace is slow, and it picks up on command. The exercise is stopped at a signal from the coach, at which time, private instruction with the attendant master runner can go on at each three-to-four-person station. At a signal from the coach, the exercise resumes. This procedure, used more often at the beginning of a "season," and periodically later on to review fundamentals, may be a satisfactory method to teach technique and yet not take too much time from the conditioning process, which is what most coaching of running is about.

BIBLIOGRAPHY

1. Dintiman, George B., *Sprinting Speed,* Charles C. Thomas, Springfield, Ill., 1971.
2. Dyson, Geoffrey H. G., *The Mechanics of Athletics,* University of London Press, London, 1973.
3. Ecker, Tom, Fred Wilt, and Jim Hay, *Olympic Track and Field Techniques,* Parker, West Nyack, N.Y., 1974.
4. Hopper, B. J., "Rotation—A Vital Factor in Athletic Technique," *Track Technique, 10* (December 1962).
5. James, Stanley L., and Clifford E. Brubaker, "Biomechanical and Neuromuscular Aspects of Running," in *Exercise and Sport Sciences Reviews,* Vol. 1, edited by J. H. Wilmore, Academic Press New York 1973.
6. Römpötti, Kalevi, "The 5000—10,000 m Stride," in *Olympic Track and Field Techniques,* edited by Tom Ecker, Fred Wilt, and Jim Hay, Parker, West Nyack, N.Y., 1974.
7. Slocum, Donald B., and W. Bowerman, "The Biomechanics of Running," *Clinical Orthopaedics, 23,* 39 (1962).
8. Slocum, Donald B., and Stanley L. James, "The Biomechanics of Running," *Journal of the American Medical Association, 205,* 721 (September 9 1968).

Chapter 13

Sprints and Relays

The fundamental mechanics of running are developed by habit patterns at an early age, and correct sprint technique is primarily a problem of improved individual efficiency. Analyzing and applying the technique of champions and superimposing desirable changes on the basic stereotype of human locomotion is a common approach to the science of the event, but it is undesirable if individual differences are not considered.

The power requirements of the sprints necessitate minimizing trunk rotation in a horizontal (transverse) plane and lengthening the stride while maintaining a rapid cadence. Stride length must somehow be achieved by the driving force of the supporting leg, without encountering the braking action of overstriding when the recovery leg makes contact with the track and becomes the support leg again. As the sprinter's starting acceleration reaches maximum velocity, posture becomes more upright, with the recovery leg grounding directly below the center of gravity. Any mechanical effort to lean at this point is inefficient and tiring.

Maintaining velocity is best accomplished through controlled relaxation and smooth, well-defined arm action. In running, the arms normally follow and compli-

Figure 55. The sprint start by Harry Jerome, Canada. PR :10.0, :20.3. Courtesy of Toni Nett, West Germany.

ment leg action, but in sprinting they are carried in more parallel planes and actively assist stride characteristics. High knee action is directly in opposition with the top of forward arm swing, and touchdown of the lead foot is coordinated with the rear limit of arm swing. Excessive backswing of the arm can only encourage overstriding. The emphasis of arm and leg action must be horizontal, with sufficient vertical-force component for the "nonbounding," airborne, flight phase of the stride. Time and force spent running up and down cannot improve flat running time. Perhaps the most important item in the constant-velocity sprinting stride is the tall posture of the sprinter, which facilitates the grounding of the foot to powerfully drive the center of gravity forward.

The Start (Figure 55, frames 1-12)

Anatomical differences among sprinters and hurdlers allow for many variations of block spacing and hand placement in relation to the starting line for the crouch start. The best combination for each individual provides for optimum acceleration to reach maximum sprinting speed in the shortest time. Although the standing start received some attention after Union of South Africa sprinter, Paul Nash, ran :10.1 for 100 m in 1967, subsequent research has failed to confirm its superiority over the traditional crouch style. The primary advantage of the crouch is because of the application of the best combination of horizontal and vertical forces and their moment (lever) arms to achieve optimum static balance in the set position and dynamic balance while accelerating. In the "set" position, the crouch also allows

stretching of muscles that will be used explosively when leaving the blocks. When the standing start is used, there is some difficulty in assuming the required motionless "set" position with the center of gravity above (or ahead of) the front foot.

Appreciation of the approximate distribution of force components in relation to the quality and quantity of the sprinter's musculature will emphasize the importance of foot and hand placement. Figure 54, page 210, illustrates the necessary horizontal force ($F1$) to compliment the moment arm ($M1$) and produce the torque ($T1$) to match corresponding vertical counterparts and provide for balance during the first stride. If $F1$ is not available in the quantity illustrated, the sprinter will either stumble in an effort to become more upright, because of the limited amount of horizontal force available, or will fall (4).

The purpose of the crouch start is to facilitate rapid clearance from the blocks and acceleration to maximum speed. In the "set" position, the distance between the hands and the front foot should allow for about 90 degrees of knee flexion, with most of the body weight supported by the hands and the front foot. The average spacing between blocks for the bunch, medium, and elongated starts is about 30.5, 45.5, and 58.5 cm (12, 18, and 23 in.), respectively, allowing for a larger knee angle of the back leg determined by the body build of the sprinter. The hips are higher than the shoulders with the arms extended and spaced wide enough apart to accomodate the placement of the legs. With the head held in a comfortable position, the eyes are focused either directly downward or a very short distance ahead of the starting line. Immediately on leaving the blocks, the described starting position should enable the sprinter to involuntarily demonstrate whatever body lean is dictated by the runner's ability to accelerate.

Figure 56. The 400-m stride of Lee Evans, USA. PR :43.86. Courtesy of Toni Nett, West Germany.

Response Time and Starting. The relations between reaction, reflex, response, and movement time are important factors contributing to the skill and speed of the individual in sprint starting. **Reaction** and **reflex time** are the conscious and unconscious interval, respectively, between the stimulus (gun) and the initial response. **Movement time** is the interval between the start and the completion of physical movement, while **response time** is the sum of reaction and movement time. Response time is faster when the crouch is used and, although May found no difference between standing and crouch-start velocity, there was no correlation between standing or crouch-response time and velocity (7). This means that maximum velocity cannot be achieved until the sprinter is almost erect, but it can be reached more quickly with the pronounced lean produced by the acceleration, enhanced by the initial crouch position.

In sprinting and hurdling, should the athlete concentrate on thinking about starting or solely on the report of the gun? Dougherty indicates that a slower reaction will result if attention is on the gun (3), and Henry and Rogers' Memory Drum theory of neuromotor reaction suggests that, if an athlete takes time to think about movement, the opportunity to succeed may be lost (6). Perhaps the best policy is to train the athlete to avoid thinking, to respond to the commands with animal instinct, and react only to the gun (9).

400-Meter Sprinting (Figure 56, frames 1–5)

This kind of sprinting differs little from shorter events but primarily requires more anaerobic endurance and psychological persistance acquired from conditioning and tactical experience. This longest dash requires a greater degree of relaxed sprint pacing to meter out available anaerobic metabolism. Biomechanically, the heel of the grounded foot will be in contact with the track for a longer time than it is in the shorter sprints, while the knee eccentrically flexes to a greater extent, allowing for more relaxed pivoting over the foot. Arm action, although still exhibiting sprint form, is more relaxed with correspondingly less kickback in the initial part of the recovery leg action.

TEACHING THE SPRINTS

For as long as coaches have been coaching, it has been said that "sprinters are born, not made." There may be more than a casual element of truth in this maxim, but should it not also be applied to distance runners, shot putters, and high jumpers? If this approach is taken, coaching becomes management exclusively, and anyone of less than championship caliber must be content with mediocrity or retire. Obviously, when coaches look for sprinters, they seek the quickest individuals with the best leg speed. When looking for shot putters, the 98-pound weakling is probably passed over in favor of candidates with good bulk and explosiveness or the potential to display these qualities. There are many ways that coaches can teach better technique, correct flaws in form, and build strength in areas of weakness to help an athlete in any event perform better. This applies to sprinting as well!

Foot Placement, Arm Carriage, and Upper Body Carriage

FOOT PLACEMENT.   Initially, it is better to work on foot placement in relation to stride length. Instruct the runner to stand naturally and draw a line across the toes to illustrate the importance of correct foot placement. If the runner toes out, the repositioning of the foot to a straight-ahead alignment should place the toes anywhere from 2.5 to 10 cm (1 to 4 in.) ahead of the previous stance. Simple arithmetic should provide the incentive for the runner to develop a new habit pattern of foot placement, if this is anatomically possible! If the runner takes 47 strides in a 100-meter dash and adds 2.5 cm per stride by correct foot placement, this places him 1.19 m (45 in.) closer to the tape. The 1.19 m may be equated to about a tenth of a second, and converts a 10.5 hundred-meter dash to 10.4. It is worth the effort to persist and make the change, if possible.

ARM CARRIAGE.   Mechanically sound arm carriage requires that:

1.   The angle of the elbow change constantly [i.e., when the knees are closest together, the arm opposite the support leg is almost straight (elbow angle is about 180 degrees). In its most forward position, it is bent slightly more than in its farthest position to the rear].

2. The thumbs are kept up, with the wrist and hand relaxed.

3. The arm is moved by driving the elbow forward and backward.

4. Although arm action will come across the body to a limited extent, the hand should never pass the midline of the body. Additionally, the hand should never go higher than eye level on its forward swing or back further than 15 to 30 cm (6 to 12 in.) behind the hips on the return.

5. Arm action should be accomplished with as little shoulder or trunk rotation as possible. The runner should visualize the trunk as a stationary board going down the track with the arms mounted on ball bearings. As arm action is expedited, the board remains stationary with no visible sway or rotation.

HEAD AND BODY (TRUNK) CARRIAGE.   Once the acceleration out of the starting blocks (with its induced lean) has been completed, correct head and trunk posture is accomplished by:

1. Being as tall as possible with no visible lean (i.e., imagine that the runner is hanging from a "sky hook").

2. Keeping the shoulders relaxed.

3. Directing the eyes and head straight ahead, with the chin up and the jaw loose.

4. Keeping the shoulders directly above the hips.

LEG LIFT AND THE STRIDE.   To enhance legitimate increases in stride length, the knees should be driven forward/upward for correct leg lift. No attempt should be made to artificially overemphasize leg reach by snapping the foreleg forward and incorrectly introducing a braking action, regardless of any intention to expedite a pawing motion of the foot. The momentum of the latter part of the recovery stride is sufficient to naturally swing the foreleg into position for foot strike. Although the runner should emphasize an active landing on the ball of the foot, the heel will ground during the support phase. This is a natural phenomenon and, as pointed out in the science section, is a mechanical as well as a physical necessity. Similarly, one should not try to artificially increase impulse by attempting to drive longer with the support leg at takeoff. This will only cause further embarrassment and contribute to injury and loss of power. Drills for enhancement of foot placement, arm carriage, and upper body carriage can be found in the foundation training and conditioning program for sprinters.

TEACHING THE START

The Standing Start
This style is occasionally employed for sprint races, universally used for the distances, and may be a desirable alternative for the weak youngster who is not

inclined to achieve the best sprinting speed from the crouch start. Starting commands for the longer races (800 m and up) require that steps 1 and 2 discussed below be expedited all at one time. The traditional three commands for sprints suggest the following routine.

1). At the command, "on your marks," the right-handed runner should step up to the line and place the left foot just behind it. The right foot is placed no more than 61 cm (2 ft) from the line. Hold the trunk erect, allow the arms to hang loose, and keep the knees slightly flexed.

2). At the command, "set," the runner will assume a standing crouch with the hips flexed, placing the head and shoulders directly above the front foot. The knees are flexed a little more, the right arm is moved forward, and the left arm is moved just behind the left hip. Look a comfortable distance down the track, and remain motionless with all parts of the body.

3). At the sound of the gun, drive forward off of the front foot, while the right arm drives back. Sprint naturally in a straight line down the track, and do not artificially shorten or crimp the stride pattern in a vain attempt to feel faster. As acceleration dictates, the trunk will naturally become more erect as the race progresses.

The Crouch Start
Since the superiority of the crouch start for sprint races has been validated by research and mechanics, here we will suggest a teaching procedure for beginners. No attempt is made to describe commonly known bunch, medium, and long foot spacing. This evolves naturally from requirements imposed by the proportions and build of the athlete, length of arms and legs and, within limits, the angles of these segments largely determined by geometry and mechanics to take advantage of available force.

The instructor should demonstrate several times in front of the group, going over each of the steps itemized below before the candidates are allowed to try the routine at the instructor's command. After some proficiency is attained, line up the candidates behind each other, and work with each one individually, making adjustment of hands, arms, legs, head, and trunk positions.

Face a number of candidates who are lined up along a starting line, and instruct them as follows:

On Your Marks

1). With the feet pointing straight ahead, place one foot ahead of the other, the left foot forward if the athlete is right-handed, etc. Occasionally a right-handed candidate will start better with the right leg forward. This adjustment can easily be attended to after some experimentation.

2). With the insteps 5 to 8 cm (2 to 3 1/4 in.) apart, align the toe of the back foot with the heel of the front foot.

3). Without moving the feet and with the arms hanging freely, kneel down and, with the back kept straight, rest the knee of the back leg on the ground. The rear knee should now be slightly ahead of or even with the toe of the front foot.

4). Keeping the back as straight as possible, flex from the hips, and allow the freely suspended arms to swing forward along the outside of the thighs until the fingers touch the ground ahead of the lead knee (the one not touching the track).

5). The elbows should be straight but not locked. Locked elbows will only increase reaction time when they have to be unlocked at the gun. The arms are just far enough apart to make room for the legs and should be slightly ahead of, or even with, the front of the forward (left) knee.

6). The bridged thumb and index finger should be parallel with wherever the starting line is. It is not necessary at this time to have the fingers behind the line.

7). Relax the back, and ask the runner to either look at the ground no more than a meter in front of him or directly down.

Set

8). Without moving the feet, ask the runners to assume a set position, with the hips a little higher than the head, leaning enough so that a little more than half their weight is supported by the hands, with the rest distributed about 60 to 40 percent on the front and back feet, respectively. The angle of the left knee should be about 90 degrees. The angle of the right knee will be greater than this.

Each individual's position should be adjusted to assure that the angle at the front and rear knees is about 90 and 120 degrees, respectively, when the sprinter is in the "set" position. Additional slight whole body position movements forward or backward may also be needed to properly position arms and hands behind the starting line.

Go

9). At the signal "go" drive forward, keeping the head steady. Push back with the forward leg while driving back with the opposite arm. Keep arm action reasonably "square" with arm-swing amplitude from the back of the hips to just below the shoulders.

10). Encourage the candidates to run forward as fast as they can, down a straight line limed on the grass or track, without overstriding or understriding.

Now that the basics have been taught, and runners have had a chance to practice and perfect a starting routine, the candidates are ready to move into starting blocks and can be taught the importance of their use.

STARTING BLOCKS.   The key to good starting is attention to starting block detail, good mechanics, a "correct" combination of muscle tension and relaxation, and the learned or natural ability to react to the sound of the starter's gun, hooter, or whatever signal is used. This is *the* time to emphasize the rules of the start and the concept that the best start is obtained by reacting to the stimulus and not attempting to beat it. As soon as the novice thinks he or she is supposed to "beat the gun," he will develop a habit and continue to think about leaving—too soon or too late!

1).   Based on the foot placement and starting position developed without blocks, measurements should be made of the distances from the back of the starting line to the front of each foot.

2).   Next place the blocks on the track, and set them according to the measurements. Continue to make minor adjustments in the positioning of the block facings to assure the advised knee angles in the set position as well as correct arm and hand placement to attain this feeling.

3).   In most instances, a right-handed runner will want to set the front block for the left foot about 61 cm (2 ft) behind the starting line, allowing an additional 35 to 41 cm (14 to 16 in.) to the front edge of the back block for the right foot.

4).   Instruct the sprinter to back into the blocks from a standing position ahead of the starting line. Place the hands on the track and back first into the front and then into the rear block, with the toes touching the track.

5).   Rest the knee of the rear (right) leg on the track, and move the fingers behind the starting line.

Generally, the instructions suggested for the basic crouch start can be followed from this point. It is very important that the runner develop a "mind-set" for relaxed responsive tension in the relatively uncomfortable "on your mark" and "set" positions.

FOUNDATION TRAINING PROGRAM FOR SPRINTERS (AND RUNNERS)

Until recently, workout patterns for the dash events were largely based on, first, finding the best sprint candidates and then teaching them the start, after which practice consisted of easy running, stretching, philosophizing, and an occasional time trial. Contemporary procedures for sprinters include drills for flexibility-agility, plyometrics, and weight training for strength and power, sprint-assisted and resistive drills for improvement of stride length and cadence, and various plans for what basically remains interval-type anaerobic conditioning (see chapter 3). A minimal amount of aerobic conditioning is usually included to indirectly assist improvement of the intensity components of metabolism and the ability to endure or sustain practice. Attention is also directed to the teaching, correction, and refinement of biomechanical technique and running strategy, with philosophy continuing to make its important contribution.

I. Warm-up and Warm-down

The suggested warm-up should be expedited without fail before every practice session at all seasons of the training program. Initially, the work load may have to be reduced to accommodate the varying capabilities of unconditioned individuals. Run 800 in three minutes. Exercise for 8 to 10 minutes with purposeful flexibility-agility exercises. Without wasting time, continue the warm-up (i.e., understand that fatigue is part of the warm-up) with four to six 60-m windsprints, accelerating gradually, three to four overemphasis drills, and three to four block starts that are optional. Proceed directly into the regular workout. Initially, the coach and athletes may find that fatigue will be overwhelming but, as condition improves, the warm-up will be less stressful while providing the foundation for regular, daily activity.

A warm-down need not be as lengthy as a warm-up. A suggested procedure might be to include an easy 1500 m in 8 minutes, either stopping occasionally for flexibility-agility exercises or doing them at the end of the run.

II. Flexibility-Agility

Incorporate activities from the flexibility-agility exercises discussed in Chapter 4 as an integral part of the warm-up and warm-down procedures.

III. Weight Training

The following exercises are examples from the more complete list found in Chapter 3 that relate to the developmental and physiological needs of sprinters and may be arranged in any sequence or program to meet the requirements of the individual.

A. Hip, knee, and ankle exercises.
  1. Squats with heel rise, 50 percent.
  2. Jumping heel rise.
  3. Straight leg dead lift.
  4. Knee rise or hip flexor exercise wearing iron boot, with knee flexed.
  5. Hamstring curl or knee flexor exercise on a table, prone position.
  6. Knee extension or quadriceps exercise on table, supine position or sitting.
  7. Bouncing split squats.

8. Single (abduction) and double (abduction and adduction) leg raise sideways with boot.
B. Elbow and shoulder exercises.
   1. Curls done alternately with dumbbell.
   2. Sprint arm exercises with dumbbells, striving for "flat" amplitude.
   3. Bench press with dumbbells, alternating the arm action.
   4. Overhead press with dumbbells, alternating arm action, seated or standing.
   5. Straight and bent arm pullovers, from the floor initially, and a bench finally, to systematically increase amplitude and flexibility.
   6. Upright rowing with barbell.
   7. Shoulder shrugs with bent or straight leg dead lift.
   8. Lateral raises with dumbbells while in a prone and supine position on a bench. This may also be done seated or standing.
   9. Chin-ups.
   10. Swinging and stationary dips on parallel bars.
C. Torso exercises.
   1. Bent and straight leg sit-ups holding a plate behind the head. Do these initially from the floor and finally from an inclined bench with and without trunk twisting.
   2. Side bender with barbell or dumbbells.
   3. Torso twist exercise with barbell. Spotter is necessary to check excessive amplitude of swing.
   4. Back hyperextension from a bench with a barbell and stabilization to hold individual down.
   5. Isometric stick body exercises. Rest the back of the head on a partner's knee. With the heels on the floor, keep the body rigidly extended for 30 seconds. The exercise may be done wearing a weighted vest or carrying a plate on the abdomen.

IV. Overemphasis Exercises
Discussed in detail in Chapter 4, these activities are valuable for the sprinter.

V. Running Activities (Anaerobic-Aerobic Training)
An entire anaerobic-aerobic workout may be an hour of Fartlek, consisting of a well- preplanned schedule of warm-up, stretching, aerobic, and anaerobic running activities and a warm-down. As suggested in Chapter 3, rest-to-work ratios for short-sprint training should be about 3:1, with the work bouts ranging from 5 to 6 seconds in length for development of strength and alact anaerobic capacity. Although events up to 100 m do not produce much lactic acid, the work bouts may be lengthened as much as 45 seconds for longer sprints. The decision of whether the rest should be complete or active, the number of sets and repetitions to employ,

and the variation of a drill to use is relative to the needs of the individual. Drills that accentuate anaerobic development include:

1. *Pickup sprints.* Jog, stride, sprint, walk an equal increment. Repeat.

2. *Hollow sprints.* Sprint, jog, sprint, walk an equal increment. Repeat.

3. *Interval sprints.* Sprint prescribed increments at a percentage effort with active rest, usually on a 3:1 rest-work basis.

4. *Repetition sprints.* A full effort, interval sprint with complete rest between repetitions.

5. *Distance run/pickup sprints.* If the distance is 1500 m, sprint 4 × 50 to 60 m per 400, jogging for rest. Complete the 1500 m in some predetermined goal, between 5, 6, or more minutes.

6. *Run ladders.* Variations include up the ladder, down the ladder, and up and down the ladder. Run and jog or walk/rest the increasing or decreasing increments (e.g., 200 run, 200 jog, 300 run, 300 jog, etc.).

7. *Acceleration drill.* Jog one, stride two, sprint three times the increment, walk two times the increment, repeat the cycle a prescribed number of times (e.g., if the increment is 50 m, jog 50, stride 100, sprint 150, and walk 100).

8. *Shuttle relays.* The author used this simple interval workout as a foundation for anaerobic and aerobic conditioning during indoor sessions at Bloom Township High School, Chicago Heights, Illinois. Only a long hallway and at least three runners are required. The best results are obtained when matched teams compete with each other. Initially two members of each team are stationed at one end of a long hallway with the remaining member at the opposite end. A leadoff runner runs to and tags off this member and rests briefly until tagged off for a return repetition, etc. If more rest is desired, simply add more runners to a team. The stress may be maximal for the amount of rest obtained, or it may be a prescribed sprint, 400 or 800 pace. The distance can be controlled, and each runner is reponsible for keeping his or her own total. In a 10 × 80 m relay, for instance, each runner of a three- four- or five-person team will run 80 m. The longer the assignment, the more aerobic the workout becomes (e.g., a four-person 30 × 80 m shuttle relay might feature 80's run in 0:12 (:60 400-m pace), rest for about 0:24, completing a total run of 2400 m for each individual.

VI. Plyometrics
Sprinters will find the bouncing, bounding, skipping, and endurance hopping exercises suggested for high jumpers to be beneficial.

VII. Forced and Resistive Training

Forced training attempts to improve stride length and cadence by repeatedly influencing existing motor patterns. If one has a treadmill capable of producing sprint velocities, its repeated use by the athlete under carefully controlled conditions is thought to improve cadence without shortening stride (2). If local conditions permit, sprinting down a low percentage grade hill may accomplish the same objective. The opposite resistive method of running up a grade on either a treadmill or a hill, climbing stairs, pulling harnessed loads, or wearing weighted clothing is discouraged by Dintiman (2), but encouraged by Bush (1). One authority says it has a tendency to slow cadence and reduce stride length, while the other feels it develops both, through progressive-resistance concepts, paying dividends when the athlete runs on the flat. Very likely, gifted athletes may prosper from any reasonable training idea in which they believe. Novices may also benefit, but represent a challenge, since their vascillating motivation and educability require closer supervision and attention.

Supervision is certainly a very important factor if the towing variety of force training with an auto is employed for its reported improvement of stride and cadence, even though the arms and shoulders cannot effectively become a part of the pseudomotor system-training concept (8). It is difficult to postulate that cadence in sprinting can be seriously altered, but perhaps a fiercely conscious effort to improve cadence in practice sprinting can become a conditioned reaction. If accomplished on the flat, it may be more fruitful, with or without the tow procedure, than on the only downgrade in town, which happens to be too steep.

Resistive Exergenie work requires special equipment, but it is a specific, isometric-isotonic (isokinetic) weight-training approach that may be a valuable adjunct to the less innovative, and sometimes boring weight-training program.

SAMPLE WEEKLY PROGRAMS

The suggestions found here for the 100 and 200 m (100, 220 yd) are general and intended for the novice athlete. The conceptual basis for workouts has been developed in Chapter 3 and is amplified here.

OFF SEASON

Unless specified, all workouts begin with the warm-up and conclude with a warm-down. The learning drill discussed in Chapter 12 may be periodically injected into the practice plan throughout off- and early season training.

MONDAY—*Weight training, even-numbered exercises for arms and legs, and all torso exercises. Employ the endurance and flexibility concepts.*
Learning drill.
TUESDAY—*Pickup sprints, 6 to 8 × 100 m.*
Plyometric bounding, 4 × 40 m, on grass if possible.
WEDNESDAY—*Weight training, odd-numbered exercises for arms and legs, and*

all torso exercises. Employ the power concept, 2 sets, 5 to 6
repetitions. Learning drill. Run 1 × 500 m at 80- to
90-percent effort.

THURSDAY—*Fartlek run for one hour:*
   1. Jog for 10 minutes.
   2. Flexibility-agility stretching exercises for 10 minutes.
   3. Run 800 m at 75-percent effort (2:25 to 2:45).
   4. Run 3 accelerations with the increment set at 55 m, sprint at
      75-percent effort.
   5. Plyometrics, 3 to 4 × 50 m.
   6. Run 1500 m in 6:45 to 7 minutes.
   7. Walk for 5 minutes.
   8. Sprint 3 × 150 m up a slight grade at 70- to 80-percent effort,
      jog down, 3:1 rest-work ratio.
   9. Repeat 8, running downhill.
   10. Jog 1500 m.

FRIDAY—*Learning drill.*
   Repetition sprints, 3 × 200 m at 85 percent effort, or shuttle
      relay, 3 to 4 man, 8 × 70 m.
   Weight training, all exercises for legs. Employ the strength
      concept, 2 sets, 3 to 4 repetitions.

SATURDAY—*Learning drill.*
   Repetition sprints, 2 × 300 m at 85-percent effort, or distance
      run 800 m pickup sprints. 4 × 50 m per 400 m. 6-minute
      goal.
   Weight training, all exercises for arms and shoulders. Employ the
      strength concept, 2 sets, 3 to 4 repetitions.

EARLY SEASON

Again, begin each workout with a warm-up and conclude with warm-down.
Warm-up may now be a 1500-m run, divided equally into jog, slow run, and faster
run, or it may be a sprint relay team baton passing drill over the same distance at
similar intensity. Either run is followed by the flexibility-agility exercises, wind
sprints, and overemphasis exercises.

MONDAY—*6 × 60 m from starting blocks with adequate rest.*
   Pickup sprints, 100-m increment, stride at 70-percent and sprint
      at 90-percent effort. Repeat the cycle four times while
      circling the track. May be done with other members of the
      sprint-relay group.
   Plyometric bounding, 4 × 70 m on grass.

TUESDAY—*Learning drill.*
   Run ladder, 150, 300, 100 m at 90-percent effort.
   Weight training, select weakest exercises for arms, shoulders,

> *legs, and trunk. Employ the power concept, 2 sets, 5 to 6 repetitions.*

WEDNESDAY—*Repetition sprints, 4 × 150 to 200 m, 95-percent effort. Remember, rest should not exceed 15 minutes.*
Or Hollow sprints, 150- to 200-m increments, repeat the cycle 4 times at 90-percent effort.
Plyometric bounding, 2 × 80 m.

THURSDAY—*Distance run 1500-m pickup sprint. Run 4 × 50 m each 400. Plan to complete the 1500 m in under 6 minutes.*
Weight training. See Tuesday, lift 1 set only.

FRIDAY—*Warm-up.*

SATURDAY—*Competition.*

LATER SEASON
As with any event near the conclusion of the season, the emphasis is on maintenance of a high level of condition, avoidance of injury, and heightened concern with quality rather than quantity in practice procedures.

MONDAY—*6 × 60 to 70 m sprint starts with gun and ample rest.*
Weight training, power concept, weakest exercises, 1 set, 4 to 5 repetitions.
Plyometric bounding, 4 to 6 × 50 m.

TUESDAY—*2400-m pickup sprint, 4 × 70 m each 400, 90-percent effort, goal of 8:15.*
Hollow sprints, increment 150 to 200 m, 95-percent effort, 4 cycles.

WEDNESDAY—*Run sprint relay for full-speed baton practice.*
3 × 150 m or 2 × 250 m interval sprints at 95-percent effort, with shoulder shrugs through a finish tape.

THURSDAY—*Acceleration drill, increment, 50 m, 1 cycle.*

FRIDAY—*Warm-up.*

SATURDAY—*Competition.*

TEACHING THE 400-METER (440 YARD) SPRINT.
Teaching the technique and strategy for the longest sprint is predicated on the physiological fact that, although it is impossible for anyone to run the entire race as an all-out sprint, psychology of the event requires a mental set or sense of readiness to consider it a sprint, sustained by willpower and fortified by a formidable training and conditioning foundation. Although the term "float," once popular for the less than all out effort of the quarter-miler is no longer appropriate, the runner must sprint with a greater sense of relaxation, metering out energy to sustain the distance. Split times for the 200's are a clue to the energy stores available, as well as the plan for strategic management of the race. In most cases, regardless of level of competition, top efforts reveal that the second 200 is about 11.5 percent,

or 3 seconds, slower than the first (i.e., a :50 400 m in :23.5 and :26.5). A picturesque suggestion to solution of the problem after the sprint start is to cruise (run) as if the runner has an overdrive, enabling him to move rapidly with his "engine" turning over slower than his trasmission gears.

With this empathetic understanding, technique is vitally important in the management of the race. As discussed in the science section, arm action is more relaxed, with correspondingly less kickback in the initial part of the recovery leg action. The heel of the grounded foot may be in contact with the track for a slightly longer period of time, and there is a little more "give" as the knee flexes, allowing relaxed pivoting over the foot. This adaptation of the sprint stride may be discussed, demonstrated, and finally practiced in the learning drill (Chapter 12).

FOUNDATION TRAINING PROGRAM FOR THE 400-METER SPRINT

Practice patterns for the long sprints include all of the training and conditioning procedures outlined for the shorter dashes. Increments and repeats are correspondingly lengthened for development of anaerobic endurance. As in the short dashes, there is a great emphasis on beginning work gradually, always stressing the concepts of relaxation while working any percentage effort, including 100 percent! It takes great reserve strength and condition to be relaxed without depreciating the quality of the effort. Consequently, emphasis is again placed on preseason activity to provide the solid foundation for injury-free quality work later on.

SAMPLE WEEKLY PROGRAM
OFF SEASON
Warm-up and warm-down procedures will be similar to those recommended for the shorter sprints. If the individual is a member of the 4 × 200 or 4 × 400 relay team, warm-up may be two laps of easy running, baton passing for the same distance, followed by the exercises for flexibility-agility, wind sprints, and overemphasis exercises.

MONDAY—*Hollow sprints, use an increment of 100 m and execute 4 cycles.*
Plyometric bounding, 2 to 3 × 50 m, preferably on grass.
Weight training. See Monday, short sprint schedule.
TUESDAY—*Shuttle relay, four-person teams, 8 × 70 m with 400 stride.*
Down the ladder, 500, 400, 300 m, 75- to 80-percent effort, or 400, 300, 200 m.
WEDNESDAY—*If a long, low percentage-grade grass hill is available, run 4 × 150 m intervals at 75- to 80-percent effort uphill. 3:1 rest-work ratio.*
Repeat hill assignment running downhill, emphasize cadence without reduction of stride length.
Weight training, power concept. See Wednesday schedule for short sprints.

THURSDAY—*Up and down the ladder, 300, 500, 200 m or 100, 200, 300, 100 m. Run with 80- to 85-percent effort.*

FRIDAY—*6 × 200 m interval workout at 75- to 80-percent effort with 3:1 rest-work ratio.*

Weight training, power concept, 1 set, 4 to 5 repetitions, even-numbered arm and leg, and all torso exercises.

Plyometric bounding, 4 × 50 m.

SATURDAY—*Fartlek. See procedure described in short sprint section, and alter for longer intervals.*

EARLY SEASON

MONDAY—*Repetition sprints, 6 to 10 × 100 m at 85- to 90-percent effort, rest should not exceed 1 minute between repetitions.*

TUESDAY—*Repetition running, 2 × 400 or 2 × 600 m at 85- to 90-percent effort. Rest should not exceed 5 to 7 minutes.*

Weight training. See Tuesday schedule for short sprints.

Plyometric bounding, 2 to 3 × 70 m.

WEDNESDAY—*4 × 30 to 60 m starts, adequate rest.*

5 × 200 m interval sprints, 85- to 90-percent effort, 3:1 rest-work ratio.

THURSDAY—*Up and down the ladder, 100, 200, 300, 100 m at 85- to 90-percent effort with adequate rest.*

FRIDAY—*Warm-up.*

SATURDAY—*Competition.*

LATER SEASON

MONDAY—*Down the ladder, 500, 300, 250, or 300, 250, 200 m at 95-percent effort with ample rest.*

TUESDAY—*5 × 200 m pace interval sprints, start-finish, alternate, etc., with 3:1 rest-work ratio.*

WEDNESDAY—*4 × 60 m starts with gun, adequate rest.*

Up and down the ladder, 150, 300, 200 m at 95-percent effort with ample rest.

THURSDAY—*4 × 150 m at race pace, start-finish, alternate, etc.*

FRIDAY—*Warm-up.*

SATURDAY—*Competition.*

SUNDAY—*Weight lifting, rest, plyometric bounding, or easy running according to need.*

THE SCIENCE AND INSTRUCTION OF RELAY RUNNING

Success in the relays, all things being equal, depends on an intelligent running order and, particularly in the sprint relays, on proficiency in passing the baton. The runners must be placed in slots commensurate with their physical and mental

Figure 57 A. The sprint relay backhand pass, palm up. Peter Radford to Ron Jones, Great Britain, at Tokyo Olympic Games. :39.6. Courtesy of Toni Nett, West Germany.

capabilities. If a good starter, the best curve runner should run the leadoff leg. The idea is to facilitate the exchange by avoiding the congestion that often occurs in the first zone. The second best overall sprinter should run the second leg, the next best turn sprinter the third leg, and the best competitor the anchor leg. The second and third runners should be particularly reliable and consistent passers, since they are involved with two other runners on the exchange.

There are a number of techniques for passing and receiving the baton. The two most generally used are the backhand pass, palm up [(Figure 57 A, frames 1–5), the safer and more efficient of the two] and the backhand pass, palm down (Figure 57 B, frames 1–9). Each runner carries and passes the baton in the hand in which it was received. The first and third turn runners run as close to the lane line as possible, with the baton held in the right hand. The second and fourth straightaway runners run in the outer half of their lanes with the baton carried in the left hand.

Figure 57 B. Renate Stecher of East Germany accepts the baton from Doris Maletzki with a backhand pass, palm down. European Championships, Rome, 1974. :42.51. Courtesy of Helmar Hommel, West Germany.

When properly executed, this type of exchange provides the advantage of "free distance" during the time the takeoff runner is still accelerating and the incoming runner is closing at a fast but naturally decelerating pace. The "free distance" is provided by the outstretched hand and arm of the donor passing the baton into the outstretched hand of the receiver, with neither runner speeding up or slowing down.

Another advantage of this pass is the "least distance" concept. Since the turn runners carry the baton in their right hand, never changing it from one hand to the other, they run a shorter distance by staying on the inside of the lane.

To be more systematic regarding the placement of runners, it is suggested that relay trials be run several times with each candidate taking a turn at *each* leg of the relay. The leadoff leg is run from the blocks through the end of the passing zone. Subsequent trials for each of the remaining three legs are run from the beginning of the acceleration zone through the end of the next passing zone, with each candidate being timed for the entire distance from the acceleration line to precisely where the next exchange will take place.

Timing may be of greater value for the donor (incoming runner) from the acceleration mark to where the exchange is to occur, and for the receiver (outgoing runner) from the acceleration line to this point plus a meter or two (to account for the "free distance" aspect). This procedure will provide the coach with a better understanding of the acceleration and deceleration characteristics of the runners in the exchanges.

Ecker, emphasizing the necessity of the free distance in relay running, *suggests* a formula that can be applied to determine the "go" mark easily rather than using up many practice sessions in arriving at the solution (5). The essence of the formula, allowing the concept of free distance to be applied wherever the coach wishes the takeover in the zone to occur, is:

$$\text{GO mark (meters)} = \frac{\text{constant } (T_2 - T_1)}{T_1}$$

$$\text{Constant} = \frac{\text{acceleration zone + takeover zone " give away" distance}}{\text{acceleration zone + take over zone distance}} \times \frac{100}{3.3} \text{ *}$$

T_2 — receiver's acceleration zone + takeover zone "take" distance time.

T_1 — donor's acceleration zone + takeover zone "give away" distance time.

* metric conversion factor

The 1 or 2 free distance is determined by the difference in "give away" and "take" distance.

EXAMPLE

$$\text{Constant} \quad \frac{10 + 15 \text{ m}}{30 \text{ m}} \times \frac{100}{3.3} = 25.25 \text{ m}$$

$T_2 = 3.5$ seconds for the first 25 m of the outgoing relay leg.
$T_1 = 2.8$ seconds for the last 24 m of the incoming relay leg.

$$\text{GO mark} = \frac{25.25 (3.5 - 2.8)}{2.8} = 6.3 \text{ m}$$

235 Chapter 13. Sprints and Relays

Standard technique in the 4 × 100 m relay requires the use of a "ready" or "lean" line about 8.5 to 10.5 m (28 to 35 ft) back of the acceleration zone line, and the "leave" or "go" mark between 3.6 to 6 m (12 to 20 ft) back, depending on the acceleration of the receiver. Although the same procedures are used for the 4 × 200 m relay, the check marks have to be scaled down in proportion to the greater deceleration of the sprinters at the conclusion of each relay leg.

If the backhand pass, palm up is desired exchange, the receiver should assume a two-point stance, with the feet pointing straight ahead, looking over the shoulder to locate the incoming runner. As this runner reaches the "ready" line, the receiver leans. When any part of the donor hits the vertical plane of the "go" mark, the receiver accelerates with normal sprint action, never to look back again. When a specific place in the zone is reached, or upon command by the donor, normal sprint arm action is altered momentarily as the receiver's arm is extended backward and held, palm up, in a stationary position above the line of the hip. The donor, in a precisely timed movement, extends the passing arm and, without reaching, places the baton into the receiver's hand with downward wrist action. Any upward or downward swinging of the extended arm should be avoided. Normal sprint arm action is immediately resumed by the recriver. The donor always explodes, under control, through and beyond the zone (i.e., the leg is not considered complete until the runner has gone 5 to 10 m beyond the zone).

The leadoff runner has a number of ways in which to hold the baton at the start. We prefer a two-finger grip with the baton pinched between the thumb and the index finger, the little finger also on the track, and the middle two fingers wrapped around the end of the baton. There are a number of other personal items that have to be agreed upon and executed consistently by members of the team. Will the receiving hand exhibit the fingers open or closed? Will the baton be aimed for the "V" between the thumb and the index finger, or will the thumb be closed and the hand cupped? There is also the option of slanting the baton to the left for the runner receiving with the left and to the right for the runner receiving with the right. When using the backhand pass, palm down, the procedure and mechanics are identical *except* that the receiver's palm is directed down and the donor employs upward wrist action while directing the baton to the "V" between the thumb and the index finger of the receiver.

A valuable, progressive teaching-training drill for relay exchanges is to have the four runners simulate normal sprint arm action while standing still in an offset position corresponding to their positions in the relay. Using the vocal signal, in turn, the runners may successively pass the baton from the first to the fourth person. After the procedure is perfected, it may be done from a jog, gradually progressing to faster paces. The ultimate practice is running people against each other at full speed in zones on the track.

The 4 × 400 m relay rarely makes use of the blind pass in the true sense of the word. It *may* be used, but it must be preceded by a visual "ready" and "go" procedure. If check marks are used, they must be placed at shorter distances than in the 4 × 100 and 4 × 200 m relays.

Many teams prefer to use the inside visual exchange, which is also excellent for indoor running where the exchange is *always* made from right to left hands. The second and third runners in this type of exchange must transfer the baton from the left to the right hand in preparation for the next pass. Some coaches dislike this transfer for fear of having the baton dropped or time lost through the momentary disruption of the natural arm action. As an alternative, the coach may have the runner keep the baton in the receiving hand with the next runner looking over the left or right shoulder, accordingly, to accept it. Exchanges should be made either from left to right or vice versa, never from right to right or left to left. The safest exchange is a completely visual one. The incoming runner can place the baton into the receiver's upwardly cupped palm or into the "V" formed by the thumb and the index finger, with a downward thrust of the wrist.

In indoor running, many coaches prefer to have the leadoff runner, in particular, and pole position runners subsequently, carry and pass the baton on the inside to protect it from being hit and lost. The outgoing runner should always be alert to the conditions of the race and to the baton hand of the incoming teammate so that he can assume the appropriate left or right shoulder visual posture.

Relays such as the sprint medley necessitate much practice, since the second person may leave before the leadoff 400 runner arrives, or a "slow" 800 anchor runner may be overrun by a fast incoming sprinter. There should never be any overlapping, or running away. Distance must be saved and the runners must discharge their incoming and outgoing responsibilities to maintain a constant team momentum.

BIBLIOGRAPHY

1. Bush, Jim, "The 440 Yard Dash at U.C.L.A," *Track and Field Quarterly Review, 3,* 34 (1975).
2. Dintiman, George B., *Sprinting Speed,* Charles C. Thomas, Springfield, Ill., 1971.
3. Doherty, J. Kenneth, "Training the Mind-body in Track and Field," *Track Technique, 4* (June 1961).
4. Dyson, Geoffrey H. G., *The Mechanics of Athletics,* University of London Press, London, 1973.
5. Ecker, Tom, *Track and Field Technique Through Dynamics,* Track and Field News Press, Los Altos, CA, 1976.
6. Henry, Franklin M., and D. E. Rogers, "Increased Response Latency for Complicated Movements and a 'Memory Drum' Theory of Neuromotor Reaction," *Research Quarterly, 31,* 448 (1960).

7. May, Robert E., "A Comparison of the Standing and Crouch Track Starts on Response Time and Velocity over the Initial Fifteen Yards," Unpublished thesis, Louisiana State University, 1972.

8. Sandwick, Charles M., "Pacing Machine," *Athletic Journal, 47,* 36 (January 1967).

9. Steben, Ralph E., "When it Comes to Starting, Don't Think," *Athletic Journal, 54,* 25 (February 1974).

Chapter 14

Middle Distance

800 and 1500 Meters (See Figure 53, page 000)

Compared with the running-stride mechanics of the sprints, rear-leg kickup and lead-leg knee lift are reduced for events in the 800- to 1500-m category to correspond with the less deliberate arm action. The forearms move toward the midline of the body, ready at an instant to recover sprint action. Body lean is nonexistent at constant velocity, with foot plant occuring 15 to 30 cm (6 to 12 in.) ahead of the runner's center of gravity.

3000 Meters and Steeplechase (Figure 58, frames 1-12)

As the events become longer, the shoulders move with the arms, absorbing the reaction of leg action. Arm action becomes more economical with the forearms directed to the midline of the body, coordinated with less dramatic rear-leg kickback and lead-leg knee lift. Posture is upright, with the center of gravity above the support leg when grounded. Perhaps the key to successful running at these distances is "quiet," relaxed, but powerful, arm action ready to respond instantly to challenges.

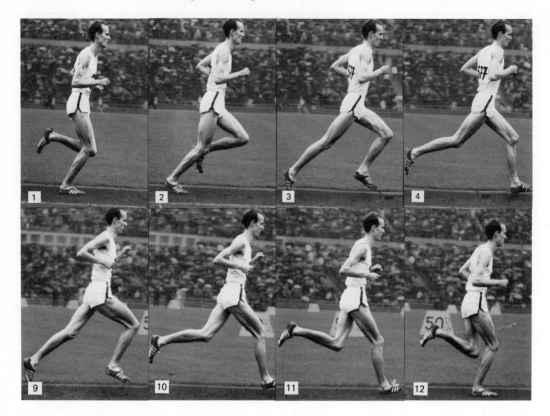

Figure 58. The 3000-m stride of Harold Norpoth, West Germany. PR 7:49.6. Courtesy of Toni Nett, West Germany.

Steeplechase Water Jump Stepping and Hurdling Science (Figure 59, frames 1-11)

The 3000-m steeplechase might be dubbed a "cross-country run on the track" but, like other continually improving events, it is evolving into a rapidly paced, middle-distance, intermediate hurdle race. The distance must be paced rapidly not only to assure continuation of momentum over the hurdles and water jump barrier but also to meet the challenge of the "sprinter" being attracted to the event.

If hurdling implies that the lead leg is *not* placed on top of the hurdle and the trail leg displays a horizontal orientation during the hip circle, propelling may be an appropriate term for the stepping action at the water jump. It denotes placement of the lead-leg foot on the barrier, absence of hurdle-style, trail-leg clearance, and implies a driving, not a pulling action. For analytical study, the following phases are suggested for propelling the water jump.

1.) Approach. From the brisk, middle-distance pace of the event, accelerate into a takeoff point placed about 1.5 m from the water-jump barrier. Attack the barrier with a slightly shortened last stride, pivoting forward over the takeoff leg to initiate the dive into the rail.

2.) Takeoff. Achieve a good split and drive off the trail leg, with the lead leg partially flexed, and aim for the highest point of the trajectory just prior to the rail.

3). Pivot landing. Come off the high point of the trajectory with the body in a simulated, crouch-start posture, placing the foot of the flexed lead leg on the top front half of the rail with a pawing motion. This posture decreases the body's moment of inertia, increases the speed of the pivot, and maintains the momentum achieved by the effective drive of the split, accomplished by the trail leg. To continue momentum at the strike, the center of gravity should be above the lead-leg foot.

4). Pivot takeoff. The trail leg is brought through, leading the flexed knee up to the chest under the returning lead arm. The hip circle (or exaggerated trail-leg, layout interphase) of hurdle racing is absent or only slightly evident. Although this tends to raise the center of gravity, the crouch position, assumed through all but the push-off of the pivot, offsets any disadvantage. The pivot foot is kept in contact with the rail for as long as possible as the trail leg is brought through in a high-stepping recovery phase.

5). The **outward drive** off the rail should be the natural result of momentum maintained by a correct takeoff, split, and dynamic pawing pivot in a crouch position. Avoid any concerted effort to forcefully push off that would unnecessarily tire the runner. For full recovery the trail leg is brought up to and off of the chest and, for effective follow-through and immediate recovery to a normal, middle-distance stride, it lands at the water's edge just below and slightly behind the runner's center of gravity. Although it is profitable to learn how to use either leg when pivoting on the rail, the leg that would ordinarily be used by the runner for takeoff in a high or long jump should be used. Arm action is strong, resembling that in intermediate hurdling; as close to normal as possible, but wide enough to stabilize the more upright trunk.

Hurdle barriers should be negotiated with technique quite similar to that used for intermediate hurdles. The hurdles may be propelled, but this places another stride in the race and slows the runner. Logically, since the pace is slower in spite

Figure 59. The propelling action of Tapio Kantanen, Finland at the water jump of the steeplechase. PR 8:12.6. Courtesy of Toni Nett, West Germany.

of accelerating into the hurdles, the takeoff is closer to the barrier with the touchdown also proportionately reduced. The more relaxed hurdle action, necessitated by the pace and the distance, must be practiced as seriously as middle-distance-run training, if success is to be achieved in the steeplechase.

TRAINING AND CONDITIONING FOR MIDDLE DISTANCE

Unfortunately, in spite of what scientists and physical educators know about human physiology of exercise, its primary practical value is restricted to the selection of prospects or testing the improvement of subjects, instead of developing a superior system of training. Some may wonder why a reliable and valid testing system cannot be developed to study an athlete's long-term improvement with various training methods. It could be developed, if researchers were given many willing subjects to study over a period of years! However, the control elements for such an experiment are presently unobtainable. Separating, studying, and synthesizing methods that have developed during the modern era of running competition and applying them to human beings with minds and emotions of their own is as much an art as a science at this time.

A sophisticated overload system that avoids great concentrations of lactic acid while training for endurance has recently been developed by East German physiologists.* The athlete is asked to run a specific distance at a comfortable 60–percent (aerobic) effort, and again, after some rest, at a 90–percent (aerobic-anaerobic) effort. After each workout, blood is drawn and analyzed for partial pressure of oxygen and carbon dioxide, pH, and lactic acid. The data are

*This information was obtained personnally from Alois Mader, M.D., former Chairman of the Sports Medicine Department for the East German Program in Leipzig from 1964–1974. He is presently the Sports Medicine Supervisor at the University for Elite Athletes of West Germany in Cologne and participated in a seminar at the L.I.F.E Clinic, Brandon, Florida, April 1977.

fed into a computer programmed to determine the optimum pace for athletes during training and predict the optimum pace for competion. This is facilitated by relating the amount of lactate produced during the two tests efforts to the pace at which they were negotiated. An exponential curve that can be used to chart future progress, prescribe training paces, and determine the level af stress incurred is developed for each athlete. The German conditioning program is based on this constantly monitored lactate-pace curve. Initial aerobic interval training is expedited at low-acidosis/slow-pace levels, followed three months later with six weeks of more extensive work featuring moderate acidosis and faster paces. In the latter part of the conditioning season, prior to competition, intensive interval work is undertaken twice a week at the 90–percent level with aerobic training interspersed on other days. With testing protocol repeated periodically, fluctuations in lactate at prescribed paces reveal whether the athlete is working too much or too little, and if the quality and quantity of work need to be altered. With adaptations, the method can be used for intensity athletes or any individual using interval training procedures. The method does not suggest what length the rest periods should be between daily repetitions and sets — apparently this is left up to the perception of the trainer and athlete.

East German scientific philosophy does not advocate heart-rate monitoring, suggesting that the return of heart rate to some baseline figure does not automatically indicate that lactate levels are comparably reduced. The greatest advantage of the concept is that constant monitoring of the stress an athlete can endure prevents overtraining or undertraining. It would appear that the DDR athlete is optimally trained, and that this system precludes a simplistic approach to modern day athletes and their training.

Conditioning for events from the 800- to the 10,000-m run, cross-country, and the marathon necessitates a knowledge of the proportionate use of energy systems discussed in Chapter 3. Although the majority of sprint conditioning is anaerobic and strength oriented because of the shortness of the event, longer races provide time for increased extraction of O_2 from the blood by the muscles and the slower mechanism of aerobic metabolism. The runner's mechanical skill (training) further refines and determines the speed of the run by reducing unnecessary movement and conserving fuel. Although available aerobic chemistry may be a limiting factor in the marathon, the slower pace for the long haul depends, to a greater extent, on reserves of glucose, electrolytic fluid, and the control of body temperature.

Middle-distance events such as the 800, 1500, 3 km, and the 3000-m steeplechase rely on anaerobic/aerobic proportions ranging from 65/35 to 10/90 depending on set physical criteria. Logically, conditioning should reflect these requirements, allowing for the available time and training-load capabilities of the young novice junior high-school and high-school athlete. "How they train" type descriptions of outstanding high-school and world-class athletes are abundantly available. Although they obviously cannot be applied verbatum to average young candidates, they reflect various methods and schools of thought, predicated primarily on the personal likes and dislikes of the athlete and coach involved. It is not our purpose to dwell on history, but a very brief review of methods and schools of training may be useful.

Freeman, Ward, and others have excellent discussions of various methods, but a major contribution lies in describing physiological and psychological values (4,5). Basically, the advantages of each system are:

1). *Interval* is a valuable method because of its administrative ease in measuring work and recovery. It provides a good heart stimulus, 160 to 180 beats per minute (bpm) for the "slow" (aerobic) variety and 180 to 200 bpm for the "fast" (anaerobic) work. Depending on the type (i.e., aerobic or anaerobic), interval allows the completion of more work at appropriate paces than continuous running.

2). *Fartlek,* of the *Holmer* variety, synthesizes interval and distance work over interesting terrain, while hopefully developing individual resourcefulness. Heart rate will vary depending on which phase of the workout the athlete is in.

Lydiard Fartlek, misnamed if Fartlek means "speed play" and similar to long-distance training, is a progressive, slow-distance workout in which an easy pace is endured for longer and longer distances over a period of several weeks or months. Heart rate is in the 130 to 150 bpm range.

3. *Long-distance training* is a good general conditioner from a physical fitness standpoint and improves muscle capillarization. The candidate's confidence in eventually negotiating very long distances is enhanced, even if the pace is slow (6:45 to 7:45 1500-m pace). It evokes a 130 to 150 bpm heart rate.

4). *Speed endurance, tempo* (a variety of interval allowing little recovery) has greater applicability to middle-distance training, is anaerobic in concept, incurs an oxygen debt, promotes resistance to great stress, and takes less practice time. Heart rate rises to 180+ bpm, and repeats are resumed before the rate returns to the 120 to 140 range.

5). *Speed training*, an endurance brand of repetition training, is a variety of rapid-pace interval with longer recovery periods. Intervals and overall assignments are necessarily short (50, 60, 70) because of the stress incurred. Heart rate rises to 180 bpm. Repeats resume when and if the rate returns to the 120- to 140-bpm range in 90 seconds. In this way, the workout is said to remain "aerobic" with little, if any, oxygen debt incurred.

6). *Eclectic/holistic* training (cafeteria style/individually oriented) synthesizes the above systems physiologically for the proportions of anaerobic/aerobic metabolism that a particular running event and the athlete's physical and mental state require throughout the season.

Schools of thought are as prolific as eminently successful distance coaches. Generally, a "school" is a way of expediting known methods of training. The *Swedish School* emphasizes Fartlek. The *Stampfl School* progressively increases the degree of difficulty of interval as condition improves and makes use of the repetition concept, while running close to or better than race pace, with adequate rest. *Igloi* introduced rugged, short-length interval training while the *Russian School* is characterized by very hard-volume, interval, and distance training. *Cerutty's philosophy* reflected a Spartan aspect, immunizing successful advocates to pain while *Lydiard* popularized "marathon" heavy-mileage training, utilizing well-thought-out periodicity, gradually increasing intensity and volume of anaerobic/aerobic methods. Synthesis methods of more recent origin include the *Oregon* and *Villanova* Schools, respectively emphasizing low- and high-pressure approaches to the quality and quantity of anaerobic and aerobic methods.

Rational middle-distance formats for novices should acknowledge varying degrees of physical and mental ability. "Gang" workouts are easy to expedite but may simultaneously overtrain some and undertrain others, while hitting it just right for a few. In addition, in considering the concepts of frequency, volume, and duration of training defined and explained in Chapter 3, we must recognize that some individuals do better with two workouts a day, others thrive on one, and many may have time for no more than one a day.

Two-per-day workouts are characterized by an easy, aerobic-effort run early in the morning, with various combinations of hard, easy, or long aerobic/anaerobic assignments in the afternoon. One-a-day workouts will also reflect a weekly cycle; examples include long, hard, easy, hard, long, easy, hard, or long, easy, hard, long, long, easy, hard, or any other combination that physiologically and psychologically prepares the athlete effectively for competition.

Whatever method of training or school of thought is followed, if the athlete is progressively stressed, believes in what he or she is doing, and is individually allowed enough time for physical and mental recovery, the results will be gratifying.

FOUNDATION TRAINING PROGRAM FOR MIDDLE DISTANCE

I. Warm-up and Warm-down

Depending on the body of the assignment, warm-up may vary. If some variety of interval is the principal assignment, the warm-up will usually be reflected in terms of running 2 to 3 km easily, followed by stretching. If the principal workout is continuous, the warm-up may be the initial part of the run or a 1- to 3-km Fartlek of either the Lydiard or Holmer variety, with or without stretching. To avoid soreness, stretching should also be done at the end of the workout to assist in flushing waste metabolites from the muscles.

II. Running Activities

A). *Continuous Running.* Endurance is acquired by running close to aerobic capacity while taxing anaerobic metabolism to a limited extent. Steady, hard runs of up to 60 minutes, adjusted to negotiate courses, are best suited for its development. This work, used during the cross-country season, is ideal preparation for the more arduous, aerobic and anaerobic training scheduled for the early part of the track season.

B). *Fartlek.* A preseason, Holmer variety Fartlek plan for sprinters was outlined in Chapter 13. Similar but longer programs featuring more running can be devised for distance runners. The variety is subject only to the imagination (including the infusion of the controlled Fartlek aspect)—but a plan must be developed in advance! Fartlek can be abused by lack of direction and ambition. The casual instruction to "go out and run some Fartlek" can degrade into a workout that would not develop moderate levels of physical fitness for a physical-education class. Holmer Fartlek combines long slow distance, aerobic and anaerobic interval, as well as flexibility-agility, plyometric bounding, and overemphasis exercises, primarily borrowed from sprinting. The workout is supposed to stress the individual in an *enjoyable* manner over stimulating terrain.

Lydiard Fartlek, as previously discussed, is a variety of long, slow-distance, continuous running over varying terrain. While more appropriate for preseason work, it can rehabilitate the psyche or the physique during other phases of the season.

C). *Interval.* The variables of interval-type training are commonly understood to include:

1. The length or duration of the run or workout in terms of the distance or the amount of time consumed.

2. The intensity or pace at which the run is expedited to attain a prescribed heart rate.

3. The number of times the workbout is repeated, at either exactly the same pace for assignments (e.g., 10 × 400 m) or flexible paces premised on the base time in the case of ladder drills (e.g., up the ladder, down the ladder, and up and down the ladder).

4. The length of the rest interval is based on:

   (a) Coach's and athlete's perception.

   (b) Return of the heart rate to some predetermined base.

   (c) Rest:work ratios (i.e., rest for some multiple of the time it took to expedite the run).

5. The disposition of the recovery phase (i.e., complete rest or active rest accomplished either by walking or jogging).

Aerobic (slow) interval. The key to success here is to work at a pace that can be tolerated and that either does not incur an (anaerobic component) oxygen debt or acquires one that can be repaid in a short recovery period between repeats (workbouts). Aerobic-interval workbouts can be as short as 15 to 30 seconds with recovery of equal or less time, but generally the workbouts range from 1 to 5 minutes. Heart rate raised to 75 percent of the heart rate range (160 to 180 bpm) should return to 120 to 140 bpm during the recovery period before resumption of the next workbout.

The following acceptable distances for this work are usually expedited in sets, with rest periods between them:

100; 150; 200; 300; 400; 600; 800; 1000:

1200; 1500; and 1600 meters.

Ladder drills may be constructed. The pace may be uniform or developed on a *cutdown* basis, each interval run at a previously determined base pace, plus or minus several seconds. After sessions, the runner should feel that he or she has had a hard workout. In aerobic interval, Daniels recommends that the total time for workbouts should be greater than cumulative time for rest (2). This may seem to be a demanding requirement, but the reader should be reminded that aerobic interval is run quite close to the current race pace of the individual. The advantage of the method is that more work is completed close to race pace than could be done by trying to run the same total distance continuously (i.e., 10 × 400 at an individual's current 1500-m pace splits can be tolerated by means of interval, but certainly not for 4 km run continuosly!)

Runners and coaches are frequently interested in more concrete suggestions relating to interval length and the pace at which workbouts should be run, as well as the amount and kind of rest during the recovery period. Because individuals vary, it is difficult to do this unless the best running start effort or basepace of each runner for a particular distance is known. When this has been determined, the following guide, adapted from Wilt, may be used (7).

1. *Add* 4 seconds to the best 100 time, *positive aerobic splits* (PAS). Run several sets of the desired number of repetitions. Active recovery will be 3 × the workbout time, *standard rest ratio* (SRR—3:1, rest: work ratio).* Allow 2 to 3 minutes between sets.

2. *Add* 6 seconds to the best 200 time PAS. Run several sets of the desired number of repetitions. Active recovery will be 2, 2 1/2, or 3 × the workbout time (SRR —2:1, 2 1/2:1, 3:1, rest:work ratio).* Allow about 3 minutes between sets.

3. Determine the average 400 time or "split" for an 800, 1500, 3-km or 3000-m steeplechase. *Add* 4 seconds to this split time (PAS), and run several sets of the desired number of repetitions. Active recovery will be 1 to 1 1/2 × the workbout time (SRR—1:1 to 1 1/2:1, rest:work ratio) between repetitions, and 5 to 6 minutes between sets. Here the total work time may be equal to the cumulative recovery time.

All of the above suggestions are appropriate for a homogenous group of runners (i.e., of comparable ability). If *heart rate monitoring* (HRM) is used, the athletes can take their own pulse for 10 seconds immediately after running to assure that the rate has raised to 180. If not, the pace is too slow and should be accelerated. Running is resumed for the next repetition and for the next set when the heart rate has returned to the 140 to 120 and 120 to 100 range, respectively. Since it is unlikely that a group of runners will all recover in the same amount of time, administrative planning can solve the problem by positioning a low-cost, oversized "drug store" clock with a sweep second hand where it can be easily seen by each runner.

Knowing how to effectively manipulate the variables of interval is further complicated by the enigma of the runner who does better in practice than in meets, and vice versa. The peer group problem may also assert itself; a younger runner may feel he or she is not supposed to keep up with or even run ahead of more experienced athletes! Other than using individual counseling, these problems may be partially overcome by strategy drills and the tentative formation of buddy

*Note that the cumulative recovery time here will be greater than the total work time. This is a result of determining a challenging aerobic pace for short distance based on best time (base pace). The coach and athlete may experiment with shorter recovery periods, validated by suggested heart-rate monitoring augmented by perception.

groups, each with their own level of proficiency. A coach could use one of the simple bench test, indirect oxygen-uptake tests to place people of current equivalent oxygen uptake, but this would not take into account individual ambition nor adjust for the level of condition and efficiency at the time of the test! However, these problems may be partially solved by adjusting the membership of the scientifically arranged groups after studying the runners and their performances.

Ecker presents an interesting plan for interval work that attempts to take some of the guesswork out of how far the individual should cumulatively run in a workout (3). Keeping the longest repeat at one-half the competitive race distance, do not stipulate the number of repeats in a set. Keep running the repeats at race pace until HRM fails to return to 120 from 180 within two minutes—then run one more repeat at maximum effort! If the total cumulative distance of the repeats is less than one and one-half (1 1/2) times the competitive race distance, the pace is too fast and should be moderated, but not so much that it is possible to run more than three times the race distance.

Anaerobic (fast) interval. Conditioning for the development of this aspect must be more intense. Because of the greater stress, interval distances are shorter (100, 150, 200, 300, 400), total work time is less, and recovery is increased. Variations include ladder drills at uniform or cutdown pace formulated from base paces. A pace-rest scheme to develop anaerobic endurance for a fast variety of interval recommends that workbout heart rates should exceed 180 bpm (190 to 200 bpm is common) (7). The work may be arranged in sets of repetitions with rest between them.

1. *Add 1 1/2 to 2 1/2 seconds to the best 100. positive anaerobic splits (PANAS). Run several sets of the desired number of repetitions. Active recovery will be 3 × the workbout time (SRR—3:1, rest:work ratio). Allow 4 to 5 minutes between sets.*

2. *Add* 3 to 5 seconds to the best 200 (PANAS). Run several sets of the desired number of repetitions. Active recovery will be 2, 2 1/2 or 3 × the workbout time (SRR—2:1, 2 1/2:1, 3:1, rest:work ratio). Allow 5 to 6 minutes between sets.

3. Determine the 400-m split for the 800, 1500, 3000, or 3000-m steeplechase. *Subtract* 1 to 4 seconds from this time, *negative anaerobic splits* (NANAS) and run several sets of the desired number of repetitions. Active recovery will be 1 to 1 1/2 × the workbout time (SRR—1:1, 1 1/2:1, rest:work ratio). Allow about 5 minutes between sets.

4. Longer distance runners, who wish to inject this kind of work into their regimen, may subtract 3 to 4 seconds from split 800 and 1500-m NANAS times of 5000 and 10,000-m races. Active recovery will be 1/2 to 1 × the workbout time. (SRR—1/2:1, 1:1, rest:work ratio). Sets of repetitions are also appropriate here.

D). *Speed Endurance and Speed Training* are varieties of interval. In speed "aerobic" endurance, long "sprint" distances (100 m to 2 km) run near an all-out effort, are purposely repeated with inadequate rest. Speed training is comparable, but conducted over much shorter distances (50, 60, 70) repeating every 90 seconds if the heart rate returns to 120 to 140 in that time.

E). *Repetition Running.* Repetition running is one of the more arduous types of conditioning for anaerobic power. A minimal number of repeats are negotiated over shorter distances at 0 to 3 seconds faster than race pace, with adequate rest to assure good recovery. Six to eight 150's at maximum effort, three to four hard 400's, or ladder workouts with the longest repeat set at 600 m (600, 500, 400, 300), with full recovery (5 to 20 minutes), are examples of this kind of conditioning workout. Heart rates should exceed 180 bpm, and time for recovery will be generous before resumption of the next workbout.

Although a runner is exerting effort to develop and condition the body, attention must also be directed toward training for efficiency (i.e., improvement of running mechanics and strategy of running). As the athlete is conditioning, he or she must always strive for relaxation, maintaining the pace with upright posture and head control, appropriate arm action, absence of overstriding, and straight-ahead, heel-to-ball foot action.

III. Strategy and Tactics

Strategy is planning for a race ahead of time, and tactics are adjustments needed to meet challenges during the race. Whether an athlete is a *front runner* or a *follower* by strategy or temperment, each type should attempt to run the splits as close to even pace as possible in order to stay within energy-expenditure capabilities. Perhaps the winner will be the more efficient of the two, but the fact that it doesn't take long for a runner to develop a reputation lends itself well to changes in tactics while the overall strategy is being expedited. An athlete should include practice work to train for both kinds of running. The following drills are recommended for change of pace response and learning how to keep out of danger and remain in contention.

    A. Varied pace drills.
        1. *Gradual accelerations to pickup pace.* Run 100's, 150's, and 200's, 1 to 2 seconds over race pace, pick up pace for next equal increment to race pace, pick up again to 1 to 2 seconds under race pace. When 3 × the increment have been run, jog a 200 in 1 minute and repeat the set. The number of sets are elective and determined by condition, need, time of season, etc.
        2. *Quick accelerations to meet challenges.* Using increments as discussed above, run the first half of each increment 1 to 2 seconds over race pace, and quickly pick up to race or under race pace the second half, jog an equal increment, and repeat as condition and need require.

Variations include running the first half at race pace and speeding up, running the second half 1 to 2 seconds better than race pace.

3. *Accelerate-pace-accelerate.* Run 1 to 2 seconds under race pace for an increment, pace the next, shift "gears," and accelerate to 1 to 2 seconds under race pace again, jog 200. Repeat.

4. *Sprinters versus middle-distance and distance runners' repeat relays.* Select three 8 × 100 or 8 × 200 m relay teams in the membership categories suggested above. [Assign runners from each category to the leadoff and exchange stations, and continue the running until all runners have run two or three intervals (100 or 200)]. The drill is helpful in learning to run against runners of varying speciality. Speed is generally neutralized by the endurance requirements of the relay.

B. Situation drills. (They can be expedited on the track, or during a cross-country Fartlek workout.)

1. *Box drill.* With two runners abreast and one in tandem behind the outside runner, assign the fourth runner to the box position behind the inside runner. Run intervals of 50 m with a jog of equal distance, rotating and repeating until all runners have had their turn in the box position. The purpose of the drill is to get out of the box and pass the runners without fouling.

2. *Tandem drill* (Indian file, the Cunningham). Place several runners in tandem. The last runner in line accelerates and passes to the front. As soon as this runner gains the pole position, the last in line peels off and moves to the front. Keep the group tight at a specified pace, and require that passing be done within 50- to 60-m increments. Close contact over the total distance assigned is required to facilitate the anaerobic bouts within the demanding aerobic pace.

3. *Phalanx or Peek-a-boo drill.* Place two runners abreast and one behind. Nonverbally, the pole runner signals for the phalanx to momentarily open on the pole position, or in the middle. The rear runner should recognize the opportunity and accelerate through the opening. Jog 50 m. Again run at a specified pace, rotating and repeating. Require that passing be done within 50-m increments.

C. Opponent simulation "buddy" drill. Pair equivalent runners with the understanding that one will simulate tactics of the next opponent. In interval or repetition format, challenges will be arranged at various points with the other runner reacting to the tactic by either becoming the lead runner or maintaining appropriate contact. The drill is not only valuable for introducing novices to the importance of race plans and learning how to cope but also in making preparations for the next opponent or anticipated race conditions (this may necessitate several more runners, all role playing for the principal benefactor).

SAMPLE WEEKLY PROGRAMS

The sample seasonal plans are only suggestions for "average" high-school runners. Since such programs may be the most controversial area of any track book, the reader is urged to amend workout patterns for the individual in terms of quality and quantity, hard and easy, or any sequence that is necessary to satisfy the personality, without ignoring the understood physiological requirements of the runner.

The foundation program is basic to the plans, amendments that appear in the assignments are conceptually the same but are explained in some detail if they do not appear specifically in the foundation. Warm-up and warm-down procedures for each day are provided, since they contribute to the volumetric load of the practice session and will serve as a model for plans of longer events.

800-METER PLANS
OFF-SEASON

MONDAY—*Warm-up, 2-km Fartlek and stretching.*
Continuous running, 5 to 6 km at 6:30 to 6:45 (per 1600 m).
Warm-down with a 1600-m light jog.
Weight training. High rep—low poundage. Select exercises found in Chapter 3.

TUESDAY—*Warm-up, 2 to 3 km of slow, steady running, 7:00 pace.*
Aerobic interval, 6 × 300 PAS with 3:1 SRR.
Warm-down with 1600-m light jog.

WEDNESDAY—*6 to 8 km at 6:30 pace.*
Warm-down with stretching.
Weight training, select exercises not done on Monday.

THURSDAY—*Warm-up, 1600-m Fartlek and stretching.*
Aerobic interval, 3 to 4 × 600 PAS. Determine 400 split pace baseline and add 6 seconds, with 1 1/2: 1 SRR.
Warm-down with 1600-m light jog and stretching.

FRIDAY—*8 to 10 km of 6:30 pace running on a hilly course. (Include stair climbing if hills are not available.)*
Warm-down with stretching.
Weight training. Select exercises that differ from those done Monday and Wednesday.

SATURDAY AND
SUNDAY—*On either day, run 5 to 6 km of Fartlek or 6 to 8 km of continuous running, averaging 6:30 or better with either assignment.*

EARLY SEASON

MONDAY—*Warm-up, 2 km of slow, steady running and stretching.*
Aerobic interval, 10 to 12 × 200 PAS with 2:1 to 3:1 SRR.

Warm-down with light 1600-m jog.
Weight training.
TUESDAY—*Warm-up, 2- to 3-km Fartlek.*
Situation drills, box, tandem, or phalanx, 4 × 400 with 5
minutes recovery between repetitions.
Warm-down with 1600-m easy run.
WEDNESDAY—*Warm-up, 2 to 3 km of slow, steady running and stretching.*
Anaerobic interval up the ladder, 100, 200, 300, 400, 600
PANAS.
Run 100 in best time plus 1 1/2 to 2 1/2 seconds, 200 in
best time plus 3 to 5 seconds, 300 in best time plus 5 to 6
seconds, 400 in best 800 pace time minus 1 to 4 seconds,
and 600 in best 800 pace time minus 2 to 5 seconds.
Base recovery on HRM, or follow SRR suggestions for
respective pace-distance requirements.
Warm-down with 1600-m light jog and stretching.
THURSDAY—*Continuous running, easy 5 to 6 km and stretching.*
Varied pace drills, 4 × 400 slow accelerations or 2 × 400 fast
accelerations employing 50-m increments.
Warm-down with 1600-m light jog.
Weight training.
FRIDAY—*Warm-up with an easy 2 km.*
4 to 6 × 100 "off the curve" accelerations to about 90-percent
speed. This may be done on an anaerobic interval or
repetition basis regarding recovery.
1600-m easy jog and stretching.
SATURDAY—*Competition.*
SUNDAY—*Rest or 5 to 6 km easy shakeout type of run.*

LATER SEASON

MONDAY—*Warm-up, 1 1/2 to 2 km easy running and stretching.*
Repetition running, 2 to 3 × 600 in 800-pace time with repeats
every 5 minutes.
1 1/2 to 3 km easy running.
Varied pace drills, slow accelerations, 2 to 3 × 400.
Pool running (as suggested in hurdle training) or 1600-m easy
running with stretching at the end.
TUESDAY—*2- to 3-km Fartlek with stretching at the end.*
Ladder drill, anaerobic interval cutdowns. Base recovery time for
reps and sets on SRR or HRM system.
2 × 400 in 800 race pace minus 2 seconds,
2 × 300 in 800 race pace minus 3 seconds,
2 × 200 in 800 race pace minus 4 seconds,

> *2 × 100 in 800 race pace minus 2 to 2 1/2 seconds.*
> *Warm-down with pool running or 1600 m of easy running with stretching at the end.*

WEDNESDAY—*Warm-up with 1 1/2 to 2 km easy running and stretching.*
> *Aerobic interval up the ladder. 100, 200, 300, 400, 600, at 800 race pace for all intervals with SRR or HRM.*
> *Warm-down with 1600-m light jog.*
> *Weight training.*

THURSDAY—*Warm-up with 1 1/2 to 2 km of easy running and stretching.*
> *Situation drills.*
> *Easy 5 to 6 km on the grass with stretching at the end.*

FRIDAY—*Warm-up with easy running and stretching.*

SATURDAY—*Competition.*

SUNDAY—*Rest or run 5- to 6-km shakedown as needed.*

1500-METER PLANS

Warm-up and warm-down as suggested in the foundation program and as applied in the 800 plans is assumed, although the distance run and time consumed may be longer. Off-season plans are *not* included, since most 1500-m runners participate in cross-country described in Chapter 15.

EARLY SEASON

Warm-up may vary with the body of the workout but generally should be 3 to 4 km with the pace gradually accelerated from 7:00 for the first 1500 to 6:45 for the second, etc., in place of the morning aerobic run. If there is a morning workout, more anaerobic interval can be substituted in the afternoon.

MONDAY—*Warm-up.*
> *Anaerobic interval, 4 to 5 × 400 in NANAS time with recovery determined by SRR or HRM.*
> *4 to 5 × 200 in PANAS with recovery determined by SRR or HRM.*
> *Warm-down.*

TUESDAY—*Warm-up.*
> *Varied pace drill. Accelerate-pace-accelerate drill, 100's. (Accelerate 100, pace 100, accelerate 100, jog 200) × 4.*
> *Warm-down with 5 to 6 km and stretching.*

WEDNESDAY—*Warm-up.*
> *Repetition running. 1000, 600, 500, at 2 to 4 seconds faster than current race pace, rest 10 minutes per repetition.*
> *Warm-down.*

THURSDAY—*Warm-up.*
> *7- to 8-km Fartlek. 1500 steady at 6:00; second 1500 variable with two 600-m runs at race pace; third 1500 steady at*

5:30 to 6:00; fourth 1500 variable with four 200's at 90-percent effort; fifth and last 1500 warm-down and stretching.

FRIDAY—*Warm-up.*

SATURDAY—*Competition.*

SUNDAY—*Rest or a steady, continuous 8- to 10-km run, as needed.*

LATER SEASON

Warm-up and warm-down procedures are continued as previously suggested. Some athletes may wish to reduce the length of these activities. Although one can afford to be pragmatic about the length of the warm-down, it should not be neglected.

MONDAY—*Warm-up.*
Aerobic interval, 8 to 10 × 400 at race pace. SRR or HRM.
Weight training.
Warm-down.

TUESDAY—*Warm-up.*
Ladder drill, anaerobic interval, variety sets, SRR–HRM, active repetition and set recovery. (Pace the jog of the active recovery distance to correspond with SRR time, or use HRM at the end of the jog.)
2 × 100 at PANAS, 100 jog recovery between reps.
200 jog set recovery.
2 × 200 at PANAS, 100 jog recovery between reps.
200 jog set recovery.
2 × 400 at NANAS, 100 jog recovery between reps.
200 jog set recovery.
2 × 300 at PANAS (add 4 to 6 seconds to current best 300)
100 jog recovery between reps.
Warm-down.

WEDNESDAY—*Warm-up.*
Varied pace drills, gradual accelerations, three sets of 200 increments. Quick accelerations (race pace to negative race pace) 4 × 100 increment.
Warm-down.

THURSDAY—*Warm-up.*
5 to 6 km of varied Holmer Fartlek, including two to three 90-percent speed 200's and one or two 90-percent 800's.

FRIDAY—*Warm-up.*

SATURDAY—*Competition*

SUNDAY—*Rest or easy 6 to 8 km, as needed.*

3000-METER PLANS

It is extremely difficult to effectively train for competition in this event without two workouts a day. Plans for the 800 did not include a morning workout or cross-country as Fall training, while the 1500 workouts assumed the cross-country season but implied the optional nature of the morning run. If the athletes have the time and the coaches have the inclination, morning-aerobic runs can greatly facilitate afternoon-practice plans. There is usually a break of several weeks between the end of the cross-country and the official start of indoor or outdoor track. It will be assumed that all 3000-m runners will train and compete in the cross-country season. The off-season plans suggested reflect these circumstances.

OFF-SEASON

MONDAY—A.M.—*Continuous running, 8 to 12 km.*
P.M.—*Warm-up, 2 to 3 km as needed, followed by stretching.*
Aerobic interval, 3 to 4 × 800. Add 4 to 8 seconds to best-known 800 splits of 3000-m run. Recovery may be HRM or less than the time it takes to run the interval.
Warm-down.
TUESDAY—A.M.—*Same.*
P.M.—*11 to 16 km at 6:15 to 6:20 pace.*
Stretching.
WEDNESDAY—A.M.—*Same.*
P.M.—*12 to 18 km of Fartlek.*
Stretching or pool running.
THURSDAY—A.M.—*Same.*
P.M.—*11 to 16 km at a challenging pace.*
FRIDAY—A.M.—*Same.*
P.M.—*8 to 11 km, easy.*
SATURDAY AND
SUNDAY—*Run 16 to 19 km easy on one day and 6 to 8 km of semihard Fartlek the other day.*

EARLY SEASON

A morning run for 30 to 60 minutes at an easy pace with one 400-m pickup per 1600, and a 2- to 3-km warm-up, at an easy pace, for the afternoon session followed by stretching-flexibility-agility exercises will be assumed. A 1- to 2-km warm-down may follow practice. If the body of the workout is a variety of continuous running, conclude the practice with stretching-flexibility-agility exercises.

MONDAY—*Repetition running. 5 to 6 at current 400-m split-base pace, with active rest for 5 minutes.*
Weight training—select exercises found in Chapter 3, using the endurance concept.
TUESDAY—*Continuous running, 12 to 16 km with hills.*

WEDNESDAY—*Aerobic interval, 3 × 1500 m PAS, 1:1 SRR, or HRM.*
Weight training, select alternate exercises from the Monday workout, using the endurance concept.

THURSDAY—*Continuous running, 12 to 16 km on the flat at a challenging pace.*

FRIDAY—*Aerobic interval, 8 to 10 × 400 PAS, 2 1/2:1 SRR, or HRM.*
Weight training, one set each of weakest exercises, using the power concept.
If there is a Saturday meet, rest or run only in the morning.

SATURDAY AND

SUNDAY—*No A.M. run. One long, easy-pace run, 16 to 19 km, or 8 to 10 km semihard Fartlek, with one pickup of 400 in the first 1600, one 800 in the last 1500. Include accelerations at 100 and 200 m every 1500, on the flat and up hills. Rest or slow 6 to 7 km (do not jog) as needed, on day of choice.*

LATER SEASON
The morning run and warm-up/warm-down routine described for early season will be continued.

MONDAY—*Anaerobic interval, 6 to 8 × 400 PANAS, 1/2:1 SRR, or HRM.*

TUESDAY—*Continuous run, 8 to 10 km on grass at challenging pace.*
Weight training. Select weak exercises using endurance concept.

WEDNESDAY—*Ladder drill, aerobic interval, 1500, 800, 400, 200, 100 at race pace (note change here) and SRR or HRM appropriate with interval just completed.*

THURSDAY—*Continuous run, 8 to 10 km with frequent 50- and 100-m accelerations on grass, or select varied pace drills and work on the track. Accumulate enough distance in this work to equal 3 to 4 km. Finish with an easy, continuous run of 4 to 5 km on grass.*

FRIDAY—*Morning run only and rest in afternoon, or complete rest.*

SATURDAY—*Competition.*

SUNDAY—*Continuous run, 10 km hard, 6- to 8-km Fartlek as described for early season, or rest as needed.*

Again, remember to be neither hypercritical nor completely compliant with the workout suggestions, which primarily reflect a concept to alternate hard with easy days, work the anaerobic and aerobic aspect, retain some strength activity, and acknowledge the necessity of strategy and speed work. The plan may be too ambitious or too easy for the specific individual involved. No attempt has been made to suggest rigid pace times or recovery patterns. The coach and athlete should work out plans, taking into consideration the current, base-pace capabilities of the runner and known weakness in any of the variables mentioned.

TEACHING THE STEEPLECHASE

Unfortunately, from an international developmental standpoint, it is unlikely that this event will soon be included in the high-school order of events. Current, conservative, administrative logic presents as much of a deterrent to adopt this event as it does to retain the javelin and discus in some states or substitute intermediate for low hurdles, lengthen cross-country distances or introduce the hammer in others. This is an "associated values" problem, with most attention being directed to "more important" athletic issues.

A shorter steeplechase could solve some of the "educative" problems, but the matter of capital investment for water-jump and hurdle-barrier equipment remains. Coaching also has its "endurance factor," and it is conceivable that conscientiousness, initiative, and persistence can overcome these obstacles.

As suggested by Bowerman, the elements of the steeplechase can be taught by laying natural barriers (such as logs) at various points along the periphery of grass athletic fields (1). Following suggestions in the science section, the technique of propelling or stepping for water-jump preparation can be easily learned on the logs. Regular hurdles, set at lower heights, could be placed at other stations along a cross-country run to encourage hurdle-technique development. Instruction in propelling and hurdling should be planned and administered to assure that the candidates will know what they are doing.

A plan for propelling could closely follow the hurdle-teaching program (Chapter 16). An instructor or expert can demonstrate propelling on a log with discussion covering the following elements.

Learning Drill

1. Line up the runners behind the leader.

2. From an easy pace, gradually accelerate into the log.

3. Lean into the log, and drive off the back leg, with the lead leg bent at the knee. Don't forget to achieve a good split between the two legs and lead with the correct arm.

4. In a semicrouch position, land at the front half of the log with a pawing action of the lead leg.

5. Drive forward, with the lead foot in contact with the log as long as possible. While pivoting, bring the trail leg through to the chest and under the returning, lead arm.

6. Drive off the log, leaning forward with the entire body extended, landing on what was the recovery leg.

7. Continue the run to the next log and repeat.

8. The coach or an assistant can stand beside the log and either help those who need individual assistance, or note who they are and individualize later.

Individual Circuit Drill

Work on a track may take the form suggested by Watts (6). Place regular hurdles at the four places usually designated for the hurdle barriers (i.e., going into and coming out of one turn and near the ends of the straightaways at the other turn —the middle of which ordinarily has the water jump). A log or other sturdy, available barrier 91.7 cm (3 ft) high can be substituted for the water jump. Progress in 400- or 800-m hurdle repetitions can be monitored by timing candidates from 10 m before the hurdle or log, to 10 m beyond it in addition to total time.

Gang Hurdling

When and if legal barriers are available, the circuit drill should be expedited with comparable groups of runners, all hurdling and propelling at about the same time —give a half stride or two. This helps the runner experience hindering and perhaps teaches the lesson that the lead position is best, although other positions are tenable as long as one plans and protects himself.

Hurdle Drills

Hurdle drills may be borrowed from the intermediate hurdle section of Chapter 16 and adapted to the requirements of the steeplechase. In the absence of official equipment, substitute regular hurdles and the log—with or without the water!

1. *Back-half drill.* 200-m repeats of the backstretch hurdle, the water jump, and the last hurdle on the straightaway into the finish.

2. *Front-half drill.* 200-m repeats of the two hurdles on the turn and one on the backstretch.

3. *Five hurdle drill repeats.* Set up five high, intermediate, or low hurdles 78 m apart on a 400-m track for interval or repetition work.

Plyometric Exercises of the bounding, leaping and skipping variety, with and without box drill-concepts, are quite valuable and applicable to the requirements of this event.

TRAINING AND CONDITIONING FOR THE STEEPLECHASE

This race might be called a cross-country race on the track although, in reality, it is a long-intermediate hurdle event. Training requires attention to middle-distance running and intermediate hurdling technique, while conditioning is a combination of work including speed, strength, flexibility-agility, aerobics and anaerobics.

Since the candidate will probably have a cross-country background in the Fall, off-season work would include the following suggestions. A morning 6- to 9-km aerobic run and an afternoon warm-up and warm-down similar to the one described for the 3000-m runners are recommended.

SAMPLE WEEKLY PROGRAMS
OFF-SEASON

MONDAY—*Learning drill.*
Five hurdle-drill repeats, 6 to 8 × 400 repeats over low hurdles. Rest 5 minutes between repeats.
Weight training. Similar to that for the 3000 runner.
TUESDAY—*Continuous running, 9 to 10 km at a steady pace with a 400-m pickup each 1500 m.*
WEDNESDAY—*Learning drill.*
Aerobic interval ladder. 1200, 1000, 800, 600 based on splits for 3000-m run at PAS and 1:1 SRR, or HRM.
Weight training, alternate exercises.
THURSDAY—*Fartlek, 9 to 10 km including hills and propelling logs on the course.*
FRIDAY—*Aerobic interval, 2 sets of 8 to 10 × 200 at PAS and SRR.*
Weight training, work with the power concept on the weakest exercises.
SATURDAY AND
SUNDAY—*10 to 12 km continuous running at an easy pace one day, 8- to 10-km Fartlek or rest the other day.*

EARLY SEASON
Morning run, warm-up, and warm-down are assumed.

MONDAY—*Anaerobic interval, 8 to 10 × 400 at PANAS and SRR, or HRM.*
Weight training, endurance concept, weak exercises, 3 sets.
TUESDAY—*Continuous running, 8 to 10 km at a challenging pace.*
WEDNESDAY—*Individual circuit drill or the five-hurdle drill. Repeat 10 × 400 with the hurdles at PAS pace, 2:1 to 1:1 SRR, or HRM. Time the runner for the 20-m increments over hurdles.*
Weight training, power concept, weak exercises, 1 set.
THURSDAY—*Continuous running, 10 to 12 km at an easy pace.*
FRIDAY—*Warm-up or rest.*
SATURDAY—*Competition or time trial.*
SUNDAY—*Continuous running, 10 to 12 km hard.*

LATER SEASON

MONDAY—*Anaerobic-interval ladder (step up), 200, 400, 800, 1200 in PANAS at SRR or HRM recovery.*
TUESDAY—*Continuous running, 8 to 9 km at a challenging pace.*
Weight training, endurance concept, weak exercises, 2 sets.

WEDNESDAY—*Gang hurdle, back-half, and front-half drills. 2 × 400 to 5 ×*
200 m, 1 set back half, the other set front half.
THURSDAY—*Continuous running, 8 to 10 km easy pace.*
FRIDAY—*Warm-up or rest.*
SATURDAY—*Competition.*
SUNDAY—*Continuous running or Fartlek, 8 to 10 km hard.*

BIBLIOGRAPHY

1. Bowerman, William, *Coaching Track and Field,* Houghton Mifflin, Boston 1974.
2. Daniels, Jack, "Success in Endurance Running: Aerobic and Anaerobic Consideration," *Track and Field Quarterly Review, 3,* 146 (1974).
3. Ecker, Tom, "Progressive Interval Training, The Workout Program that Eliminates the Guessing." *Athletic Journal, 57,* 22, April, 1977.
4. Freeman, William H., "Distance Training Methods, Past and Present," *Track and Field Quarterly Review, 4,* 4 (1975).
5. Ward, A. P., *Middle Distance Running,* Amateur Athletic Association, London 1967.
6. Watts, D., "Hints on Steeplechasing," *Track Technique, 41* (September 1970).
7. Wilt, Fred, "Training for Competitive Running," in *Exercise Physiology,* edited by Harold B. Falls, Academic Press, New York, 1968.

Chapter 15

Distance Events

Perhaps no activity in track and field, or in other realms of athletics for that matter, offers as much enjoyment, personal satisfaction, and long-lasting physiological and psychological value as distance running. As echoed by Åstrand (2), Chapter 3, and countless others in their own way, it is probably true that the aerobic ability of a runner depends more on inheritance than on stress training and improvement of mechanical efficiency. If this approach is taken at face value, however, the philosophy of much of our American physical-education, teacher-training curriculum would have to be reassessed for the development of a new set of educational "values."

There has probably been more material written about distance running than any other area of track and field. Despite all of this writing, some of which is based on research, there is still much disagreement about the "best" way to reach success. Young coaches seem to follow the word of internationally known coaches and the programs of world-class runners, and they do not spend enough time examining the plans and philosophy behind them. Even though Lindgren (11), as a graduated high-school senior, trained as much as 400 km (250 miles) in a one-week period

Figure 60. The running stride of Lasse Viren, Finland. PR 13:16.4, 27:38.4. Courtesy of Toni Nett, West Germany.

during the summer before the Tokyo Olympics, and Shorter (19) included :67 track interval 400's in his training on the premise that he would never run at a slower pace, the authors do not suggest such ambitious quality or quantity work for novice high-school runners. Instead, coaches should examine their own physical environment and the maturity level of the people they are coaching. Much scientific data is available on the subject—in fact, so much that, to try to digest it all is confusing and frequently leads to complete bewilderment.

Distance running, particularly if subdivided by sex, age, and ability, can be the greatest gift to cardiovascular health in the country while, at the same time, providing the opportunity for the evolution of champions who pursue a more competitive, long duration high steady state energy expenditure regimen. Correspondingly, in defense of biomechanics and exercise physiologists and those interested in putting the best American on the track in international competition, our current set of "values" in educational athletics should be reevaluated somewhat in terms of applying scientific principles to the selection and training of the elite.

Here, we want to apply the running techniques discussed earlier to the distance events and explore some basic training and conditioning principles.

5000 (3 MILE) AND 10,000 (6 MILE) METER RUNS
Some enthusiastic coaches may think, in terms of biomechanics and physiology, that these events belong in the middle-distance category, and this may be valid *if* the marathon is regarded as the true distance event. Perhaps the secret of running these distances is to find a way to improve efficiency and carry the arms as economically as possible, without sacrificing ground-gaining progress. Fox and Costill, estimating cardiorespiratory responses during long-distance running, found marathon runners to be about 10 percent more efficient than middle-distance runners (4). Conserving oxygen consumption, in these cases, is reflected in using

less oxygen to maintain a given pace and retaining a metabolic reserve for the finish.

An academic exercise on the subject would conclude that the trunk should be upright; little vertical and lateral oscillation should occur during the phases of the stride; and foot plant is initially on the heel, with the progress to the rear initiated before the strike. The recovery leg is active with respect to reduced "moment of inertia," swinging through a reasonable range of motion rapidly without reaching, and arm action is directed toward the midline of the body with backward excursion terminated when the elbow approaches the line of the shoulder (Figure 60, frames 1-9). One must exercise unusual mental discipline in a running style that is predisposed to relaxed cruising so as not to be overcome by the monotony of the run and the desire to "take it easy." Although these suggestions echo those mentioned earlier in connection with the faster paces of middle-distance events, they are softened because of the added distance.

Individual structural differences in runners cannot be changed in most instances, and research confirms that after hundreds of miles logged by an individual, an efficiency characteristic of the individual evolves in terms of decreased stride length and support times, with stride rate increased as strength increases (15). Runners may simply run and become efficient. Perhaps there is an element of truth in this statement but it is actually an oversimplification of the problem and an excuse to coach by telling the runners to "hurry back."

A case in point involves appropriate arm action while running turns and straightaways. How many runners forget to realign themselves on the straightaway after correctly anticipating a turn by leaning into it with the outside shoulder ahead of the inside one, moving the subsequently raised right arm toward the midline of the body with greater amplitude than the slightly lowered left arm?

CROSS-COUNTRY

Generally the distance for this event approximates that of the 5 and 10,000-m runs with the primary difference being the change of running geography. This challenge in itself may account for the increasing popularity of the sport. In some individuals, times for comparable distances may well be faster for cross-country than for flat, circular counterparts! Variety in what an individual is experiencing can be a definite asset in endurance running. Pace remains important, and runners must be able to judge this, regardless of the terrain, weather, and spectators. Hours of running on marked practice courses of varying topography, changing running technique to run up hill and downhill, on the straight and around numerous curves, on narrow trails through wooded areas, over smooth and rough ground, contribute to the thinking athlete's feel of pace. Efficient running style features brevity of stride coordinated with economical arm and shoulder carriage and aerobic capacity enhanced by a body devoid of excess weight. A serious approach is required in productive, competitive running, although many athletes participate with more *élan* in the activity when absolved of this responsibility while preparing and conditioning. A brief synopsis of successful cross-country includes:

1). *Examination of the course.* This is valuable in helping one determine a plan of action for the race. The procedure will be easier if the team can devise a similar home course to practice on. If this is not the case, imagination combined with study of a map of the competition course and a careful look at the first and last 800 to 1000 m during the warm-up on the day of the meet will have to replace practice experience. Carefully consider the length of the initial straightaway, tightness of turns, single-file trails, logs, streams, pavement, rough ground, hills, legitimate shortcuts, and the effect weather might have on the course.

2). *Contending with the terrain.* Many courses, unfortunately, include numerous turns and repeats of loops to attain the required distance. Taking turns correctly, as described earlier, can significantly improve performance. Practice sessions should include interval or Fartlek work negotiating turns with other team members. Turns may be tight, gentle, narrow, wide, encountered while going up, cresting, or at the bottom of a steep or low, percentage-grade hill. Team approaches help determine whether the best strategy is to run lead, follow others, or take the turn wide while attempting to maintain pace in a crowded field of runners.

Perhaps as a result of personal experience, Higdon recommends a flatfoot run uphill, with erect to slightly reclining posture (9). Only when the hill is quite steep should the runner lean into the hill like an accelerating sprinter. Downgrades are negotiated with controlled acceleration, requiring forward lean and a sprint-style stride. However, the recent findings and conclusions of Henson's treadmill grade-running experiment prove and confirm that the runner will lean slightly forward when running uphill and slightly backward downhill (8). At racing speed, up grade or downgrade, foot placement is closer to the ball of the foot. As the positive grade increases, frequency of stride should increase more than stride length. If running downhill slowly, increase the frequency, but lengthen the stride if negotiating the downgrade rapidly. As expected, although energy is conserved by downhill running, the saving is less than the additional amount necessary to run up the same incline at the same speed.

A map can provide some assistance in the orienteering of obstacles such as logs, streams, and puddles, which obviously cannot all be anticipated without a careful look at the entire course. Although the strategy can be plotted beforehand, quick, tactical decisions have to be made enroute. Stepping logs and felled trees is probably better than running around them and may actually help the pace by breaking a rhythm that may be becoming slower by the minute.

Rough ground is best negotiated with a flatfoot run—and a good pair of shoes. Many American manufacturers are now successfully competing with European footwear companies, marketing lightweight shoes that protect the entire leg by building in strong, elevated, wide soles and heels without decreasing flexibility, arch, or shank support. The principal problem seems to be the price! But when one considers that even with correct running mechanics, improper or worn footwear can cause a myriad of foot, knee, hip, and lower back problems after thousands of practice kilometers, cost is the preferable alternative.

The Competition

Football and basketball teams work most of the practice week against offensive and defensive variations of the opponent, and cross-country runners should devote part of their preparation to a study of the physical and psychological characteristics of their competition. The best approach is a rational realization of a team's potentiality on the course in question, taking into consideration the number of athletes involved. Ultimately, success in cross-country team running depends on pace judgment, gang running, and confidence in the ability of the team to break contact with important, competitive runners enroute. Rational instead of empassioned coaching in regard to the start, turns, hills, obstacles, and narrow trails during the week and just before lining up for the race should suffice. Weather and personnel can change rapidly, and the team should be mentally ready for anything. The advice, "don't think, it takes too much time" may be appropriate for some intensity events, but it does not add to the effectiveness of a long-distance runner. If one takes a rational and tough approach, stress and the pain of fatigue can be controlled or subdued by persistent, positive thinking.

TRAINING AND CONDITIONING FOR DISTANCE EVENTS

What is the best way to condition for endurance runs? Considering the time factor (i.e., approximately 13 to 30 minutes for runs of varying distances), over 90 to 95 percent of the practice and weekly schedule should be aerobic. This may be accomplished with continuous, Fartlek, or slow-interval training. The balance of the workout procedure may be anaerobic or strength oriented. Many will disagree with this overly simplistic approach and point out that, although it makes sense to run a steady, aerobic pace at about 75 percent of one's aerobic capacity, the competitive race itself is uneconomically run with anaerobic spurts throughout. Lothar Hirsch, national distance coach for the West German Athletic Federation, has made the same observation and suggests a preseason aerobic approach, with occasional and gradual increase of anaerobic components (10). In the competitive season, there should be a change in the relationship between volume and intensity, with the ratio of aerobic to anaerobic work 50:50.

Ernst Van Aaken of West Germany, however, supports the great volume, long, slow-run approach with walking breaks (20). About 5 percent of the workout employs the tempo or speed endurance concept at best effort racing pace, with ample time for active rest. He also ludicrously recommends that a runner lower body weight *20 percent* below normal, evidently to improve oxygen-uptake parameters! Although a reduction of body fat to below 10 percent would be more valid physiologically, a gross reduction of weight would decrease muscle mass also, and correspondingly lower the VO_2 variable (3). Athletes should adjust mileage and length of tempo runs to distances longer than their usual event, with the longer runs performed at the beginning or the end of the week (6).

Van Aaken contends that years of progressive buildup are necessary for complete preparation in distance running (20). This is applicable to all runners, regardless of age, sex, and ability. The inference is to avoid immediate exposure to arduous workouts, allowing ample time to overcome the general body stress of many kilometers. After a good level of physical fitness has been established, any of the previous methods of training may be tailored to the needs of an individual or homogeneous group of runners, with race-pace interval or tempo reserved for the latter part of the reduced-volume, competitive season. As in most athletic training, it is wise to alternate hard with easier days of practice, regardless of the time of year, and to allow for occasional and sequential days of complete absence from practice responsibilites.

This advice may suggest underdevelopment. However, once the foundation has been established by a daily 7:00 to 7:15 1600-m pace run for 50 to 60 minutes, the tempo should pick up gradually for work at a more demanding pace to challenge the oxygen uptake and lactic-acid tolerance parameters. This does not seem to connote or suggest an easy workout arrangement!

It is important to train the body by training the mind because, unfortunately, it is very easy to learn incorrectly. Although it is impossible to alter inherited characteristics and tendencies, the central nervous system contains parts within the voluntary jurisdiction of the athlete that initiate not only gross but also the more discrete skill-related contractions of muscle. In other words, one of the subdivisions of the voluntary nervous apparatus is responsible for the general mechanics of a running stride, while the other refines its execution. Eventually, with continued practice and concentration on correct technique, assisted by feedback arrangements from muscle to the brain to refine movement, trace patterns for habitual or subconscious movement are established in the sensory part of the brain. Some learned human movements, however, are too fast for sensory-feedback adjustment, and their trace patterns are stored in the motor portion of the brain. Thus, the correctly learned stride will become habitual, with further training becoming a problem of improved efficiency and conditioning. Correspondingly, incorrectly learned technique will be very difficult to alter, requiring unusual patience and time to effect changes in the stored information. The coaching point of this discussion should be apparent. Distance running requires positive thought, psychologically; intellectual thought, biomechanically; and a tough attitude, physiologically!

FOUNDATION PROGRAM FOR ENDURANCE RUNNING

Essentially, advice for novice athletes regarding the correct way to train for long distance runs should be based on the events that are actually available for them. Although the incidence of 10,000 m, road racing, and marathon running is increasing among young runners, the majority will continue to regard cross-country, with distances ranging from 3 to 5000 m, as the longest event. Basically, whether this distance is run on the track or the cross-country trail, the training is similar, and all of the work is submaximal to maximal aerobic in nature, with most of it done off the track.

The Basic Foundation

A prime requirement for novice training in endurance running is a good aerobic or physical-fitness foundation. Elementary, junior high, and beginning high school candidates should be instructed and encouraged to follow a relaxed program of summer running. Slow-pace volume work should be emphasized, beginning with a run, walk, jog, hike approach, once a day for 5 to 6 days a week throughout the first half of the vacation period. Initially, the pace is not important, but finishing what you start is! Generally, a sub to seven minute 1600-m pace for a total of 5 to 6 km one day and 10 to 12 km the next is recommended. The work may be done without a stopwatch, and 45 minutes to an hour of running with short, active breaks will usually fulfill the basic requirements. A watch may be used occasionally to recognize and learn pace.

Unfortunately, this work is boring, and the candidate should be instructed to vary the course of his running to modify this factor. Generally, it is unwise to recommend serious Fartlek or interval, since it encourages anaerobic work and injury before the athlete is ready for the limited, required amount of this capacity. Fartlek and interval of a slow nature is advisable, however, and would include a limited amount of hill work below race pace and walking or jogging recovery periods before resuming flat running.

More mature distance runners will work out twice a day as a regular routine. The second workout is generally used to increase the endurance base that can be built from running many miles over a long period of time at a steady pace. It is important that the amount of work prescribed for the secondary workout is such that it does not detract from the primary workout.

Sample Programs for a week during each half of the summer are provided. Each coach must adopt a suitable program that fits the individual situation. The work is amenable to change, should be done off the track, and can be expedited more enjoyably with running companions.

A representative program for a week in June

MONDAY—*2 to 3 km followed by 15 minutes of stretching.*
10 to 12 km with 3 km of it at a sub 7:00 pace.
TUESDAY—*6 to 8 km of Lydiard Fartlek.*
15 minutes of endurance weight training.
WEDNESDAY—*4 sets, 4 × 800 m on a marked, cross-country course at a sub 3:30 pace, jog or walk 1 to 2 minutes between repetitions, and stretch for 2 to 3 minutes between sets.*
THURSDAY—*6 to 8 km with the last 3 km at a sub-7:00 pace.*
15 minutes of endurance weight training.
FRIDAY—*10 to 12 km slow Holmer Fartlek with hill work and three 5-minute stretching sessions interspersed.*
SATURDAY AND
SUNDAY—*Either rest one day of choice or recreate. Use the other day for an uninterrupted run of 14 to 16 km at a steady pace.*

A representative program for a week in July
Warm-up procedure to be followed each day
Run 1600 m in 7:00 to 7:15.
15 minutes stretching.

MONDAY—A.M.—*5 to 8 km at a 7:00 pace.*
P.M.—*Run 10 to 12 km with the last 3 to 4 km at 6:45 to 7:00 pace. 10 minutes of endurance weight training.*
TUESDAY—AM—*Morning run.*
PM—*4 × 1600 m at 6:30 to sub 7:00 pace on a marked, cross-country course, with 2 to 3 minutes of stretching and active rest between repetitions.*
WEDNESDAY—A.M.—*Morning run.*

> P.M.—*6 to 7 km Lydiard Fartlek, including work stepping or propelling logs and steeplechase hurdles. 10 minutes of endurance weight training.*
>
> THURSDAY—A.M.—*Morning run.*
>
> P.M.—*6 to 8 km at 6:45 pace over varying terrain including hills, tight turns, and narrow trails.*
> *15 minutes of stretching.*
>
> FRIDAY—A.M.—*Morning run.*
>
> P.M.—*10 to 12 km at a steady pace.*
> *10 minutes of endurance weight training.*
>
> SATURDAY—A.M.—*Morning run.*
>
> P.M.—*12 to 15 km at steady pace with one pickup of 400 m each 3 km at current race pace.*
>
> SUNDAY—A.M.—*Morning run.*
>
> P.M.—*Rest or recreate.*

Weight Training. Endurance runners have little need for serious, progressive-resistance weight training but may profit from the low-resistance, endurance-repetition variety. Strength gained from this type of lifting will improve local endurance of muscle groups and help to improve the efficiency of running technique. All large muscle groups of the body need attention, although hill running with the obvious aid of gravity provides a simulated weight-training experience for the legs. A 10 to 15 minute workout with any of the exercises for these parts of the body developed in previous chapters will suffice. The important thing is the selection of a reasonable resistance, correct technique for lifting, and maintenance of a rapid tempo for 15 to 20 repetitions per set to stimulate the muscle. Naturally, when this load becomes easy to handle, the resistance should be progressively increased by small increments, or the number of repetitions should be increased, or a maintenance program is substituted if a desired strength level has been reached. Although there is a difference of opinion, perhaps it is best to do this work after running, on a split routine basis, when the athletes are fatigued and less apt to assume the heavier loads which could lead to injury.

Flexibility. Weight training itself will help to improve flexibility if the technique is correct and the athlete lifts through a complete range of movement at the joint involved. Flexibility, however, is better enhanced by a 15 to 20 minute period of serious stretching after 5 to 10 minutes of easy running. Any of the flexibility-agility exercises described in Chapter 4 are applicable. Particular attention should be directed to loosening up the tight hamstring and gastrocnemius-soleus muscle groups. Distance runners are particularly susceptible to injuries of these muscles, along with Achilles tendon injuries, as a result of their great volume running. Certainly, all antagonistic or contralateral muscle groups along with the movers most involved should be developed to prevent muscle imbalance, but both groups should also be stretched. The best way for any runner to stretch the hamstrings is to lie in a supine (face up) position with the lower back supported and flex the hip unilaterally (one leg at a time) to its limit and hold it for 5 to 10 seconds with the knee extended to prevent pelvic tip. Remain in the supine position, and pull slowly and steadily on a towel or strap wrapped around the foot to stretch the gastrocnemius and soleus (calf) muscles.

Nutrition.   Generally, distance candidates are thin or of the ectomorphic variety, although many heavily muscled high-school runners who are devoid of body fat do a creditable job in endurance activity. However, great volume work will burn up enough energy to require a substantial intake of food to maintain the metabolism and allow for growth. Essentially, a well-balanced diet, including commonly suggested portions of the basic food groups with a reasonable emphasis on extra carbohydrate, satisfies these energy needs, maintains blood sugar levels, and keeps the individual lean for optimal total oxygen uptake and body weight relationships. It is not necessary to fortify the diet with various heavily advertised and usually expensive food supplements for which endorsements are customarily made by highly imaginative and often overzealous well-known athletes. The "secret" ingredients of bee pollen, protein tablets, super sugars, for instance, are also found in the basic food groups and at less expense. It is valuable to include a replacement of electrolyte containing fluids in the diet, but again, fruit juices, along with food will usually accommodate very nicely. Distance runners should be advised about the problems of heat exhaustion and replacement of body fluid and electrolyte, particularly during the hot, humid summer months.

Prescription for running

Workouts for this section will be characterized primarily, but not exclusively, by submaximal aerobic activity incurring increasingly larger but tolerable amounts of lactic acid. The remaining balance of earlier season workout plans will include best effort racing pace activity. Greater amounts of this, as well as anaerobic assignments will make a stronger contribution from the winter on (5).

Some specialized language used in the sample programs needs definition for the concept described above. Pace will not depend as much on any suggested times as it will on heart rate range/oxygen uptake characteristics.

Swing tempo will be used to denote a pace requiring 60 to 75 percent of the heart rate range and 50 to 60 percent oxygen uptake, respectively.

Quick tempo, a more accelerated pace, should require 75 to 80 percent of the heart rate range and, correspondingly, 65 to 75 percent of the oxygen uptake.

Race pace efforts will enlist greater heart-rate/oxygen-uptake parameters and will approach the limit of aerobic activity.

If a runner is instructed in the simple art of taking the pulse while resting and after intensive activity, running at 75 percent of the heart-rate range will usually stimulate aerobic mechanisms while running at less than race pace. Occasionally checking the pulse immediately after a submaximal run will verify the correct stress level.

Naturally, resting pulse will progressively drop after months of work. So will the maximal pulse! Consequently, new pulse bench marks occasionally have to be determined. In other words, as an athlete develops, he will use less cardiovascular and oxygen uptake capacity to do what was previously a chore. To continue development, more stress must be progressively added by stepping up the pace to regain the 75-percent, heart-rate level.

Recreation

Like all athletes, distance runners need to break the tedious monotony of daily workouts with activitiy that will help them return to running with enthusiasm. However, the danger of injury while vigorously doing something that requires unusual stresses must be weighed against the theraputic value of participating in the activity. The choice is elective dependent on philosophy. Swimming and water polo, however, are activities that will help runners discover they have other muscle groups with a minimal likelihood of injury.

Injury Prevention

We all recognize that the best cure for injury is prevention. The basic foundation (with good footwear) will help establish this. Attention to flexibility work and strength improvement is also important. Add careful administration of anaerobic "speed" work, and the cycle should be complete. But in spite of this, injury will occur, and when it does the best procedure is to treat it without workouts. Most injuries will mend within a week or two, and this respite rarely lowers aerobic capacity. Injuries that persist should be referred to a physician for X ray and, if results are negative, this may be enough to stimulate a return to activity. If not, the problem may be psychological, but it should not be so regarded at the initial report of injury!

Motivation, Strategy and Tactics

Developing the positive attitute toward competition is best accomplished during the preseason and regular-season workout sessions. Frequent approval of the progress of an athlete is helpful, even when the subject is on a plateau. Some coaches find that "devices" (T-shirts, certificates, ability group minimeets, attention directed to the plodders as well as the top men) are most helpful. Other, more complete suggestions regarding "devices" are enumerated in Chapter 2, dealing with the organization and administration of a program.

Practice sessions with exercises for strategy and tactics are found in Chapter 14 and are briefly listed here for reinforcement: varied pace drills, box drill, tandem drill, peek-a-boo drill, and simulation buddy drill, including "drafting", a technique whereby one runner runs behind another to take advantage of a wind-breaking effect. In all of these drills or exercises, emphasis should be placed not only on the aspect of physical contact but on the concept of mental contact as well. An excellent activity for this concept is controlled Fartlek, a procedure employed at

Indiana University that is similar to the "buddy" drill discussed in Chapter 14. The purpose of controlled Fartlek is to teach variety of pace and the role of concentration regarding physical contact in racing. Runners of a group take turns at leading and setting the pace for a group attempting to maintain close contact at all times. This very tough workout emphasizes the mental alertness necessary in distance running.

Also, concentrate on running up and down hills, and practice taking turns as discussed earlier (pages 266-7). Motivation is best served on the day of the meet by simply reviewing strategy for the race. Although running and competing should be fun, if the groundwork has been laid in previous weeks, the fiery oration before the meet and exortation to "stretch out" and "get on your toes" should be avoided during the run.

SAMPLE WEEKLY PROGRAMS

In the United States, high schools are basically on types of track programs that require peak performance two or three times a year for cross-country, indoor and outdoor seasons. The sample programs provided are correspondingly developed to meet these requirements if a running base has been developed by summer training. They are not intended to be regarded as a "gospel" but should be adapted into plans that fit individual and group needs. The type of terrain locally available will also affect and influence the pace and volume of work. It may take as much energy to run 10 km at a 6:00 1600 m pace on hills as it does to run 13 km at a slightly faster pace on the flat. The alert coach should always be aware of, and adjust to conditions and variables that can alter prepared programs.

Throughout the entire, long-range program, always include a daily second run of 8 to 10 km, preferably in the morning. Precede each afternoon session with a warm-up run of 3 to 4 km followed by stretching-flexibility exercises, and conclude with 2 × 100 m of easy pickup style runs to current race pace.

Stress of continuous running assignments in the body of the workout will be determined by the heart-rate/oxygen-uptake guidelines discussed in the foundation program. Active rest periods of 1 to 5 minutes will provide recovery between assignments not covered by interval SRR or HRM procedures.

Warm down or cool off after each session with an easy 1200-m run and additional stretching. Lightweight endurance-style weight training, when scheduled, will always be done after the warm-down. All PANAS and NANAS assignments (Chapter 14) are based on current best available race-pace criteria utilizing SRR or HRM for recovery. Frequently, interval assignments of short distance repeats will be suggested. They are to be expedited at race pace with attention directed to technique. Rest may be either SRR or HRM.

OFF-SEASON, CROSS-COUNTRY (late summer and early fall)

MONDAY—*5 km, swing tempo.*
Active rest, 1 to 5 minutes according to need.

3 km, crisp tempo.
10 × 100 m current race pace intervals, SRR or HRM recovery.
Weight training.
TUESDAY—12 to 14 km, swing tempo.
WEDNESDAY—10 minutes of running, swing tempo.
10 minutes, crisp tempo.
10 minutes, swing tempo.
Varied pace drills, either gradual accelerations to pick up pace
or quick accelerations to meet challenges (page 250-1),
10 minutes, swing tempo.
5 minutes, crisp tempo.
Weight training.
THURSDAY—10 to 12 km of running, swing tempo.
FRIDAY—10 minutes, swing tempo.
10 minutes, Holmer Fartlek.
10 minutes, swing tempo.
10 minutes, crisp tempo.
10 × 100 m current race-pace intervals.
Weight training.
SATURDAY—8 to 10 km, swing tempo.
SUNDAY—10 to 18 km, swing tempo.

EARLY SEASON, CROSS-COUNTRY

MONDAY—10 minutes, swing tempo.
10 minutes, controlled Fartlek.
10 minutes, swing tempo.
10 minutes, controlled Fartlek.
10 minutes, swing tempo.
12 × 100 m current race-pace intervals.
Weight training.
TUESDAY—10 to 14 km, swing tempo.
WEDNESDAY—Situation drills, box, tandem, or buddy.`
4 × 800 m on a cross-country trail at race pace. Run a cycle of
4:30 (i.e., start to start of the 800's).
5 km, swing tempo.
Weight training.
THURSDAY—4 km, swing tempo.
2 km, crisp tempo.
4 km, swing tempo.
10 × 10 m current race-pace intervals.
FRIDAY—No warm-up or warm-down. Run 7 to 10 km at an easy, relaxed
pace.

SATURDAY—*Competition.*
SUNDAY—*12 to 20 km, swing tempo.*

LATER SEASON, CROSS-COUNTRY

MONDAY—*5 km, gradually accelerate from swing to crisp tempo.*
    3 × 400 m, 1 second faster than race pace. Run a cycle of 2:40
      (i.e., start another 400 at 2:40).
    3 × 400 m as above with the cycle set at 2:30.
    Weight training.
TUESDAY—*8 to 12 km, swing tempo.*
    4 × 200 m, 2 seconds faster than race pace.
WEDNESDAY—*4 to 5 km, swing tempo.*
    2 × 800 m at 2 seconds faster than race pace.
    10 minutes controlled Fartlek.
THURSDAY—*8 to 12 km at an easy, relaxed pace.*
FRIDAY—*3 to 4 × 100 m pickups at race pace.*
SATURDAY—*Competition.*
SUNDAY—*12 to 20 km, swing tempo.*

OFF-SEASON, TRACK PROGRAM (late fall-early winter)

MONDAY—*2 × 400 m PANAS with SRR or HRM (Chapter 14).*
    2 × 800 m PANAS.
    2 × 200 m NANAS.
    Active rest, 5 minutes following return of HRM to acceptable
      level.
    3 to 5 km, swing tempo.
    Weight training.
TUESDAY—*50 minutes of swing tempo with a faster 400 m every 1600 m.*
WEDNESDAY—*20 minutes, swing tempo.*
    20 minutes, Holmer Fartlek.
    10 minutes, swing tempo.
    Weight training.
THURSDAY—*40 minutes, swing tempo.*
FRIDAY—*Anaerobic ladder drill, 200, 400, 600, 800, 600, 400, 200 m.*
SATURDAY—*20 minutes, swing tempo.*
    No rest.
    15 minutes, Holmer Fartlek.
    No rest.
    20 minutes, swing tempo.
SUNDAY—*1 hour run, swing tempo.*

If indoor competition is scheduled for Friday or Saturday, the weekly workout pattern should be altered to taper off by Thursday.

EARLY OUTDOOR SEASON

MONDAY—*3 × 400 m, NANAS.*
2 × 600 m, NANAS.
2 × 150 m, quick tempo.
5 km, swing tempo.
Weight training.

TUESDAY—*45 minutes of running, 15 minutes at swing followed by 30 minutes at quick tempo with an accelerated 100 m every 400 m.*

WEDNESDAY—*Anaerobic ladder drill. 2 × 200 PANAS, 1 × 800 NANAS, 2 × 200 PANAS, 1 × 800 NANAS, and 2 × 400 NANAS.*
2 to 5 km, swing tempo.
Weight training.

THURSDAY—*30 minutes, swing tempo.*
3 × 150 m, NANAS.
10 minutes of easy, relaxed running.

FRIDAY—*4 to 6 km at an easy, relaxed pace.*
2 to 3 × 100 m current race-pace intervals.

SATURDAY—*Competition.*

SUNDAY—*50 to 60 minutes at swing tempo.*

LATER TRACK SEASON

MONDAY—*2 sets, 4 × 800 m NANAS.*
4 to 6 × 150 m, at current race pace.

TUESDAY—*35 to 40 minutes, swing tempo.*
Weight training.

WEDNESDAY—*2 × 200 m, NANAS.*
4 × 600 m, NANAS.
2 to 5 × 150, hard.
3 to 6 km, swing tempo.

THURSDAY—*30 minutes of easy, relaxed running.*
2 × 400 m at race pace.

FRIDAY—*6 to 8 km, easy, relaxed running.*

SATURDAY—*Competition.*

SUNDAY—*45 to 50 minutes, swing tempo.*

THE ADMINISTRATION OF CROSS-COUNTRY COMPETITION

As with any activity that is being initiated or reorganized, the process of administration requires planning, followed by organizing, directing, coordinating, and controlling. This approach should include a problem-based/problem-solving concept to systematically anticipate problems and constantly reevaluate the process and the program. Since Chapter 2 outlines suggestions regarding the administration of track-and-field and cross-country programs, our principal concern here will be the informational and organizational aspects of conducting a meet.

Information

Before a meet, information, instructions, and a map of the course should be sent to the visiting schools. Briefly, essential information includes:

1. The name of the meet.

2. A brief, introductory paragraph or listing denoting who the meet is for, including the time and place of the event.

3. If the meeting features separate runs for various categories of runners (age, grade, sex), an order of events should be given with the staging and starting times and the distance each group will run.

4. Specific instructions should be provided regarding the numbering and scoring system to be used.

5. Briefly describe the nature of the awards and how they will be dispensed after the meet.

6. If an entry blank is included with return expected, provide specific information regarding how it is to be completed and when and to whom it is to be returned.

7. Include a well-drawn map of the marked course, with instructions of its location, how to get there, and where to check in at the designated time.

The Course

Prior to the meet, the course should be adequately marked identically with the instructions on the map. Rule book procedures may be used, but there are acceptable alternatives, including the use of traffic cones with limed arrows around them to indicate the direction of the run turns. Check marks should be designated for each 1600 m for pacing and timing purposes.

A funnel-shaped chute, narrowing to the width of one runner and long enough to accommodate at least a third of the field should be set up at the finish. Again, the high-school rule book provides adequate information, but two by fours, 1.20 to 1.52 m (4 to 5 ft) long, painted red, sunk 31 cm (1 ft) into the ground, and strung with clothesline rope should be adequate. It may be advisable to pad the posts at the constriction of the funnel with sponge rubber or polyurathane to protect competing runners at the narrow entrance.

Clerks and scoring tables should be set up at the end of the chute and enclosed to keep all but the necessary officials out of the area. A tent roof to cover the workers is a wise advance precaution in case of inclement weather.

The Officials

The minimum requirements would include:

1. A clerk of the course with registration materials.

2. The head scorer with two assistants to read numbers as runners file by and to assist with and validate the scoring.

3. A starter, who may also serve as the referee to arbitrate disputes.

4. (A) Several judges placed strategically on the course to keep the race progressing smoothly.
(B) Two timers and a recorder listing the sequential times for every runner by checking them off on a sheet to be matched with the finish list later.

5. Several marshalls distributed along the chute to keep the runners in line and moving toward the end of the chute.

6. An announcer with a power megaphone to issue basic instructions prior to the meet, announce progress of the run, and give results.

7. An awards clerk for dispensing any awards that may be given.

8. One or two police officers to handle any difficult crossings that involve vehicular traffic.

9. Several marshals patrolling a wide extension of the chute to keep visitors from interfering with the runners coming down the final stretch.

Number of Contestants and Scoring Alternatives

Any number of athletes may run in a cross-country meet, although a minimum of five runners per team must finish to be additively scored. The usual full compliment includes two additional runners who score indirectly when they finish ahead of any of the first five runners of the opposition, thereby increasing their additive score.

There are a number of alternatives for registering runners.

1). *Entry blank.* In major meets, an entry blank is returned prior to the meet, with 10 to 12 runners listed in the order of their anticipated finish. They are assigned a specific, sequential series of numbers identifying the school. Before the run, the coach will pick up a packet containing the numbers (with names on them) from the clerk's table and distribute them to the seven who are finally selected to run. The number is placed on the front of the runner's jersey. Attached to this number with a staple is a smaller punched card with the number repeated, the name of the school, and a place for the finish judge to mark the finish position. The card is torn off as the runner walks through the end of the chute, the place is marked on it, and it is handed to a score clerk who in turn places it on a board under the name of the school. When the last team runner has walked through the chute, the scoring is completed. Runners from schools without a team entry are easily identified by the color-coded card on their jersey number, the card is torn off, and the last previous team runner's finish is marked on it, plus a hyphen and a letter of the alphabet or a number. For example, if the fifth runner of team A places 50th and the next runner represents an incomplete team, his place is 50-A or 50-1, etc. These are sequentially placed on another board. It is relatively easy for the awards clerk to determine who the medalists are, and typing the results after the meet is simplified. [See Joe Newton's *The Long Green Line* for a related system utilizing paper clips for carrying the cards and a masterboard or sandwich board equipped with jumbo clips to hold the turned in cards carried by a manager. (16)].

2). *Nonentry blank.* Alternatives to this seemingly sophisticated method require that the coach, upon early arrival, report to the clerk's table and register seven runners, marking the assigned numbers on the back of each runner's right hand with a marking pen. Runners from *incomplete* teams are assigned distinctive numbers or letters to be encircled.

(Alternative A) As the athletes finish the run and walk through the end of the chute, the numbers are read off by a clerk and the scorer records them. Some time must be taken after the last runner files through to number the list, omitting the athletes from incomplete teams, and to locate the sequence numbers per school and tally up the score.

(Alternative B) Scoring may be expedited by handing out place cards to the team athletes as they file through the chute. These are handed by the athlete to his coach, who tallies them on the outside of a previously supplied envelope, encloses them, seals the envelope, and turns it in to the scorer. Individuals from incomplete teams are handed a distinctively different color-coded card on which the clerk must mark 50-1 or 50-A, as described above. This number is handed to the coach by the athlete and subsequently turned in to the scorer in a previously supplied color-coded envelope with related information recorded on the outside by the coach.

Follow-Up

The complete results should be prepared as quickly as possible and either duplicated and distributed after the meet or mailed to the respective schools. The results should include a complete, sequential listing of everyone who finished, their school affiliation, and their respective time. An additional listing displays the low five (+ two) additive scores for each school with a complete team.

Meet administration should be approached with thought directed toward future contests, improving the procedure before as well as after the meet. In larger invitational meets, the number of runners per school is usually limited to seven to facilitate scoring, although the practice of designating them just prior to the meet and renumbering the finish list will allow the physical education approach of activity for all.

Assuming that advance publicity was undertaken with the press and other media, the results should be delivered by hand as soon as possible after the meet. Perhaps the sport is sufficiently popular to have attracted the attendance of a reporter, but this is the exception rather than the rule. Regardless, the results must be prepared by the meet administrator in a form that can be published. Few sports newswriters will wish to interpret the complete results sent to the participating schools.

THE MARATHON

Running is as commonplace to a marathoner as walking was to the 1940 mailman. The compulsive "run for" nature of this super cross-country event is best facilitated by an individual style that guarantees conservation of physical and psychological energy. The better marathoners do more than shuffle along, and their characteristics are improved by tall posture, additional shoulder rotation, high, "weightless" arm carriage, and a featherweight stride.

Distance running of the marathon or long, road-race variety is increasing in popularity among both sexes and all ages. Included are 37-year-old Harry Cordellos, totally blind since age 19, and 36-year-old Dr. Joan Ullyot, with a best of 2:58:09 after only 6 years of endurance-running experience. Kenneth Young has compiled and statistically analyzed data regarding the number of people involved in distance running and finds peak participation periods between the ages of 15 to 19 and 25 to 29, respectively, for men and women (21).

Joe Henderson, speaking from great experience, acknowledges that training for the marathon is a long-term commitment (7). This must present quite a challenge for some children who have been known to run the event, as well as to the septuagenarians and octogenarians on the other end of the growing marathoner population continuum. Henderson suggests a jog, run, race program for anyone's initial marathon, which requires three months of progressive-resistance training. A six-point schedule acknowledges the suggestions made in earlier sections of this chapter regarding the gradual weekly buildup of aerobic work for distance running. The most interesting suggestion that he makes is that the novice is ready for the big event after practice runs of 24 kilometers (15 miles) at a pace that requires 2 hours. He urges that it is the total, cumulative distance in practice that counts, and this will help the fledgling, with courage and patience, to finish what he or she starts.

Tom Miller, a U.S. Marine Corps Engineer, maintains that "Every Body is Right" and utilizes the proven physiological principal that, in work against gravity, the oxygen uptake requirement per unit of weight is the same among all people, with total oxygen uptake varying with body weight in calculating height/weight ratios for realistic assessment of obtainable performance goals in the marathon (13). Unfortunately, he also recommends a belly-breathing, four-count rhythm of exhaling every other time the left foot contacts the ground, to assist in obtaining necessay oxygen-containing air, as metabolically less costly than the "gasping" method of respiration. Until substantiated by research, however, any approach toward controlled breathing should be regarded with reservation and speculation. Nature provides an excellent breathing apparatus that automatically adjusts to the stress of immediate and long-term training.

The best male and female marathoners are quite lean and average 7.5 to 15-percent body fat, respectively. It is claimed that the greater body fat of females need not be considered a disadvantage in terms of excess baggage, but as a reservoir of fatty acids to be used advantageously as a high-octane fuel (20). Theory or not, it is a fact that fatty acids are used to a far greater extent as a fuel during submaximal activity than "cleaner burning" glucose among endurance-trained individuals of both sexes (17).

Because the marathon depends on metabolic capacity or the amount of fuel available under near maximum aerobic demands, considerable research and refutation of it has been done on the practice of carbohydrate loading (1). The basic idea of the practice is to stimulate glycogen loading by exhausting these stores in the muscle with a long run a week before competition. For several days following, the diet consists of protein and fat. Carbohydrates are avoided during this time, after which unusually large amounts are added along with the fat and protein. Dr. George Sheehan, M.D., warns, however, that the practice is not for everyone (18). Some runners experience muscle breakdown, with an increase of myoglobin from the muscle cells in the blood clogging the kidneys and causing renal shutdown. Others have experienced hypoglycemic stress during the fast because of low amounts of glycogen in the blood, muscles, and the liver. The stress, characterized by loss of emotional self-control, can be pacified by ingestion of small amounts of slow-absorbing fructose.

Nathan Pritikin of the Longevity Research Institute of Santa Barbara, California, has little regard for loading, pointing out that fats, and proteins ingested during the fast are poor fuels and accumulate ketones or acid by-products that cause fatigue and lethargy (12,14). He suggest a normal diet with extra carbohydrate on a daily basis. It is also of interest here that his comments on the efficiency of fat as a fuel contrasts with Ullyot's on the female fat advantage.

In conclusion, marathon and long-distance road running requires years of gradual adjustment to a high level of endurance fitness with small amounts of speed work at race pace reserved for the fit individual. In other words, start gradually, progressively increase the volume of running, and do limited work at sensible speed when condition is mature —and do it all with a good pair of shoes!

BIBLIOGRAPHY

1. Åstrand, Per Olaf, "Diet and Athletic Performance," *Federal Proceedings, 26,* 1772 (1967); *Nutrition Today, 3,* 9 (1968).
2. Åstrand, Per Olaf, and Kaare Rodahl, *Textbook of Work Physiology,* McGraw-Hill, New York, 1970.
3. Costhill, D. L., R. Bowers, and W. F. Kammer, "Skinfold Estimates of Body Fat Among Marathon Runners," *Medicine and Science in Sport, 2,* 93 (1970).

4. Fox, Edward, L., and D. L. Costill, "Estimated Cardiorespiratory Responses during Marathon Running," *Archives of Environmental Health,* 24, 315 (1972).

5. Hellerstein, H. K., and Adler, R., "Relationships Between Percent Maximal Oxygen Uptake and Percent Maximal Heart Rate in Normals and Cardiacs," *Circulation, 43–44,* Supplement II (October 1971).

6. Henderson, Joe, "Repaying a Small Speed Debt," *Runners World, 11,* 58 (June 1976).

7. Henderson, Joe, "Training for the First One," *Runners World, 12,* 29 (February 1977).

8. Henson, Phillip L., "Pace and Grade Related to the Oxygen and Energy Requirements, and the Mechanics of Treadmill Running," Unpublished Doctoral Dissertation, Indiana University, 1976.

9. Higdon, Hal, "Taking the Fall Sport Seriously," *Runners World, 11,* 46 (September 1976).

10. Hirsch, Lothar, "Sample Aerobic to Anaerobic Ratios," *Track Technique, 64* (June 1976).

11. Lindgren, Gerry, Personal Conversation, 1964.

12. Martin, Tom, "A Personal Energy Crisis," *Runners World, 11,* 47 (August 1976).

13. Miller, Tom, "Every Body is Right," *Runners World, 11,* 46 (July 1976).

14. Monkerud, Donald, "How Diet Can Change You," *Runners World,* 11, 43 (August 1976).

15. Nelson, Richard C., and Robert J. Gregor, "Biomechanics of Distance Running: A Longitudinal Study," *Research Quarterly, 47,* 417 (October 1976).

16. Newton, Joe, and Karl Schindl, *The Long Green Line, Championship High School Cross Country,* All American Publishing Co., Oak Brook, Ill., 1969.

17. Saltin, Bengt, and J. Karlsson, "Muscle Glycogen Utilization During Work of Different Intensities," In *Muscle Metabolism During Exercise* (Advances in Experimental Medicine and Biology Series, Vol. 11), edited by Bengt Pernow and Bengt Saltin, Plenum, New York, 1971.

18. Sheehan, George, "Case Against Loading," *Runners World, 11,* 46 (August 1976).

19. Shorter, Frank, Personal Conversation, 1976.

20. Van Aaken, Ernst, "Program for Distance Runners," *Track Technique, 64* (June 1976).

21. Young, Ken, "Best of Times," *Runners World, 11,* 76 (June 1976).

22. Ziegler, Nancy, "Joan Ullyot," *Runners World, 11,* 34 (June 1976).

Chapter 16

The Hurdles

The biomechanics of hurdle technique requires that there be integration of controlled sprinting with the maintenance of dynamic equilibrium over a series of obstacles set at prescribed distances and heights. Depending on the length of the event, a rapid-stride pattern coordinated with clearance procedures is essential. A sprint-oriented hurdles coach might emphasize that the race is run and won on the ground, while the technician, agreeing that sprint speed is valuable, would emphasize hurdle form. A synthesis of their convictions would acknowledge that hurdling is continuous sprinting with clearance perceived as an exaggerated sprint stride. The sprint to the first and succeeding hurdles is not independent of their clearance.

In any hurdle event, the pathway of the center of gravity is also considered, with good technique requiring the least disruption of its moving pathway between and over the hurdles. Language used with beginners should convey this concept, emphasizing that the event is never compared with the jumps nor is clearance described as hanging or floating in the air. Terms that are applicable recognize the lead leg as the one that attacks the hurdle along with the lead arm of the opposite

Figure 61 A. The hurdle technique of Guy Drut, France. PR :13.28. Courtesy of Toni Nett, West Germany.

side of the body. The trail leg, coordinated with the opposite trail arm, which is carried in normal sprint action, is comparable to the recovery leg in sprinting.

In order to negotiate the measured 13.72 m (45 ft) to the first hurdle in eight accelerating strides in the 110-m race, most hurdlers place the lead hurdle leg back in the starting blocks. Tall athletes may benefit from a seven-stride approach, which requires opposite leg placement at the start. Depending on the physical characteristics of the athlete, the takeoff to the first and subsequent hurdles will vary from 1.98 m (7 ft) for taller individuals to 2.13 m (8 ft) for others. The landing, after clearance, will be about 1.22 m (4 ft) from the hurdle (Figure 61A, frames 1-12).

In the shorter 100-m hurdle event for women, stride patterns to the first and subsequent hurdles are comparable to those for the longer 110-m race, in spite of a reduced distance to the first hurdle [13 m (42 ft 7 3/4 in.)], and a lesser increment [8.495 m (27 ft 10 1/2 in.)] between the ten 84 cm (33 in.) hurdles. Most women take off about 30.5 cm (1 ft) and land 7 to 10 cm (3 to 4 in.) closer to the barrier than men (Figure 61B, frames 1-11).

The exaggerated sprint stride in hurdle clearance is preceded and followed by normal sprinting. By enhancing cadence, the rapidity with which the clearance stride is expedited can increase or maintain speed. Clearance can be identified in three phases: the attack or takeoff; the interphase or layout; and the escape or descent.

Attack Phase (Figure 61A, frames 1-4; Figure 61B, frames 1-5)

At takeoff, a dive is initiated at the hurdle by slightly reducing the length of the last stride, causing the body to pivot or rotate forward from the toes of the supporting or trail leg. This initial pivot, subsequently combined with full supporting leg extension, initiates the desirable leg split, promoting low clearance of the hurdle. Coincident with this action, the knee of the flexed lead leg is driven forward and upward, initiating the necessary small rise of the center of gravity of the body for

its flat pathway over the hurdle. Leading with the knee in this manner decreases the moment of inertia of the leg, correspondingly increasing the speed of its upward rotation about the hip. Once off the ground, the pathway of the center of gravity cannot be altered but will allow movement of parts of the body about it. Good technique requires that segments of the body be distributed more horizontally than vertically about the parabolic trajectory of the center of gravity.

There are a number of disadvantages to straight lead-leg hurdling. The greater moment of inertia of an extended lead leg slows down its upward rise, increases chances of hitting the hurdle on the way up, and delays its descent. The additional possibility of landing on the heel makes it more difficult to sprint off the hurdle.

To assure good balance on landing, the lead leg is driven forward and up in a median (sagittal) plane, rather than cocked to one side or wrapped around the edge of the hurdle. Coordinated arm action requires leading with the partially flexed lead arm, which is then allowed to extend naturally to avoid any twisting action of the trunk.

Near the completion of a race, particularly in negotiating the last three hurdles, all hurdlers (especially taller ones) should overemphasize the authority with which they attack the hurdle. If the race has progressed normally, the athlete will find that

Figure 61 B. Annelie Ehrhardt (R) of East Germany in the 100-m hurdles. PR :12.30. Courtesy of Helmar Hommel, West Germany.

the hurdles are getting closer, which requires a very attentive lead-leg approach to avoid hitting the hurdle while going into it.

Interphase (Figure 61A, frames 5–8; Figure 61B, frames 5–7)

In the momentary interphase of continuous action, the body assumes a layout-position. This horizontal distribution of body mass for a brief second allows clearance of the hurdle with the lead and trail leg in a sequence of dynamic equilibrium.

The high point of the trajectory of the hurdler's center of gravity is reached a little less than a meter before the rail. The partially flexed lead leg, with the foot carried at a right angle with the rail, is momentarily extended to allow the heel to clear it. Any effort to extend, point, or plantar flex the ankle would encourage collision with the rail or premature snapdown and hitting the hurdle with the back of the thigh—"riding the hurdle." The trunk, with the lead arm extended, will be directly above and parallel with the lead leg in the layout position. Simultaneously, the trail leg, with the toe pointing up and out to the side, begins to flex at the knee and move out of its sagittal plane in a circular forward/upward transverse manner—"hip circle." This will provide high clearance of the trail leg, knee, and ankle in the escape phase, eliminate hitting the rail, and place the athlete in a better position for the next hurdle.

Although used successfully by the great Forrest Towns in 1936, the double-arm thrust advertised to assure a quick return to the ground while keeping the shoulders square and the side profile low should be avoided (4). Although this technique provides an apparently desirable layout, it places the arms in uncoordinated positions and retards the sprint concept. The trail arm should be kept close to the trunk, either describing a small circle carried in an abbreviated sprint action, or held slightly behind the trunk in a stationary manner for maintenance of balance.

Escape Phase (Figure 61A, frames 9–12; Figure 61B, frames 7–11)

In the descent or escape phase, the snapdown of the flexed, lead leg is a natural reaction to the action circling of the trail leg around and up to the midline of the chest. This upward rotation of the active trail leg not only assists the reaction return of the lead leg to the track but also places the hurdler in a better running position for the next hurdle. The knee of the trail leg should laterally catch up with the hip above the rail, momentarily assuming a parallel layout position. The heel is tucked behind the buttucks with the toe pointing outward. Undue emphasis on purposely snapping the lead leg down and hastening the travel of the trail leg should be avoided. Premature and overzealous lead-leg action will raise the trunk by reaction and correspondingly lower the trail leg into the hurdle. Accelerating the advance of the trail leg will add to this problem as well as result in a cramped position resembling a hop.

At the moment of touchdown, the landing is executed with the center of gravity directly above or slightly ahead of the backward pawing grounded foot. The trail-leg hip circle is returned to the median plane, and the knee drives into the next stride. The relatively quiet trail arm now drives forward in concert with the lead arm, moving back in vigorous sprint action.

Body Planes and Rotations

It is evident that the technique of hurdling requires many necessary rotations of body parts that can cause a loss of balance if not countered by action-reaction principles. The analysis just described may be enhanced by a knowledge of the cardinal planes and axes of the body. Although a beginner does not have to know much about them, the *coach* should perceive their spatial usefulness so he or she

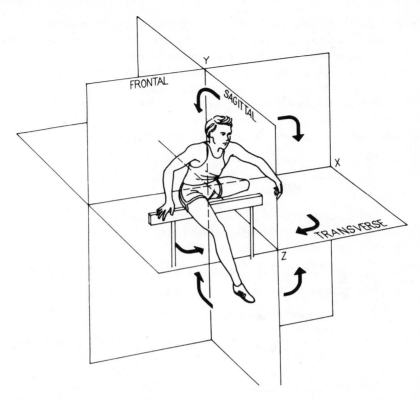

Figure 62. Rotations of the hurdler's arms, legs, and trunk occuring simultaneously in three planes during the "escape" phase. *X* axis bisects the saggital plane.

Y axis bisects the transverse plane.

Z axis bisects the frontal plane.

In the sagittal plane the trunk rotates up as the lead leg moves down; in the transverse plane the trunk twists to meet the trail leg moving forward; in the frontal plane the trunk and lead leg rotate toward each other on the right. Based on G. H. Ġ. Dyson, *The Mechanics of Athletics.* University of London Press, London, 1973.

can teach correct techniques and reduce problems created by excessive body rotation.

Figure 62 illustrates a hurdler in the descent phase superimposed on the cardinal planes and their companion axes. Note that they all intersect at the hurdler's center of gravity. Rotation of parts of the body will occur *within* planes and *about* axes at right angles to the planes. A clockwise rotation within a plane and about its axis on one side of the body will always be countered by an opposite (counterclockwise) rotation on the other side of the body. This rotary action-reaction, also known as torque-countertorque, occurs simultaneously in all three planes and about all three axes during hurdling. The ability to study and analyze technique is enhanced by recognizing the following imaginary planes and axes that go with the hurdler, regardless of changing position.

Sagittal Plane. This vertical, medial plane bisects the body into left and right sides. Its companion axis about which rotation occurs is the *X* lateral axis.

Frontal Plane. Another vertical plane divides the body into anterior (front) and posterior (back) "halves." Rotation occurs about the *Z* anterior-posterior axis.

Transverse Plane. This is a horizontal plane separating the superior (upper) from the inferior (lower) segments of the anatomy. A vertical or longitudinal *Y* axis provides the focal point for rotation.

During the **attack phase,** the following rotary activity may be recognized.

1). Within the *sagittal* plane about the lateral *X* axis, the trunk cames down as the flexed lead leg goes up. The lead arm reaches forward in a semiflexed position and the supporting leg is fully extended, driving off the track.

2). Within the *frontal* plane about the anterior-posterior *Z* axis, the trunk is stable with the shoulders level. There is no effort to throw the lead arm away from the body or prematurely lay out the leg.

3). Within the *transverse* plane about the vertical *Y* axis, the lead arm and leg tend to rotate toward each other with the arm required to rotate more, since its mass is less.

During the **interphase:**

1). In the *sagittal plane-X axis,* the knee of the maximally raised lead leg is momentarily extended at the top of its swing. By reaction, the trail leg is extended (indicative of a good takeoff) and begins to initiate the knee drive of the hip circle. The lead arm is extended, and the trail arm describes a short sprint arm stride ahead of the hip. The trunk is as far down as it will go, with the head in a low position.

2). In the *frontal plane-Z axis,* the shoulders are still square, the trail arm is close to the hip, and the lead arm is directed straight ahead, parallel with the lead leg. There is no evidence of a premature layout of the trail leg.

3). In the *transverse plane-Y axis,* the entire body is in an elongated layout position. Although the legs are maximally split, there is some evidence of the trail-leg knee beginning to flex for the forward/upward/lateral hip circle.

During the **descent phase:**

1). In the *sagittal plane-X axis,* with the knee flexed to assure landing on the spikes, the lead leg descends and, by reaction, the trunk rises. The trail leg, in its pull-up to the chest, is momentarily laid out parallel to the rail and passes under the extended backward moving lead arm.

2). In the *frontal plane-Z axis,* the trunk and lead leg move toward each other on the trail leg side of the body.

3). In the *transverse plane-Y axis,* the flexed trail leg moves upward to the chest and under the lead arm from its layout position, countered by the generally extended lead arm moving out, down, and back.

LOW HURDLE SCIENCE

Although low hurdles for males require less hurdling technique, it is still difficult to maintain balance, since the layout, which slows down adverse rotations in high hurdling, is rejected in favor of speed. The hurdles are so much lower that the center of gravity is raised very little, if at all, by some long-legged runners who use a sprint stride that requires less modification than in high hurdling. The suggested stride pattern is nine to the first hurdle and seven between the remaining six, which are spaced every 18.29 m (20 yd) from start to finish. The barriers are cleared relatively high to allow the center of gravity to remain constant throughout the race and, consequently, the high moment of inertia low profile, or dive, essential for high hurdling, is not advised and may actually slow down the runner. Emphasis of wider, sprint-style arm action with less reaching by the lead arm is the best means of pacifying embarrasing rotations.

INTERMEDIATE HURDLE SCIENCE (Figure 63, frames 1–8)

The low hurdles are rapidly being replaced in scholastic circles by a race with low or intermediate hurdles at intermediate spacing. Technique of intermediate hurdle clearance is similar to the mechanics reviewed for high hurdling, but with less emphasis on the layout that so effectively softens rotations in all three planes.

Intermediate hurdling features an additional set of challenges because of the longer distances negotiated (300 to 400 m) and is partial to an alternating stride pattern. While all hurdlers are not as strong as Edwin Moses who can run 13 strides between hurdless for the entire distance nor as flexible and perceptive as John Akii Bua who can instinctively relate between fatigue and stride length before the next hurdle, it is suggested that all beginning hurdlers be taught to attack an intermediate hurdle with either leg. Although some world-class athletes use 19 to 20 strides, normally 21 to 22 are recommended for the 45 m to the first hurdle. (Odd-number stride patterns require placing the lead leg forward in the starting blocks.) After initial hurdle clearance, beginners may employ a safe, but more time-consuming 17-stride pattern for the 35-m intervals, but should gradually adopt 15 strides as the standard. Accomplished hurdlers will attempt to either use 13 strides all the way, or change to 15 when necessary during the race. Highly skilled people may alternate and use 13 and 14 during the same race without any discernable loss of rhythm.

The 400-m hurdle event for women has recently been added to competition schedules, although it is not yet contested in the Olympic Games. Specifications for the race differ only in the height of the hurdle [76 cm (30 in.)]. The stride pattern between them may differ with 22 to 26 strides to the first hurdle, and 17 to 19 strides between them.

Figure 63. Geoff Vanderstock, USA, running the intermediate hurdles. PR :49.06. Courtesy of Toni Nett, West Germany.

Leading with the left leg is advisable for most hurdlers, since this approach best facilitates leaning into the turn. With a right-leg lead, there is a tendency to land too far to the right in the lane, which necessitates an adjustment that requires the hurdler to take off slightly to the outside of the middle of the lane and land slightly inside of the center after coming off the hurdle. Oncoming fatigue and changing wind conditions may necessitate changes in the stride pattern, but plans should be made for this occurence before the race begins! Some hurdlers can intuitively adjust as unexpected conditions arise, but this comes only after great experience.

Novice hurdlers tend to allow the trail leg to "hang" over the edge of the rail. Rules require that all of the body be within the plane of the lane, and teaching technique should acknowledge this. It is easier to run in the outer lanes of the track, although assignment to the inside lane will happen to anyone sometime. Practice in this lane to adjust available strength and speed with necessary lean and stride × frequency requirements is a necessary and wise precaution.

TEACHING THE HURDLES

Teaching technique in this interesting event can lead to good results in a short period of time with a minium of equipment and instruction. Basic requirements include a half dozen easily constructed *L* base 61-cm (24 in.) hurdles and two instructors. A stepwise procedure would initially include groundwork discussion emphasizing that hurdling is sprinting and not jumping, with aggressiveness, flexibility, some speed, and attention to detail being the chief essentials for success.

With a group of novices seated before the instructor and with more observation than commentary, have an assistant or master hurdler run through several flights of hurdles. Instruction then begins with the following suggested format.

Ground Hurdling.   Demonstrating first, ask the candidates to assume the hurdler's spread on the ground. The lead leg should be defined and expressed as the one that naturally comes up and goes over the hurdle first. The trail leg is identified as the one that will lay out while passing over the hurdle. Since novices will not

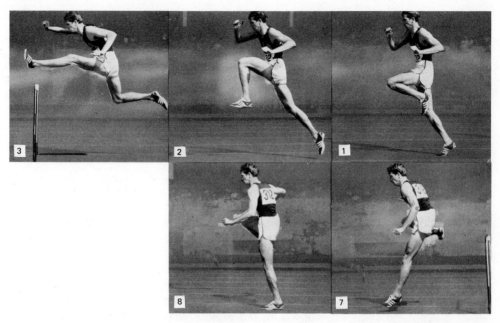

know which leg is "natural," alternate turns with the right and left leg in each position. To avoid tipping, instruction should indicate that the lead arm, which is opposite the lead leg, should be thrust parallel to, and not at the foot of the lead leg. The other arm should not be placed on the ground for support but held slightly ahead of the hip in a position known as an "arm and a half." Keeping it off the ground emphasizes the need for future flexibility training.

Ecker, in describing high hurdle arm action options, points out that there are several ways to use the lead arm to allow trunk adjustment for the trail leg swinging forward (1).

1. Employ normal, sprint arm action (i.e., lead arm forward, trail arm back).

2. Sweep the extended lead arm down and back.

3. With the partially flexed lead arm held high in front of the body rather than straight ahead, sweep it down and back.

The latter method, used by Milburn and others, features a rather high initial position of the arm that may prove troublesome for some hurdlers. Advise the novice to avoid this wraparound lead arm. The best mechanics entail an increased moment of inertia of the lead arm about a vertical axis so that the trial leg will not twist the upper body. This can be best accomplished with a more horizontal trunk lean and an extended straight-ahead lead arm.

The instructor and assistant should circulate through the group, lending assistance in this basic drill and emphasizing:

1. The knee of the lead leg need not be completely extended.

2. Laterally, the trail leg should be at a 90-degree angle with the lead leg. The knee is flexed, the heel tucked behind the buttocks, with the toe pointing outward.

3. The lead arm should be directed parallel with the lead leg, the trail arm slightly ahead of the hip in the "arm and a half" position. Pump the arms back and forth, reaching with the lead arm as the trunk is brought down toward the thigh of the lead leg.

4. Repeat the drill with the opposite leg as the lead.

Follow the Leader-Walking. Line up the young hurdlers in front of the first 61-cm hurdle, and lead them in a walking drill over several hurdles, instructing them to circle back and line up before the first hurdle after completing the flight. The hurdle flights may be set up in shuttle, with the novices walking the drill back and forth. Instruction should emphasize:

1. Leading with the favored leg, aim it straight ahead and either to the right or left of the middle of the hurdle in a sagittal plane, depending on which leg is used. Emphasize that this leg *should not* "wrap around" the hurdle (i.e., not be brought around the side of the hurdle).

2. Bending the lead leg slightly at the knee to encourage easier swinging as well as enhancing landing on the toes first.

3. Swinging the trail leg through, attempting to flatten it out as it passes over the rail. Point out that the trail leg and returning lead arm must stay within the lane described by the width of the hurdle.

4. Bringing the knee of the flexed trail leg through toward the chest, under the arm, and back to the line of the walking cadence. Avoid a wide stance coming off the hurdle, and keep the shoulders square (i.e., perpendicular to the direction of the activity).

5. Repetition of the drill, experimenting with either leg as the lead not only to find the best leg but also to emphasize the necessity of equivalent flexibility, which is valuable later for intermediate hurdle racing.

Follow the Leader-Jogging. Repeat the drill, jogging between the hurdles.

Stride-Pattern Drill. To emphasize the importance of stride consistency and the use of the same lead leg, set the hurdles at some standard distance so they can be negotiated in three, five, or seven strides. For a 10 to 11 age group, this might be 5.49, 7.32, 9.14 m (6, 8, 10 yd), respectively. The best distance can be determined by observation and quickly adjusted for the majority. As the students develop the confidence to run faster, the hurdles can gradually be moved further apart to accomodate the three- and seven-stride pattern for future work at high and low hurdles.

The procedure discussed above may be expedited in one well-organized session, with individual attention directed later to promising candidates. If the teacher knows the scientific aspects of the activity, errors can be corrected dependent on the ability of the learner to absorb simple suggestions largely related to consistency of stride, body segment placement and rotation, and application of the law of action-reaction. Obviously, some people will learn faster than others, just as some will work with greater diligence than others.

Powell employs a sticks and bricks concept that some teachers may prefer (3). Essentially, after proving to the learners that they can stand astride or straddle the hurdle without touching it, the candidates are graded in height and placed in pairs of lanes to train up and down a straightaway. Emphasis is placed immediately on proper placement of the legs in the start and top speed to negotiate the initial 13.73 m (15 yd) in seven or eight strides without any obstacles in the way. Following this procedure, the three-stride pattern is studied for eventual placement of the second and third anticipated barriers. When repeated sprint and stride efforts are consistent, "hurdles" made by placing sticks on bricks are set up, starting as low as 10 cm (4 in.) gradually raising them to 45 cm (18 in.). As proficiency is gained, attention is directed to obtaining a good split, reaching the "high" point before the rail, and the stride coming off the hurdle. The use of the lead leg, trunk action, square shoulders, arm action, and the trail leg previously discussed must also be considered.

As the learner progresses and matures, concentrate on the refinement of high-hurdle technique. A 76-cm (30 in.) hurdle, with either a rubber bumper attached to or replacing the rail, may be substituted for the 61-cm barrier. We should emphasize the following items.

1). *Sagittal plane*—drive into the hurdle with the trunk down. A set of standards may be set up on either side of the hurdle with a string or other fragile crosspiece set in place above the hurdle to encourage bringing the head and trunk down. Come off the hurdle with the trunk reverting to upright sprint posture as the lead leg returns to the ground, with the center of gravity directly above or ahead of the foot of the lead leg.

2). *Frontal plane*—as one looks at a left lead-leg hurdler approaching, the leg tends to rotate up counterclockwise, and the trunk tends to rotate down toward it clockwise. This action is reversed coming off the hurdle. In each case, the closer the "arm and a half" action is to normal sprint type, including the lead arm thrust with the shoulders square, the smoother this activity will be.

3). *Transverse plane*—arm action is also the key to activity in this plane. As the trail leg is brought forward, the trunk will twist toward it. The lead-arm action previously described will smooth out any overreaction. Additionally, the trail leg should be brought up to the chest on its way back to the middle of the lane before it is returned to the track for continuance of the stride. This manuever, with emphasis again on normal sprint-style arm action, which returns the lead arm down and behind the hip without throwing it away, retains dynamic balance.

4). As suggested in the technique section, hopping can be avoided by bringing the trail leg through relatively "slowly." Any effort to unduly hurry the trail leg will disrupt the overaccentuated "normal" sprint stride over the hurdle and result in poor rhythm.

5). It is just as bad to overemphasize a quick, savage lead leg snap-down as it is to bring the trail leg through too fast. This can only result in straightening the trunk prematurely, hitting the hurdle with the trail leg, hopping, and landing while leaning back.

Starting technique for hurdling is similar to that in sprinting, with minor modifications. Generally, the leg that clears the hurdle first (lead) should be the one that is back in the blocks, which are set for a medium start. This will provide for the commonly accepted eight approach strides for the initial 13.72 m. Since few hurdlers have trouble getting upright soon enough, as with the sprinter, it is advisable to keep the head down while in the "set" position. Looking at the first hurdle will only hasten becoming erect too soon. In spite of this, the hurdler will assume an upright posture sooner than the sprinter to prepare for the takeoff into the first hurdle. Occasionally, a tall subject may have to substitute a seven-stride approach, with the lead leg forward in the blocks. This approach may appear and feel slower, but should be within the hurdler's natural pattern of acceleration. Any attempt to make a person run with a shorter stride, which *looks* faster, discounts the fact that the important thing in sprint running is natural stride length × stride frequency. Overstriding or understriding is *always* less efficient.

Items *4* and *5* above epitomize correct technique in coming off of any hurdle. A landing that facilitates a minimum of heel contact, with the center of gravity above the lead leg when landing, coordinated with a trail-leg sprint stride that lies within a sagittal plane will insure a good finish. Techniques of turning the trunk or diving at the tape may occasionally help an expert, but, even with accomplished beginners, the best advice is to sprint off the hurdle and through the finish.

TEACHING THE INTERMEDIATE AND LOW HURDLES

The basic procedure described earlier is appropriate for teaching any hurdle event to novices. However, as candidates mature and develop and graduate to standard height hurdles and distances, the problem of adaptability versus specialization begins. It would be ideal if hurdlers could specialize in an event, but this is not likely in view of team needs. Assuming the essentials of hurdle form are understood and not ignored, the most important element in teaching the 164.6-m (180 yd) high-school lows or 300-m race with 76-cm or 91.5-cm hurdles is one of rhythm and striding.

Farmer suggests a straightaway plan with the intermediate hurdler matching fifteen 1.765-m (6 ft, 10 in.) strides marked on the track for the 35 m (38 yd, 3 1/3 in.) between the hurdles (2). When this becomes easy to do, the hurdler may work on a 2.07-m (7 ft, 10 in.) stride for a 13-step pattern, progressively emphasizing arm action and knee lift. To pragmatically establish confidence, the hurdles may be set a few feet closer to each other, gradually moving them to the correct interval as progression is noted. An alternative pattern using 14 strides may be employed if the characteristics of the hurdler allow it. Women hurdlers may want to use this plan with either a 17- or 19-step pattern.

Once the straightaway procedure is mastered, attention must be directed to turn running. This is more easily executed if the hurdler uses a left leg lead, provided the trail leg is brought through completely, keeping the shoulders and hips square at all times. Right leg leading will necessitate learning an outside to inside zig-zag pattern to establish a path for the runner.

In most instances, a 164.6-m low hurdle race is run on a straightaway with the 76-cm barriers set uniformly—18.29 m (20 yd) apart from start to finish. Most hurdlers will use 10 strides to the first hurdle and 7 between the barriers. A 1.765-m stride pattern can be outlined on the track similar to the intermediate procedure discussed above, with the learner running through it first without hurdles and then with barriers introduced one at a time. If problems ensue, the hurdles may be set a little closer to the start and to each other, and gradually returned to their standard positions.

The intermediate and low hurdler spends more time in the air while negotiating the lower barrier, traveling anywhere from 3.66 to 3.96 m (12 to 13 ft) between takeoff and landing. Unfortunately, speed cannot be gained while in the air, so the primary key to success is momentum, with stability maintained by a wider swinging, sprint-style arm action caused by the more upright position of the trunk.

TRAINING AND CONDITIONING FOR HIGH HURDLING

Since most high school-age hurdlers will run both the high and low or intermediate hurdles and, invariably, the sprint or mile relay, conditioning is similar to that utilized by sprinters with corresponding flat race responsibilities. Off- or preseason training, concentrating on endurance and strength development facilitated by running and weight training, is augmented by flexibility work, which is more extensive than the work experienced by sprinters. Training, which suggests technique work, is predicated on correctly learning hurdle form and strategy. The learning drills described in the teaching section will have uncovered the best hurdle candidates who begin the conditioning process through a continuation of the learning drills. Gradually, five- and three-stride side and full hurdling exercises are introduced and used on a daily basis to emphasize establishment and maintenance of correct habit patterns. This is particularly important because of the multiple responsibilities of the event. Like other athletes, hurdlers find it difficult to simultaneously think of numerous details of technique. Therefore it is better to concentrate on one thing at a time until all the elements mesh.

The responsibility of dealing with the event as a sprint race, in spite of the obstacles in the way, requires great concentration. The hurdler must not only attend to the flight of hurdles but also compete, and he or she cannot be distracted during this work. As suggested in the previous sections, hurdling is sprinting, formalized by fixed stride patterns while periodically injecting an exaggerated sprint stride, raising the center of gravity very little for hurdle clearance. The key to success is emphasis on leading with the knees in hurdle clearance, landing with the center of gravity directly above the lead foot while moving forward with as little deviation from normal sprint arm action as possible.

FOUNDATION TRAINING PROGRAM FOR HURDLERS

I. Warm-up and Warm-down

The warm-up is absolutely essential before the body of the workout. It may start with 800 to 1200 m of jogging and easy running, followed by stretching (flexibility-agility) exercises described in the foundation training section of Chapter 4. A word of caution regarding stretching exercises is necessary. While applicable to athletes in all events, it cannot be overemphasized here. Running must always precede stretching, do not overstretch, and do not stretch any differently on the day of competition than on practice days! Previous discussions of stretching suggest replacing the dynamic variety with static or isometric stretching but, since track events are dynamic, dynamic activity must also be included.

The stretching should be gradual, progressively working toward greater flexibility, not only during each daily practice session but also cumulatively throughout the length of the season. Static routines may precede their dynamic counterparts at the beginning of each practice session or they may be used exclusively during initial phases of training, to be replaced by dynamic activity as the season develops and condition improves. To avoid unnecessary repetition, the names of the flexibility-agility exercises described in the high-jump chapter will simply be listed here.

A. High kick.
B. Wrestler's bridge.
C. Floor touch.
D. Trunk flexion.
E. Trunk extension.
F. Jack spring.
G. Agility six-count exercise.
H. Alternate splits.
I. Reverse sit-up.
J. Single and double leg swing-overs.
K. Hurdler's spread.

After the busy 15- to 20-minute stretching session, the athlete relaxes with 400 to 800 m of easy running before engaging in the body of the workout.

Special Warm-up Exercises for hurdlers include the following drills.

A. Side hurdle drill. Arrange two flights of hurdles in shuttle set, either 4.57 to

8.23 m (5 to 9 yd) apart for three-striding, or 9.15 to 10.97 m (10 to 12 yd) for five-striding. Walk first and stride later:

1. *Lead leg drill.* Present the lead leg only to the hurdle. The trail leg does not go over the hurdle and responds naturally in an abbreviated layout. Emphasize "arm and a half" sprint-type arm action, simulate diving or lowering the trunk as the knee goes up. Come down on the toes as the trunk becomes upright.

2. *Trail leg drill.* Present the trail leg to the second flight. Emphasize driving with the flexed knee, lock the heel to the buttocks, and turn the toe out and upward to gain momentary "flat" clearance. Continue driving the flexed knee up to the chest under the relatively extended lead arm, driving down and backward. Bring the knee back to the line of walk or jog in a normal sprint-style action. The lead leg should land about 30 cm beyond the hurdle for the trail leg to come through properly.

B. Hurdle bending is similar to the hurdler's spread done on a rail while standing. A steeplechase hurdle or gymnast's balance beam offers the firmest foundation, although a hurdle may be used. Lay the trail leg on top of the rail and, without bouncing, carefully reach down and touch the floor. Repeat with the other leg.

C. Hip Circling may be done with one or two hurdles. While holding onto and leaning into a high hurdle set before the athlete, circle the trail leg repeatedly over the side of a second offset hurdle. Do this with each leg, keeping the knee flexed with the toe pointing out and up.

D. Lead Leg Circle Drill. This is similar to drill A1 done with one hurdle. Facing the long dimension of the rail, stand to the side of the hurdle, holding onto it with one hand. Swing and kick the lead leg (with a slightly flexed knee) back and forth over the rail, momentarily releasing the grip on the hurdle as the trunk is lowered with the passage of the lead leg over the rail.

E. Standing, Walking, and Ground Splits are valuable for stretching and loosening up the trunk and groin muscles. Great care must be exercised in performing this work! Static work prior to dynamic exercise is highly recommended. Vigorous bouncing back and forth or up and down should be carefully controlled, if not avoided.

Ground Splits, a favorite exercise of dance students, resembles the hurdler's spread without a layout of the trail leg.

Standing or *Walking Splits* are done while flexing the trunk into a hurdle. The athlete grips the hurdle with both hands, placing the heel of the lead leg on the hurdle rail. Driving with the trail leg, tip the hurdle by pushing with both arms and the lead leg on the rail. Hop forward and give with the lead leg and arms to return the hurdle. It is advisable to block or hinge the hurdle to keep it from moving down the track.

While the warm-down does not have to occupy the same amount of time as the warm-up, it can prepare the hurdler for a restful night and the next day's practice session. Metabolic waste products are flushed from the muscles by an easy 1600-m Fartlek run interspersed at intervals with relaxed stretching exercises.

II. Weight Training

Use the lifts recommended for sprinters with emphasis on the concept of lifting through a full range of movement with moderate weight and slower contractions at the end of each lift for development of flexibility.

III. Forced and Resistive Training

Similar to that described for sprinters, Chapter 13, this may be augmented by stadium step work with and without a weight jacket. Emphasize the power concept of high knee lift while wearing a jacket.

IV. Depth, Multiple-Triple Jump Depth, and Plyometric Exercises

Discussed earlier (Chapter 4 and 6), these exercises are valuable for eccentric-rebound strength development needed in coming off the hurdle.

V. Overemphasis Drills

Hurdlers will find these drills (Chapter 4) as valuable and necessary as they are for sprinters.

VI. Tempo, Interval, and Repetition Drills

A jog back should be sufficient rest for the tempo concept, with a walk back adequate for interval, and several minutes rest for repetition.

A). From a running start, five-stride 3 to 5 flights of three to seven hurdles set 9.14 m apart, or three-stride the hurdles set at 4.57 m, emphasizing natural lead-leg snapdown and delayed but quick trail-leg activity, always returning the knee of the trail leg back to the center of the lane.

B). From the starting blocks, three-stride 3 to 5 flights of five hurdles set a 9.14 m. Too much emphasis cannot be placed on doing either submaximal or full "practice" speed work from the blocks for perfection in the seven- or eight-stride approach pattern, coming off of each hurdle with power and sprinting through the last 13.72 m. Lazy work in this area is a waste of time. Practice must emulate competitive circumstances as much as possible.

C). Back to back 55- to 110-m (60 to 120 yd) time trials in repetition (5 minute rest) or interval (rapid walk-back rest). This procedure is not only valuable as a progress report during the early season prior to meets but also for the "endurance" aspect of qualifying in later season meets. This work should be done from the crouch start at full "practice" speed, striving for perfection.

VIII. Running Activities (Anaerobic-Aerobic Drills)

Used by sprinters, these drills can and should be employed for hurdlers as well. Many outstanding hurdlers (Davenport, Milburn, Misher, Shipp) suggest repeat 159.44 m (165 yd) during the indoor season and 300 m during the outdoor season.

The various drills discussed in Chapter 13 can be adjusted to accommodate these standard, suggested distances. An intermediate hurdler may wish to lengthen the distances proportionately.

SAMPLE WEEKLY PROGRAM—HIGH HURDLES
OFF-SEASON

All practice sessions are preceded and completed with the warm-up and warm-down discussed in the foundation program. Special exercises for hurdlers should be done every day after the warm-up (side hurdle drills; hurdle bending; hip circling; lead-leg circle drill; standing and ground splits). Assume that the teaching procedure for hurdling has been administered and practiced. Some suggestions have been drawn from the foundation program for sprinters found in Chapter 13.

MONDAY—*3- to 4-km cross-country at easy pace.*
Weight training, upper body exercises, power concept 2 to 3 sets.

TUESDAY—*Overemphasis drills (Chapter 4), 2 × 50 m per exercise; high knee lift, ankle flips, arm-action drill, rapid cadence drill, stride-length drill.*
Run down the ladder.
Repetition 300, 200, 150, 100 at 75- to 80-percent effort with no more than 5 minutes rest between repetitions.

WEDNESDAY—*Stadium climbing, up and down the steps, 5 to 6 repetitions emphasizing rapid cadence, high knee action.*
3- to 4-km cross-country at easy pace with one 75- to 80-percent pickup of 150 m per km.
Weight training, lower body exercises, power concept, 2 to 3 sets.

THURSDAY—*Overemphasis drills, 1 × 60 m per exercise.*
Shuttle hurdle relay, 4 person team, 8 × 36.58 m (13.72, 9.14, 13.72) over two hurdles.

FRIDAY—*Interval hurdle drill, 4 × 1 hurdle from the blocks, 4 × 2 hurdles from the blocks. If difficulty is encountered in striding normally, set these hurdles closer to the start and each other.*
Stadium climbing, endurance hopping up and down the stairs, occasionally alternate legs.
Weight training, upper and lower body exercises, power concept, one set.

EARLY SEASON

Precede and conclude each workout with the recommended warm-up, including special exercises, and a warm-down.

MONDAY—*Interval hurdle drill. Using a running start, five-stride 6 × 3 hurdles set at 9.14 m at 90-percent effort with a rapid walk-back rest; three-stride 6 × 3 hurdles set at 4.57 m with the same effort and rest.*
Interval sprinting. 3 × 160 m at 90-percent effort. Active recovery at 3:1 rest:work ratio.
Weight training. Similar to Monday, off-season.
TUESDAY—*Overemphasis drills for sprinters, one repetition of 70 m for each exercise, excluding endurance hopping.*
Hurdle drills. From a crouch start, three-stride 6 × 3 hurdles at full effort with no more than 5 minutes rest between repetitions.
Pool running for warm-down.
WEDNESDAY—*Shuttle hurdle relay, 4-person team, 6 × 54.86 m (13.72, 9.14, 9.14, 9.14, 13.72) over 4 hurdles.*
Pickup sprints, 4 × 200 m, jog the first 200, stride the second at 70-percent effort, and sprint the third at 90-percent effort, walk 200. Repeat.
Endurance hopping-plyometric exercises. Jump from both legs and hop off of alternate legs. 1 × 60 m; up to and off of 50-cm boxes spaced every 5 m for 60 m; over the boxes spaced every 5 m for 60 m.
Weight training. Similar to Wednesday, off-season. Pool running for warm-down.
THURSDAY—*Back to back 55-m time trials in repetition, 5 minutes rest.*
Distance run pickup sprint. Run 1500 m to 2 km, accelerating from 70 to 90 percent for 50 m. 4 × every 400. Goal under 6 minutes.
No warm-down.
FRIDAY—*Repetition hurdle drill. From a running start, five-stride 1 to 2 × 5 hurdles set at 9.14 m at 90-percent effort, 3 stride 1 to 2 × 5 hurdles set at 9.14 m at 90-percent effort.*
Light warm-down.
SATURDAY—*Competition.*
SUNDAY—*3- to 5-km Fartlek or 5- to 6-km continuous run at a challenging pace.*

LATER SEASON

Characteristically, work at this time is quality instead of quantity oriented. This does not imply any letup, merely a honing of the edge of training and conditioning. Continue the warm-up and warm-down procedures with reaffirmed attention to their value.

MONDAY—*Tempo hurdle drill. From a running start, five-stride 3 × 7 hurdles set at 9.14 m and three-stride 3 × 7 hurdles set at 9.14 m. Jog-back rest.*
Repetition sprinting, 3 × 160 m at 90-percent to full effort with no more than 5 minutes recovery.
Pool running for warm-down.

TUESDAY—*Repetition hurdle drill. From a crouch start, three-stride 3 to 5 flights of 5-hurdles at 90-percent to full effort.*
1 × 300 m at 90-percent to full effort or endurance hopping-plyometric exercises similar to Wednesday, early-season prescription.
Weight training, upper and lower body exercises, power concept, 1 set.

WEDNESDAY—*Gun starts, 4 to 6 × 3 hurdles with 3 to 5 minutes rest.*
Hollow sprints (sprint, jog, sprint, walk) 4 × 400 using 100-m increment.
Stadium climbing, 2 to 3 repetitions up and down the steps.
Pool running for warm-down.

THURSDAY—*Back to back 110-m hurdles, recovery either 5 minutes or rapid walk back elective.*

FRIDAY—*Warm-up and special exercises.*

SATURDAY—*Competition.*

SUNDAY—*Rest or 3-km Fartlek, or 4-km cross-country run as needed.*

TRAINING FOR THE LOW AND INTERMEDIATE HURDLES

Training and conditioning for the high-school low hurdle event may parallel that suggested for the sprints and high hurdles. Both the coach and the athlete, should be cautious in preparing for participation in either hurdle event. High hurdling requires closer attention to technique than low hurdling. The athlete cannot afford to forget about the layout or increased moment of inertia necessary for the highs, as opposed to the more upright, floating, decreased moment of inertia style employed in the lows, stabilized by wider swinging sprint arm action.

Training for the intermediate hurdles requires a combination of the programs for hurdles and (long) sprint training. Again, the probable lack of specialization and the incidence of doubling in hurdle events presents some problems. The sample programs that will be presented are based on specialization, and the alert coach and athlete will have to synthesize weekly practice programs to effectively deal with the specific problems of both events. Intermediate hurdling is primarily a problem of striding and sprint endurance, with the 400 m type of individual at an advantage. Preseason conditioning for the intermediate assignment should include a good deal of running and weight training. Running programs include cross-country, preferably over courses including hills. Flat land athletes may substitute stair climbing in always convenient football stadia. Farmer suggests running in the shallow end of a swimming pool as a worthwhile diversionary conclusion to some of these workouts (2).

Weight-training exercises described for sprinters are necessary several times a week, preferably near the end of a practice session. There are disadvantages to this procedure, and some coaches and athletes may prefer to include one or two "fresh" lifting sessions at the beginning of practice or as the primary assignment of a session for one or two months.

Special Running Assignments for Low and Intermediate Hurdlers

Several special arrangements for 400-m intermediate hurdle work will be described. Coaches and athletes may scale them down proportionately for 300-m intermediate and 164.6-m low hurdles.

Shuttle Hurdle Relays. These are similar in principal to flat shuttle-relay workouts. They are done at full "practice" speed, preferably from starting blocks. Emphasis is on rhythm and consistent stride with increasing fatigue.

Repetition or Interval 195 Hurdles (H) —205 *Flat(F)* from the blocks. Run the first 195 of a repeat 400 m over the hurdles and the last 205 on the flat. Repetition implies "complete" rest between repeats and interval implies less rest, usually 3 minutes for every minute of work.

Repetition or Interval 195 F—205 H. Run the first 195 of the repeat 400 m on the flat and the last 205 over hurdles.

Repetition and Interval Stepdown and Ladder Hurdling. Similar to flat work, the repeats in this exercise progressively add or subtract distances with hurdles set at standard increments.

Eleven hurdle 400 m. This is a 400-m run over one extra hurdle set 5 m from the finish.

390 F—110 H. After an initial 390, the remainder (110) of a 500 m is negotiated over three hurdles.

490 F—110 H. After an initial flat 490, the remainder (110) of a 600 m is negotiated over three hurdles.

SAMPLE WEEKLY PROGRAMS FOR INTERMEDIATE HURDLERS

The warm-up and warm-down procedure for sprinters should be recognized as an understood requirement for beginning and concluding practice in this discussion, with the workout suggestions for 400-runners followed (pages 230-31), particularly for preseason or off-season work. Coaches and athletes will also want to work in the hurdle exercises and drills discussed in the foundation program for hurdlers. Of necessity, early-season practice sessions will include more work on the striding aspects of hurdling with quality work becoming more important as the season progresses.

OFF-SEASON

MONDAY—*Special exercises for hurdlers.*
Cross-country, including hill or stadium climbing work.
Weight training. Select exercises from the sprint chapter with a schedule in mind for subsequent routines (i.e., upper body one session, lower body the next; or even-numbered exercises for both body segments one session, odd-numbered ones the next, etc.).

TUESDAY—*Down the ladder. 600, 500, 400, 300, 200 at 75- to 85-percent effort.*
Pool running for warm-down.

WEDNESDAY—*Special exercises for hurdlers.*
Shuttle hurdle relay, 4-person team, 8 × 125 m (45, 35, 45) over 2 hurdles.
Weight training.
Pool running for warm-down.

THURSDAY—*Overemphasis drills, 50 to 60 m, 60- to 70-percent effort.*
Up and down the ladder. 200, 300, 400, 200 at 80- to 85-percent effort.
Pool running for warm-down.

FRIDAY—*Special exercises for hurdlers.*
4 × 1 hurdle from blocks
2 × 300 interval workout at 75- to 80-percent effort.
Weight training.

EARLY SEASON

Substitute the warm-up and warm-down procedure suggested for hurdlers. While it differs little from the one employed for off- season, there is a greater emphasis on slightly reduced quantity of running and more hurdle oriented stretching exercises. Later off-season work should have included the straightaway plan indoors (on a track or down a hallway) or outdoors, as weather permits. Hurdle assignments should be done at full-practice effort, with no compromise of effort, which can lead to disruption of the rhythmic-stride pattern and endurance aspect so important to the event.

MONDAY—*2 to 3 × 195 H — 205 F from the blocks, between :58 to :60.*
Weight training.

TUESDAY—*2 to 3 × 195 F — 205 H, between :58 to :60.*
Pool running for warm-down.

WEDNESDAY—*Repetition hurdle stepdown from the blocks; 5, 4, 3. Rest should be adequate for near complete recovery, not to exceed 5 to 7 minutes.*
Weight training.

THURSDAY—*Interval* 3 × 300 at 75- to 90-percent effort with 2 to 3
minutes rest, followed by a set break of 10 minutes and 3 ×
200 at full "practice" speed with 2 to 3 minutes rest.
Pool running for warm-down.
FRIDAY—*3 × gun starts over 3 hurdles, 10-minute break followed by 3*
× finishes over 3 hurdles.
SATURDAY—*Competition.*

LATER SEASON
Work is progressively reduced in quantity, with quality work emphasized. The
warm-up and warm-down used for early season are continued.

MONDAY—*1 × 490 F—110 H* under 1:28, rest 5 to 7 minutes, 1 × 390 F—
110 *H* under :71.
Weight training.
Pool running.
TUESDAY—*Special exercises for hurdlers.*
Down the ladder repetition hurdling, 300, 200, 100 at
90-percent to full "practice" effort with 5 and 3 minutes
rest, respectively.
WEDNESDAY—*3 × gun starts over 3 hurdles, 10-minute break, followed by 3*
× finishes over 3 hurdles.
1.5 to 2-km distance run pickup sprints. Sprint 2 × 100 per 400
with jogging for rest. Complete the assignment between 5
and 7 1/2 minutes.
Pool running.
THURSDAY—*3 × 1 hurdle from the blocks.*
FRIDAY—*Warm-up.*
SATURDAY—*Competition.*

BIBLIOGRAPHY

1. Ecker, Tom, "High Hurdle Arm Action," *Athletic Journal, 54,* 72 (February 1974).
2. Farmer, Dixon, "Intermediate Hurdles," *Track and Field Quarterly Review, 3,* 46 (1975).
3. Powell, John, "How to Introduce Hurdling," *Track and Field Quarterly Review, 3,* 38
(1975).
4. Towns, Forrest, "The Double Arm Action in Hurdling," *Track and Field Quarterly
Review, 3,* 45 (1975).

section five

Caring for the Athlete

Chapter 17

Athletic Injury

Although the field of athletic training is very complex, most injuries that track coaches and their athletes will encounter involve the lower extremities, accompanied by the psychological problem of rehabilitating an athlete whose physical disorder is notably influenced by a hypertensive emotional state. The primary job of the trainer is to prevent injury and get the athletes back into competition as soon as possible, strengthening their physical prowess as well as their mental attitude, encouraging continued improvement of performance.

Muscle tissue has four unique characteristics: the ability to (1) shorten and (2) be stretched; (3) regain normal shape or form; and (4) respond to a stimulus (6). Normal muscle performance depends on these unique physical properties in conjunction with critical neuromuscular balances. The nervous system, although expediting the direction for intensive, skilled activity, involuntarily reacts in terms of many muscle groups. The agonists or prime movers must be energized by neuromuscular impulse simultaneously with inhibition of antagonists or oppositely located muscles. Additionally, synergists, usually located on each side of the prime movers, guide or keep the activity in a desired plane while stabilizers or anchor muscles make sure there is a significant basis of foundation for the work of the movers. Integration and coordination is further enhanced by the response of the muscles to specific stimuli, contracting a given number of muscle fibers at a frequency needed to perform the desired movement. Any increase in load will require the enlistment of a greater number of fibers, usually at a greater frequency.

Obviously, this requires an efficient, well-coordinated neuromuscular system, the work of which is enhanced by a solid foundation of preseason conditioning, adequate nutrition, sufficient warm-up (including stretching), correct technique, a balance of work and rest for the control of fatigue, and an ample supply of good luck! Unfortunately, in spite of these precautions and preparations, numerous agents may bring about an unwanted stimulus, causing an imbalance in the nature of contraction which increases the possibilities of injury. Generally, these agents range from products of fatigue, loss of electrolyte, and inadequate nutrition through structural deformities and genetic weakness, to poor condition, inadequate warm-up, sudden changes in running gait, and psychological disturbances.

LOWER EXTREMITIES

The obvious function of the lower extremities in athletic performance is propulsion and locomotion, without which the athlete becomes merely a spectator. Depending on the severity of the injury, the athlete may be sidelined for a few days or for an entire season; therefore, skilled diagnosis and treatment are critical in the longevity of the athlete.

With the present, year-round system of training in vogue, some injuries (e.g., arch problems, tendonitis, stress fracture, and chondromalacia—vague pain around the knee cap) are becoming more commonplace. Additionally, to the frustration of the coach and trainer, modern athletes are experiencing difficulty in differentiating between the soreness or normal stress of practice and the pain of injury, delaying fast, accurate diagnosis. It seems apparent that the best trainers are also psychologists and are able to extract all the necessary information from athletes who may experience difficulty in expressing themselves accurately.

Shin Splints

This term represents several different conditions that may occur singly or in combination. The problem may be minimized if detected early. When treated promptly with the various modalities* and with rest when it can be afforded, symptoms of the condition respond quickly, shortening the overall time lost.

Generally, the "shin splint" is a clinically painful and seemingly disabling condition of the lower leg and ranks high among complaints that plague the track athlete. The patient usually complains of pain and tenderness, with swelling and heat in the muscle groups situated around both the anterior and posterior aspects of the large

*Modality—a method of application or the employment of any therapeutic agent; limited usually to physical agents.

tibia bone located in the lower leg, or the soft connective tissue, interosseus membrane, attaching the fibula with the tibia. A clinical sign for a vast majority of shin splints is observed when the athlete experiences pain when asked to raise the toes toward the shin area, dorsiflexion of the ankle.

To the utter consternation of coaches, trainers, and sports physicians, the shin splint is an injury that seems to be contagious at times, with the greatest incidence occuring at the beginning of preseason work and again near the completion of the season (7). Suggested causes—and things to avoid—range from running on uneven terrain as in cross-country, changing running surfaces (an athlete can condition to any surface but should then continue to run on that surface), strenuous work on unyielding surfaces, sudden changes in direction including stopping and starting, to inadequate physical fitness, imbalanced leg length, arch problems, and a misfiring of reciprocal coordination between opposing muscles of the lower leg resulting in cocontraction, with one muscle pulling against another (2).

Unfortunately, trainers and sports physicians have not been able to agree on the specific causes of shin splints or on the best method of treatment because there are various symptoms, and treatment and response differs in each case. Constant heat in the form of whirlpool, analgesic balm packs, and ultrasound therapy have been found to give positive results with some athletes. Many trainers, however, have had the greatest success in both acute and chronic stages using ice massage. In other instances, ice massage and heat in combination during the day has had positive results. Heat before and ice massage after practice, followed by application of ice bags for two to three hours when the athlete is studying or watching TV may be the correct approach. If a clear-cut diagnosis can be made, placing a pad under the tarsals or metatarsals or supportive taping of either the ankle or the shin may also be helpful. Static stretching and exercise programs designed to develop the musculature of the involved areas should be undertaken only when the exact cause of the condition is known and further aggravation of the injury will not occur. Most of these exercises require development of posterior muscles to increase the resistance of the shin area to anterior leg syndrome by employing the heel rise type of activity, plantar flexion of the ankle.

de Vries, following a line of reasoning that recognizes the way in which muscle spindle and tendon organ proprioceptors work, suggests static stretching of the anterior or dorsiflexor muscles for prevention and treatment of shin splints (4). Eliminating any bouncing activity that would invoke the stretch reflex and more contraction of the muscle, the athlete kneels down on the extended (plantar flexed) ankle, sits down, and gently rocks back on the ankles, holding the position for about a minute. The muscle-spasm theory of muscle soreness can be applied to any muscle group to prevent as well as relieve soreness.

It is particularly important that the trainer and coach be able to differentiate between common shin splints and such entities as periostitis, an inflammatory condition involving the outer, protective covering of the bone; tenosynovitis, an inflammatory condition of the tendons; myositis, an inflammation of muscle tissue;

stress fractures of the tibia, fibular, or foot bones; muscle herniations; or acute anterior-tibial compartment syndrome, a severe swelling within the anterior fascia chamber (7). A coach familiar with each aspect of shin splints should also keep in mind that many athletes cannot or do not make the distinction between soreness and pain when reporting "shin irritation."

If the onset of the condition occurs either acutely, as in preseason preparation, or chronically, developing later and continuing throughout the competitive season, myositis or periostitis may be the correct diagnosis. Persistent, difficult to describe pain that changes its location may be caused by the stress fracture, muscle herniation, or acute anterior-tibial compartment syndrome. Prolonged shin splints should be X-rayed for evidence of these conditions, but it should be emphasized, particularly in the case of stress fractures, that X rays will be negative for the first two to four weeks (i.e., one negative X ray does not mean that the athlete is imagining things and all is well).

Muscle Contusions

A muscle contusion or bruise is an injury common to all sports and occurs in any muscle vulnerable to trauma applied by an external force. In track, the hurdler or steeplechaser is more likely to incur this injury by hitting the barriers. Bleeding may occur in any soft-tissue injury and will usually heal within 1 to 7 days, depending on the number of muscle fibers and blood vessels injured and the amount of hemorrhage that follows (1, 5, 7). The athlete will usually complain of a sharp, localized pain and, if the hemorrhage is severe, heat may be detected by lightly palpating the involved area. If there is loss of range of motion because of this hemorrhage, the treatment should be conservative, suggesting partial or complete immobilization.

The ultimate objective in treating a contusion is to terminate or minimize the bleeding and swelling. This is best accomplished by quickly applying cold compresses (ice) and continuing the treatment for 24 to 48 hours immediately following the injury (5). The involved part should also be kept elevated, compressed with a pressure bandage and movement restricted. Once the bleeding has subsided, the treatment should consist of a heated whirlpool, light massage, and gentle, active exercise to allow circulation to absorb the residue of hemorrhage. The area should be wrapped with an elastic bandage and further protected from trauma.

A contusion or other traumatic injury to muscle may be accompanied by painful clonic or alternating muscle spasm. The pain sets up a reflex pattern which, while protective in limiting or preventing further movement, causes more spasm in the afflicted muscle. Although the cycle must be halted, do not force stretching of the fibers in clonic spasm, since the accompanying stretch reflex will only cause more spasm. Ice massage, followed by moist heat of hydrocollator packs after an adequate time period is particularly effective for disrupting the cycle. Stubborn spasm may be treated by anaesthesia, injections, muscle relaxants, or electrotherapy administered by a sports physician.

Whether the contusion is the familiar "charley horse" of the anterior thigh or is located elsewhere, note that a complication known as myositis ossificans may develop if the injury is ignored, exposed to heat therapy, or improperly manipulated by the athlete. While development of this condition can and should be prevented, hemorrhage in soft tissue may calcify, producing a somewhat firm, immobile mass of ossified material deep in the involved muscle adjacent to the bone, making it difficult to either stretch the muscle or extend the joint the muscle services. Diagnosis of the injury should be confirmed by X rays, with the same caution suggested earlier regarding premature conclusions concerning negative X-ray reports. If subsequent reports are positive, surgical removal of the ossified mass may be undertaken if the function and comfort of the muscle and joint are hindered.

Muscle Pulls

The majority of movements in track and field are of a ballistic, free-wheeling nature. This to-and-fro movement of arms and legs in running and hurdling requires precise, integrated coordination of the neuromuscular system. Explosive throwing and jumping events are either preceded by running or concluded by a single effort directing and releasing the body or implement ballistically. Muscles contract explosively for a microsecond and then turn off, allowing momentum to supply the dynamic inertia.

In sprinting, the timing of these pendular movements must be so precisely timed by involuntary means that muscle strains of various degrees may occur in spite of correct preparation and condition. The tension within the rectus femorus of the anterior thigh of a sprinter's trailing leg when changing to recovery and the comparable tension-time sequence of the hamstrings in a hurdler's lead leg when attacking the barrier quickly followed by snapdown suggest opportunities for injury. The two joint muscles are particularly vulnerable to the changeover that occurs when, as movers, they must flex one joint and extend the other, and be stretched to and sometimes beyond their limit and then immediately turn off in the role of antagonists for the return movement.

When the athlete performs any movement that will forcibly stretch or violently contract an unwilled muscle, injury may occur either in the muscle itself, at the musculotendenous junction within the tendon, or at the attachment of the tendon with the bone. The latter injury, known as an avulsion, may be the result of either explosive activity or constant, chronic pulling.

Initially, it is difficult to categorize strains or pulls. The reported discomfort and initial trauma is not a valid indicator of the actual amount of damage incurred. Usually a day later the strain can be narrowed to a localized area identified by pain that is aggravated by movement or muscle tension, with failure of the desired movement. There may be swelling, bleeding, discoloration, tenderness, and a decrease in muscle function and strength (3).

Unfortunately, muscle strains tend to reoccur, which suggests that the injury should be given time to rehabilitate. When the limb has regained its normal range of motion, as well as strength for flexion and extension as compared with the uninjured, contralateral extremity, the athlete should be ready for competitive efforts. Treatment involves immediate application of ice (massage, followed by bags), compression, and elevation for a period of 48 hours. Within reason the athlete should be encouraged to use the limb as normally as possible, not only to reduce atrophy that usually begins 48 to 72 hours after any immobilization but also to minimize compensatory movements predisposing to other malfunctions resulting in lower back pain.

Following the ice, compression-elevation procedure, diathermy or ultrasound treatment is probably superior to superficial whirlpool therapy for flushing out the deep-seated residue of hemorrhage and encouraging healing. If equipment and facilities are limited to the use of a whirlpool, this therapy can be more effective if accompanied by movement of the limb during treatment. This self-massage concept discourages the formation of scar tissue. Once healing has been completed and near normal range of motion is experienced, continued rehabilitation requires that attention be focused on maintaining or regaining complete muscle strength and flexibility of the limb. Although much of the clinical rehabilitation can be done in the training room, it is normally accompanied by careful resumption of practice on the field. The athlete should cautiously increase the quality and quantity of work on the track while increasing range of motion of the limb. Premature efforts to "run out" the injury should be avoided; torn or injured fibers must be given time to heal.

Muscle Cramping

A sudden, involuntary, persistent contraction of an uninjured muscle will lead to immobilization of the limb in a painful flexed position characteristic of tonic spasm or cramping. It is now appropriate to passively apply stretch, or break the reflex pattern by extending the limb and engaging the contralateral or antagonistic muscles. According to Novich and Taylor, cramping may be the result of: (1) loss of salt as a result of increased sweating; (2) hyperventilation or blowing off an unusual amount of carbon dioxide and encouraging a condition known as respiratory alkalosis; (3) fatigued state with lactic acid buildup leading to the inability to relax; or (4) circulatory impairment resulting from a tight supportive strap, improperly fitted equipment, or shoes (7). Other reasons may include: (1) overstretched muscles; (2) tight muscles; (3) poor physical condition; (4) sudden, sharp blows causing a persistent reflex spasm but no contusion; and (5) the ever-present, unapparent reason!

Prevention of cramping is the elimination of the cause which, in most cases, requires replacement of salt, electrolytes, and fluids to the body, and is best accomplished by simply including them in the daily diet. In addition, adequate warm-down at the conclusion of practice and warm-up prior to the next day's session can flush cramp-producing lactic acid and other fatigue products out of the muscle.

Associated Injuries of the Periosteum

There are a few injuries that young junior-high and high-school age athletes may be susceptible to. Depending on the growth patterns of youngsters and the degree of immaturity of bone structure, ballistic activity can tear the attachment of muscle and tendon from its bony attachment. The avulsion was defined earlier in conjuction with the muscle pull, but it was pointed out that it may be the result of chronic pulling activity also. In other words, an activity such as long distance running may be the cause of a partial avulsion. One of the favorite sites for this type of injury is the proximal attachment of the hamstring muscle group. In due time, the injury will heal but the apophysial projection may change the mechanical disposition of the muscle sufficiently to encourage chronic malfunction. The athlete may complain of vague pain in the general area of the hip, which, when X-rayed, may reveal the inability of immature ossification centers to adequately anchor the muscle origin. An orthopedist may recommend complete rest followed weeks later by gentle exercise to allow calcification to occur normally. In most instances, therapy of other means is quite secondary to rest or normal activity until recovery is achieved.

The Osgood-Schlatter Syndrome of the knee is a typical example of this type of injury. Often, a youngster will incur such an injury, experience little pain, and never actually realize the condition occurred or know why performance may have declined. Some time later, the familiar Osgood-Schlatter calcified protrusion on the front of the femur will be an indication of having pulled or avulsed the tendenous attachment of the quadriceps muscle group from its insertion or distal attachment on the front of the femur.

An apophysis is a projection or outgrowth of bone without an independent ossification center. It may develop from a heelbruise that is a particular kind of contusion involving the periosteum membrane covering the exterior of the bone. While it is important that all athletes involved in jumping events wear heel cups or shoes with adequate heel padding, the younger athlete should be fitted with running shoes that offer built-in protection for the heel, regardless of the event. This does not imply that the heel should be built up to take tension off the Achilles tendon, which could only lead to muscular imbalances and associated foot and postural problems. If an athlete experiences a heel bruise, the treatment requires ice, followed by moist heat, support, padding, and sufficient rest to encourage healing, followed by gradual involvement in vigorous activity.

THE PSYCHOLOGY OF TRAINING

Each athletic injury is as separate and distinct as the athlete. However, while specific care should be given to properly diagnose the injury and set up a rehabilitation program, the treatment of the injury should be similar, regardless of the location or who is involved. Prevention is the key to reduction of injury, and this emphasizes proper conditioning and the learning of correct technique. A case in point is the culturally dictated gross movement of throwing a baseball, which, if applied to hurling a javelin, could only lead to disaster. Additionally, instruction in the value of a well-balanced diet without the expensive and unnecessary addition of gimmick health foods can lend to the credibility and intelligence of the athlete. A nice balance of work and rest can be scheduled by the coach, but further counseling to maintain it away from practice is also helpful.

In track and field, a sincere one-to-one relationship in dealing with the athlete is essential. Real injuries of the general class described in this chapter are *relatively* easy to diagnose and treat, or to refer to a physician. The problem of the psychogenic or psychosomatic injury, however, is more complicated. They deserve definition but are beyond the scope of this chapter, requiring diagnosis and treatment by a trained psychiatrist.

The psychogenic injury has its origin in the mind and is the result of physical and mental forces producing a condition that precludes the athlete from practice or competition. The psychosomatic injury is a disorder notably influenced by the emotional state of the individual. In other words, the psychogenic injury is initially imagined, physically does not exist, but is real in the mind of the individual. The psychosomatic injury was real to begin with, but fails to respond to treatment in the mind of the individual after healing should have occurred.

There have been attempts to superficially train prospective coaches in this difficult psychology, but they have not met with much success. Although there are differences in the charismatic posture of a coach or trainer, the best advice in coach, trainer, and athlete relationships is honesty.

From the coaching and training standpoint, there are a number of things that should be discussed with the athlete, when there is time, to improve the elements of confidence and improve performance; then, on the day of competition, rain, wind, condition of the surface, temperature, humidity, the starter, the unexpected athletes present, can be better tolerated and dealt with by the athlete, who is on the field as a single entry and has no one to turn to but himself. Instead of having athletes who excuse themselves from competition, the coach now has athletes who can take advantage of the worst conditions and feel confident of their performance because the groundwork has consistently been laid in practice.

Most track athletes are social beings and many talk with each other both before and after competition, comparing aches, pains, and training schedules. Expertly used by some individuals, this seemingly idle chatter is intended to "psych out" the opposition. Either an athlete should avoid this verbal exchange or be prepared to respond in kind, but the best advice is to contain the psychology, concentrate on the event, and perhaps psych out the opposition to a greater extent.

Best-performance lists are becoming more available on the local level in neighborhood newspapers, and they often have a disruptive effect on athletes. An individual's performance may be adversely affected if he or she is worried about competing against someone who is ahead on the list. Encourage the athlete to disregard the lists; many times they are misleading. For example, there was a national caliber 200-m runner, who was ignored because he was relatively low on the best-performer lists. There was only one problem—since this athlete did not know he could lose, he ran to win and won the NCAA, AAU, and Olympic trials in 1972.

And then there is the subject of pain. Evidently, this is what most training is about. If the trainer and coach know what the athlete's threshold of pain is, it will help them make decisions involving that extra race or attempt that could win the meet. Perhaps, of greater importance, what the threshold for pain is will enable a coach or trainer to make a realistic assessment of the athlete's progress in practice. In other words, it is important for every athlete to know there is pain on the way to superior condition and performance, although the coach must step back and put it in realistic perspective for the betterment of the athlete. It is possible for an athlete to push himself or be pushed too hard. Remember that, while an athlete is a biological machine with enduring capabilities, do not ask him or her to do what you would not ask yourself to do at the same age. Perhaps this advice does not work if you are not inclined to push yourself, but it is an attempt to deal honestly with the problem—to retain the confidence of the athlete.

There are peaks and plateaus reached during the training and performance of any athlete. The plateaus can be quite frustrating because the athlete is training hard but no improvement occurs. The coach can help the athlete become aware of this possibility and help him deal with it more effectively, with a minimum of frustration. Anticipating that, at this time, the coach knows his athlete intimately, he also probably knows something that will help trigger an improved performance. The successful coach will use this knowledge to improve the athlete's performance, still keeping his best interests in mind.

BIBLIOGRAPHY

1. American Medical Association, *Standard Nomenclature of Athletic Injuries,* American Medical Association, Chicago, 1966.
2. Arnheim, Daniel, D., *Dance Injuries—Their Prevention and Care,* C. V. Mosby Co., St. Louis, 1975.
3. Cailliet, Rene, *Knee Pain and Disability,* Davis Co., Philadelphia, 1973.
4. de Vries, H.A., "Quantitative Electromyographic Evaluation of The Spasm Theory for Muscle Pain," *American Journal of Physical Medicine, 45,* 119 (1966).
5. Dolan, Joseph P., and Lloyd Holladay, Jr., *First-Aid Management,* Interstate Printers and Publishers, Danville, Ill. 1974.
6. Greisheimer, Esther M., *Physiology and Anatomy,* Lippincott, New York, 1963.
7. Novich, Max M., and Buddy Taylor, *Training and Conditioning of Athletes,* Henry Kimpton Publishers, London, 1970.

index

Page numbers in *italics* refer to illustrations.